Our Shared Future

Our Shared Future

Windows into Canada's Reconciliation Journey

Edited by
Laura E. Reimer and Robert Chrismas

Foreword by
David Barnard

LEXINGTON BOOKS
Lanham • Boulder • New York • London

Published by Lexington Books
An imprint of The Rowman & Littlefield Publishing Group, Inc.
4501 Forbes Boulevard, Suite 200, Lanham, Maryland 20706
www.rowman.com

6 Tinworth Street, London SE11 5AL, United Kingdom

Copyright © 2020 The Rowman & Littlefield Publishing Group, Inc.

All rights reserved. No part of this book may be reproduced in any form or by any electronic or mechanical means, including information storage and retrieval systems, without written permission from the publisher, except by a reviewer who may quote passages in a review.

British Library Cataloguing in Publication Information Available

Library of Congress Cataloging-in-Publication Data

Names: Reimer, Laura E.- editor. | Chrismas, Robert- editor.
Title: Our shared future : windows into Canada's reconciliation journey / edited by Laura E. Reimer and Robert Chrismas ; foreword by David Barnard.
Description: Lanham : Lexington Books, 2020. | Includes bibliographical references and index. | Summary: "This collection provides windows into Canada's conflicted history and the innovative and courageous efforts to reconcile relationships between Indigenous people and settler descendants. The vision and deep experience of scholars and leaders from across the country offer tangible ways that Canada is working toward a peaceful shared future"—Provided by publisher.
Identifiers: LCCN 2020008017 (print) | LCCN 2020008018 (ebook) |
  ISBN 9781793603470 (Cloth : acid-free paper) | ISBN 9781793603494 (pbk)
  ISBN 9781793603487 (ePub)
Subjects: LCSH: Reconciliation—Canada. | Peace-building. | Conflict management.
Classification: LCC JZ5584.C26 O87 2020 (print) | LCC JZ5584.C26 (ebook) |
  DDC 323.1197/071—dc23
LC record available at https://lccn.loc.gov/2020008017
LC ebook record available at https://lccn.loc.gov/2020008018

∞™ The paper used in this publication meets the minimum requirements of American National Standard for Information Sciences—Permanence of Paper for Printed Library Materials, ANSI/NISO Z39.48-1992.

Contents

Foreword vii
David Barnard

Reconciliation: A Canadian Journey 1
Laura E. Reimer and Robert Chrismas

1 Our Long Road: The Story of Indigenous Relations in Canada 9
   Laura E. Reimer

2 Leadership, Reconciliation, and Friendship 35
   Paul E. Vogt

3 Walking in the Footsteps of the Peacemaker:
   A *KENIENKĒ: HAKA* Personal Odyssey of Reconciliation 47
   Brian Rice

4 Beyond Apology: Decolonizing the Jesuits 67
   Peter Bisson, S.J.

5 Reconciliation and Indigenous Adult Learners:
   Reshaping Education through a Trauma-Informed Lens 93
   Christa Yeates with Laura E. Reimer

6 Reconciliation through Education: The University of Winnipeg 121
   Annette Trimbee

7 Ago'widiwinan (Principles of Treaties) 141
   Loretta Ross

8 Reconciliation and Satellite Urban Reserves in Canada 163
   Joseph Garcea

9	Business and Reconciliation: Call to Action 92 *Ronald G. Evans*	189
10	Reconciliation and the Evolution of Canadian Policing *Dale McFee with Robert Chrismas*	205

Our Shared Future: Conclusions from the Windows 225
Robert Chrismas and Laura E. Reimer

Afterword and Dedications 229
Laura E. Reimer and Robert Chrismas

Appendix A 233

Index 237

About the Contributors 243

Foreword
David Barnard

Kaniibowit wapshki muckwa nindizhinikaaz. My spirit name is Standing White Bear. I received this name from Elder Dave Courchene, Jr.

I introduce myself this way out of respect for the ways of the people of the land where I live, and for the friendships that led to me having the name. I came to the prairies from Ontario the better part of thirty years ago, first to Saskatchewan and then to Winnipeg and the University of Manitoba (UM). I am fortunate to have developed working relationships and friendships with many Indigenous people.

I and my colleagues at UM have been deeply influenced by the realities around us. UM has long had Indigenous faculty, staff, and students in its campus community and has focused energy on welcoming Indigenous people into the University. I made a statement of apology on behalf of UM (the only university to do so) at a meeting of the Truth and Reconciliation Commission of Canada (TRC), UM successfully applied to the TRC to host the legacy research center when the Commission passed on its materials and expectations for safekeeping, UM is part of a broad collaboration with other participants in the education sector in Manitoba to improve educational outcomes for Indigenous people, and UM has just created the position of Vice-President Indigenous Engagement (as far as I know, the first in Canada).

But in spite of many good intentions in many places, not just in this province and at my institution, the gap between the life experiences and outcomes (health, economic, etc.) for Indigenous and non-Indigenous people in Canada remains unacceptable.

Many good people want to change this situation, and some of them have been working at it for a long time. These good people do not accept the inequities between the lived experiences of Indigenous people and the experiences of the large majority of Canadians. Educational outcomes, health, and other indicators of social well-being are out of balance for many Indigenous Canadians relative to the rest of the country.

This book presents a sample of the activities that some individuals and some groups have undertaken as their particular contributions to our shared future. A multifaceted approach is clearly required, but we do not yet know how effective some of the particulars will be. In this book the editors have brought together descriptions of some of the many attempts to bridge the gap between our two realities. We are not faced with two solitudes (a metaphor from Anglophone and Francophone Canadian interactions in the past) but with a more dynamic image: a shared journey, with different particular choices of what might draw us closer together as we travel.

It is natural to hope that the experiences of our children and grandchildren, of our neighbors and their children and grandchildren and of our fellow citizens more broadly considered, will be in a social context that is safer and more equitable for all people than has been the case in Canada for Indigenous people.

The approaches described here can help us to understand and to improve the circumstances of our shared journey.

Dr David Barnard, OM
President and Vice-Chancellor
University of Manitoba
Winnipeg, Manitoba, Canada

Treaty One Land and Homeland to the Métis Nation

Reconciliation
A Canadian Journey
Laura E. Reimer and Robert Chrismas

Our journey for reconciliation in Canada is, in many ways, just beginning. The future of Canada is, for us, the story of our past, present, and future lives. This is a time for courage and tenacity, a conviction that our great dreams are rooted in the strength of respectful relationships animated by our past, present, and our vision of our shared future.

Through each of the chapters ahead, readers will be provided with windows into how Canadians are making sense of our past, living our present, and striving to give shape to the future we hope for. While reconciliation is a journey that includes people, organizations, and countries, it is also a journey of the individual heart and mind. Throughout the complex processes of reconciliation, time and healing are interwoven, and for those walking the road, it is very personal.[1] Though the need for reconciliation usually flows from the actions and decisions of governments, it is not solely the work of governments to embark on the journey, nor is it the work of one individual, nor of complex organizations. Reconciliation is shared. The chapters in this volume are written by Canadian Indigenous and non-Indigenous scholars and leaders. Together, we explore reconciliation in the complex levels of conflict, while acknowledging that reconciliation is simultaneously a global struggle, a community struggle, and a deeply personal struggle. Like all conflicts, Canada's reconciliation journey is complicated.

But the Canadian world is built on relationships that began long before the founding of the country in 1867, and are now undergoing the fragile process of reconciling. At the same time, the country is becoming home to newcomers with many other experiences and stories, who bring with them a different past to graft into our future together. Canada is and always has been a place where many people can come together and learn to be together respectfully and comfortably. There are very few effective frameworks or models for action emerging from the disciplines of international relations, political science, or the social sciences in matters of reconciliation, though from these areas comes much of the literature.[2] While others take to pen to criticize us, the contributors to this volume demonstrate that in many sectors of our society, authentic and transformative change is taking place. The chapters explore practical, active responses in immediate circles of influence. The outcomes are rooted in our desires for reconciliation. This is our journey.

RECONCILIATION

When we step into the river of other people's lives, it must be with great humility. The concept of reconciliation is not a new one, though its circular depth makes it relevant to the many worldviews through which Canada has been interpreted. Acknowledged reconciliation scholar John Paul Lederach explains that reconciliation is "the place where Truth and Mercy, Justice and Peace meet."[3] These are fluid energies for and within reconciliation, and this energy is evident in the chapters of this book. When these concepts are applied to social and political situations, political and social leaders are trying to make the journey toward reconciliation operational; peace becomes a national reconciliation process, truth commissions are formed, mercy emerges in the form of national amnesty programs, and justice is incarnated as war tribunals.[4] In this way, national and international leaders design processes and procedures that they think will move conflict and injustice toward peace and justice. In all of these, the reconciliation framework "assumes that we must first establish what happened in the *past*, in order to make it possible to live together in the *present* and move together as a society into the *future*."[5] But there are broken hearts and individual lives greatly affected by Canada's past and its present. We take very seriously the knowledge that it will be through the energies of reconciliation that we can and will shape our future.

Conciliation is a collaborative problem-solving alternative dispute resolution practice;[6] a process of building positive social relationships through unassisted, cooperative decision-making among parties.[7] This seems to be where Canada needs to go, yet our contemporary political leaders have eagerly taken us not into the realm of conciliation, but have instead engaged the reconciliation narrative around the globe, including Canada, Northern Ireland, and South Africa. This is confusing because despite frequent declarations by the government of the day that Indigenous people and Indigenous relationships matter, in Canada, at least, government commissions throughout Canada's history have found that most Canadians are not particularly certain of what it is that is being reconciled.[8]

In many ways, the *Apology for Indian Residential Schools Policy*[9] of Prime Minister Stephen Harper in 2008 was a national awakening that there has been something very wrong in Canada. On that day, Canadians in all walks of life heard for the first time the candid, difficult admission from our prime minister, on behalf of all our governments over time, including the leaders of the empires that colonized us, that "we were wrong."[10] Despite the views of some critics of that apology, there is much in the criteria literature[11] to suggest that this may have been one of the earliest, authentic acknowledgements of wrongdoing, and the work of peace, mercy, justice, and truth as reconciliation began to take root in wider society.

Determining the wrongs of yesterday and today is not the end of the journey; this is where governments stop and the work of individuals begin. There must be a shared future beside and on the other side of reconciliation. It is in this context of an ethically remembered, shared future, where truth, mercy, love, and justice meet, that growing numbers of Canadians are striving to learn, understand, and respond to the needs of reconciliation around us.

EARLY CANADA

There is much evidence that despite some contests relationships among Canada's early inhabitants were characterized by respect, born in part out of the symbiotic benefits of the fur trade for both the Indigenous people and for those whose origins are typically traced to the British Isles. The early covenants depicted on the front jacket of this book, called Wampum and treaties, are evidence that early relationships were built on respectful co-existence. As covenants, they are to stand for all time. The message of the Two-Row Wampum established somewhere near modern Virginia, USA (1631) is that Europeans and Original People will travel the rivers side by side, for all time, and neither shall steer the others' water vessel; the Treaty of Niagara (1764) agreement among the growing settlements north of the 49th parallel, extended this agreement to include the Settlers. Major European and British legislation, and later the *Canadian Constitution Act*, these are the bedrock upon which Canada was founded, expanded, and stands today. But events since these covenants indicate that we now must seek reconciliation. This means that in order to do so, there must be trust, both in the systems of Canadian society and in each other; and there must be respect. This is not a linear process, and understandably it does take a long time. Scholars agree that reconciliation may take generations, in part because of the need for healing at the individual, community, and societal levels.[12] According to scholarship, for reconciliation to mature, there must be a shared future that includes security (no potential for recommencement of past violations), truth (acknowledgement of the wrongs of the past), and justice (in the form of punishment or reparations).[13] The burden of reconciliation is ours to share.

We also cannot ignore the fact that Canada was a French, and then British colony. This means that we live in a colonized state and that has had very complicated repercussions for reconciliation, and those of us that call Canada home are at different stages of embracing this reality. One scholar has stated that "decolonization recognizes that it is not an easy process but is latent with paradoxes, because the colonial mindset is too complex to dismantle fully."[14] While an extensive colonization literature review is well beyond the scope of this book, colonization does need to be briefly explained. This is not colonialism, which was the policy of total control and domination engaged by the French and British empires in the earliest days of what became Canada. Colonization occurs when one people or culture is dominated or conquered by another, the basic social structures are weakened or destroyed, and the conquered culture is replaced with that of the conquering or dominating culture.[15] A great divide is generated and established as the dominant group sees itself as superior and benevolent embodying the quintessential values, ethics, and mores of nationhood, in the quest for civilization.[16] Decolonization in Canada is required for Indigenous and non-Indigenous minds alike, and has been widely acknowledged in the literature as foundational for full reconciliation, though how that will be for Canada is the story that is now unfolding.

Indigenous academics have taken exception to the assumptions of western research to conduct research on rather than with Indigenous people; yet this is also the case with Canada in the broader context, and as Canadians we take exception.[17] Academics from Europe and the United States criticize our journey and write freely of our failures, while viewing our world through their eyes. They do not see their views and opinions as imposed on us; we are in some ways being recolonized by foreign academics. In the following chapters, readers will have opportunity to explore some of the complexities and responses of the Canadian reconciliation journey through our eyes and our great dreams for our shared future. We acknowledge that many will insist this is not enough; but the words of this book do indicate clearly that we are engaged in our journey.

David Barnard, President and Vice-Chancellor of the University of Manitoba in central Canada has written the Foreword. As home to the archives of Canada's *Truth and Reconciliation Commission of Canada* (TRC), and located on Treaty land, the University of Manitoba (meaning resting place of the Creator in our local Indigenous language) has been central to much of the recent activity of Canada's reconciliation journey.

The book jacket was created by Mikayla Leanne Plett, a Manitoba artist whose skilled pen has understood the heart of our reconciliation journey. Canada's landscape, also symbolic of the nations that call Canada home, is wrapped in two of the earliest covenants of respectful relationship; the Two-Row Wampum and the Treaty of Niagara. The three rivers flowing side by side eternally from the mountains, like the Treaty of Niagara, represent the ways of the Original People, the Europeans, and the Settlers.

Laura Reimer provides an integrated history of the evolution of the earliest relationships between Indigenous and non-Indigenous peoples through the window of public policy. The chapter flows chronologically from early encounters between Europeans and Original People in what is now North America, through to the official transfer of relationship for Original People above the 49th parallel into a colonial one, under the realm of the Canadian government and the 1869 *Indian Act*. The relationship was then characterized by the aggressive dismantling of Indigenous identity and ways of life with the abrupt imposition of a defined, structured relationship with government for the Original People as Indians. Following the actions (and inactions) of Canada's government since before the founding of the country, relevant issues and policies of government that have contributed to the current context for reconciliation are provided. This provides a foundation for understanding some of the complexities of our journey. The chapters are followed by the full text of the 2008 federal government Apology to former students of residential schools for the residential schools policy – one of the darkest chapters of Canada's history.

In his chapter entitled *Leadership, Reconciliation, and Friendship*, Paul Vogt engages readers to wrestle with the concept of what effective leadership must be like in the context of reconciliation. The issue of leadership is frequently part of any discussion of the *Truth and Reconciliation Commission Final Report* recommendations, and the resulting *Calls to Action*. The chapter explores the meanings of the *Calls*, and the responsibilities of public leaders in particular. Vogt thoughtfully invites readers to consider how leadership has been, and how it must be, in order to be effective.

The book then turns to the personal level of reconciliation as *KENIENKĒ;HAKA* (Mohawk) Scholar Brian Rice honors us by taking us with him on his personal odyssey, walking the way of the Peacemaker.[18] Rice's journey serves as a guide and we learn that reconciliation begins in the heart. Father Peter Bisson paints for us the poignant nuances of decolonizing the Jesuits in his roles as the leader of a national organization, including brutally painful personal epiphanies of the conflicts between the intentions of his heart, and external perceptions of the Catholic Church.

The book also explores what reconciliation means to suffering individuals while decolonizing education. Acknowledging the fragility of the human heart and how trauma can manifest in a classroom, teacher Christa Yeates shares how she has engaged with trauma-informed education to reshape education with empathy. Aware of the insidious impacts of trauma on teaching and learning and on teachers and students, Yeates has worked successfully for over ten years to guide inner-city Indigenous adult learners to completion of their high school education.

Annette Trimbee, president of the University of Winnipeg, presents the decolonizing of a Canadian university under her leadership. Trimbee shares with readers how her university is developing meaningful connections and relationships with Indigenous people and communities by including Indigenous perspectives and experiences in the university, recognizing and employing Indigenous talent and knowledge, and supporting future Indigenous leaders and learners at the institution.

Increasing numbers of Canadians and their organizations are enthusiastically engaged in "reconciliation," though general understandings are unclear. Through the efforts of Treaty Relations Commissioners (appointed originally by England and by Canada's central government since), most public meetings are now opened with an acknowledgment of the agreements between Indigenous people and governments for stewardship and sharing of the land beneath us. The treaties, and especially the *Numbered Treaties* of the Canadian west, are explored further in Manitoba Treaty Relations Commissioner Loretta Ross' chapter entitled *Ago'widiwinan*, a local Indigenous phrase meaning principles of treaties. Land sharing in the ongoing debate regarding satellite urban reserves as a reconciliation ideal is presented by Professor Joe Garcea.

Indigenous Chief and former provincial Grand Chief Ron Evans draws upon his broad leadership experiences to explore one of the *Truth and Reconciliation Commission's Calls to Action*, Business and Reconciliation, and applies its relevance as an agent for positive growth, development, and prosperity in Canada's northern communities.

Police Chief Dale McFee and Staff Sergeant Bob Chrismas provide a window into the very old and contested relationship between law enforcement and Indigenous Canada, and how reconciliation works in their context. The authors present practical ways police leadership in western Canadian cities can and is advancing justice and respect as contributions to Canada's reconciliation journey.

We are grateful to the contributors to this volume for the quiet efforts they have made for reconciliation by their decisions and examples among the people in their realm of influence. This is hard work that flows from a vision of great dreams for the future of our country and deep caring for our people. We trust that through the window of each chapter, readers will gain a picture of how seriously Canadians are undertaking our desire for reconciliation and a shared future. We believe that it is through the work of people like the contributors to this book that we shall be shepherded through reconciliation to the other side, where our future will be respectful and together. From the wisdom and contributions of scholar Dr John Paul Lederach to the timeless, borderless work of reconciliation, we offer the following:

To take up the journey of reconciliation, we keep our feet on the ground and our head in the clouds. Now is the time for great convictions and great dreams. Let us dream boldly. Let us dream boldly that our feet may carry us through the challenging realities that stir around us. May God grant us the innocence to dream, and the wisdom, courage, and sustenance to take up the journey.[19]

NOTES

1. John Paul Lederach, *The Journey Toward Reconciliation*, (Scottsdale, PA: Herald Press, 1999), 62.

2. Lederach, *Journey*, 64.

3. John Paul Lederach, *Building Peace: Sustainable Reconciliation in Divided Societies* (Washington, DC: United States Institute of Peace, 1997), 29.

4. Lederach, *Journey*, 64.

5. Lederach, *Journey*, 71.

6. Christopher Moore and Peter J. Woodrow, "Collaborative Problem Solving within Organizations," in *The Consensus Building Handbook: A Comprehensive Guide to Reaching Agreement*, ed. Lawrence Susskind, Sarah McKearnana, Jennifer Thomas-Larmer (Thousand Oaks, CA: Sage, 1999), 629.

7. Moore and Woodrow, "Collaborative Problem Solving within Organizations," 616, 629.

8. See *The Royal Commission on Aboriginal Peoples Final Report, 1996*. Accessed September 3, 2019. https://www.bac-lac.gc.ca/eng/discover/aboriginal-heritage/royal-commission-aboriginal-peoples/Pages/final-report.aspx

9. For the complete transcript, see The Right Honourable Prime Minister Stephen Harper, on behalf of the Government of Canada, Statement of Apology—To Former Students of Indian Residential Schools. Accessed August 30, 2019. https://www.aadnc-aandc.gc.ca/DAM/DAM-INTER-HQ/STAGING/texte-text/rqpi_apo_pdf_1322167347706_eng.pdf

10. See Appendix A.

11. For a comprehensive analysis of the criteria of "effective" public apology, see Robert R. Weyeneth, "The Power of Apology and the Process of Historical Reconciliation." *The Public Historian* 23, no. 3 (Summer, 2001), 9–38.

12. Marwan Darweish and Carol Rank, *Peacebuilding and Reconciliation: Contemporary Themes and Challenges*, ed. Marwan Darweish and Carol Rank (London, UK: Pluto Press, 2012), 5.

13. Andrew Rigby, "How Do Post-conflict Societies Deal with a Traumatic Past and Promote National Unity and Reconciliation?" in *Peace and Conflict Studies: A Reader*, ed. Charles Webel and Jorgen Johansen (New York, NY: Routlege, 2011).

14. Patricia Elgersma, "Decolonization and Reconciliation: The Colonial Dilemma of Canada's residential School Apology and Restitution," in *Peacebuilding and

Reconciliation: Contemporary Themes and Challenges, ed. Marwan Darweish and Carol Rank (London, UK: Pluto Press), 97.

15. Elgersma, "Decolonization and Reconciliation," 89.

16. Ibid., 89.

17. In 1999, Indigenous scholar Linda Tuhiwai Smith released *Decolonizing Methodologies: Research and Indigenous Peoples* (Zed Books, 1999, 2012), which remains one of the major contributions to Indigenous social justice research.

18. See Paul Wallace, *The White Roots of Peace* (Santa Fe, NM: Clear Light Publishing, 1994).

19. Paraphrased from the book of *Hebrews* in John Paul Lederach, *Journey,* 202.

BIBLIOGRAPHY

Darweish, Marwan and Carol Rank. Eds. *Peacebuilding and Reconciliation: Contemporary Themes and Challenges* (London, UK: Pluto Press, 2012).

Elgersma, Patricia. "Decolonization and Reconciliation: The Colonial Dilemma of Canada's Residential School Apology and Restitution." In *Peacebuilding and Reconciliation: Contemporary Themes and Challenges*. Edited by Marwan Darweish and Carol Rank (London, UK: Pluto Press, 2012).

Lederach, John Paul. *Building Peace: Sustainable Reconciliation in Divided Societies* (Washington, DC: United States Institute of Peace, 1997).

Lederach, John Paul. *The Journey Toward Reconciliation* (Scottsdale, PA: Herald Press, 1999).

Moore, Christopher and Peter J. Woodrow. "Collaborative Problem Solving within Organizations." In *The Consensus Building Handbook: A Comprehensive Guide to Reaching Agreement*. Edited by Lawrence Susskind, Sarah McKearnana, and Jennifer Thomas-Larmer (Thousand Oaks, CA; Sage, 1999).

Rigby, Andrew. "How Do Post-conflict Societies Deal with a Traumatic Past and Promote National Unity and Reconciliation?" In *Peace and Conflict Studies: A Reader*. Edited by Charles Webel and Jorgen Johansen (New York, NY: Routledge, 2011).

Chapter 1

Our Long Road

The Story of Indigenous Relations in Canada

Laura E. Reimer

The story of Indigenous relations in Canada is a long one. It seems that since people have been recording history either orally or in the written word, they have been recording the story of our people. Canada is located in North America, nested between the Pacific, Atlantic, and Arctic Oceans. The country is vast: one of the largest geographic regions in the world. The southern border, which closely follows the forty-ninth parallel of the earth, is shared with Canada's only neighbor, the United States. This land was once called Turtle Island by its Indigenous inhabitants. Canada is home to about 1.1 million Indigenous people; the rest of the 33 plus million people within its borders have ancestral roots all over the globe. Founded in 1867 by an Act of the British Parliament and settler groups mostly from Europe, Canada continues to welcome newcomers, refugees, and immigrants; it is and always has been a country of diversity.

But there is a mostly hidden story of Canada, and one that most Canadians did not and do not know. Our early history included policies intended to erase perhaps not the people, but certainly the cultures and traditions of people Indigenous to the country now known as Canada. In 1991, almost 350 years after first contact, *The Royal Commission on Aboriginal[1] Peoples* (RCAP) was established by the Canadian government, mandated to investigate and propose solutions to the many challenges that had grown in the relationship between Indigenous (Aboriginal) people, the Canadian government, and Canadian society as a whole. This was, in many ways, one of Canada's earliest reconciliation efforts. Sadly, it took many years and a change of governing political parties before government began to respond to the *RCAP* recommendations.

In its first of the comprehensive five-volume report, submitted to government in 1996, the Commissioners observed that history

> shows how ancient societies in this part of North America were dispossessed of their homelands and made wards of a state that sought to obliterate their cultural and political institutions. History shows too attempts to explain away this dispossession by legally ignoring Aboriginal peoples, in effect declaring the land *terra nullius*—empty of people who mattered. This is not a history of which most Canadians are aware. It is not a history of democratic participation, nor is it a history that reflects well on Canada or its sense of justice.[2]

It is here in the acknowledgment of a contested story that the healing elements of reconciliation begin. According to peace scholar John Paul Lederach, the primary goal and key contribution of reconciliation is "to seek innovative ways to create a time and a place, within various levels of the affected population, to address, integrate, and embrace the painful past and the necessary shared future as a means of dealing with the present."[3] And so the reconciliation of Canada's relationships requires that Indigenous and nonIndigenous people understand our past more fully, in order to share our future respectfully.

LONG BEFORE THERE WAS CANADA

The story of conciliation begins over 400 years ago south of what is now Canada. The original relationship was good: a partnership of respect and principled relationships. One of the pieces of that early relationship is now an understandably deeply offensive flashpoint. That is the early European use of the word "savage" to refer to Indigenous people. Without doubt, over the centuries, the meaning has changed. The origins and the current associations with this term are also significant to understanding Canada's need for reconciliation:

> To understand what the English actually meant [by referring to native people as "savages"] one has to set aside the intervening four hundred years of American racial history. Seen through the prism of those four hundred years, the English attitude looks like racism; how it could it not be? Improbably enough, the English of 1606 were not racist . . . in the conventional sense. The English did not believe that white people like themselves were innately superior and the natives innately inferior; savagery had nothing to do with biology. It also did not signify that the natives were necessarily fierce (some tribes were, some weren't) . . . savagery was only the starting point for a people's progression toward modernity. It did not render those within it less than fully human.[4]

As the evolution of the meaning of the word changed shamefully, so did the aggressive racism and superiority demonstrated by the Canadian government toward Indigenous people. The early relationship was a respectful one, and there were agreements in place to ensure it would stay that way. So what happened along the way?

One of these important agreements was the Two-Row Wampum (on the cover of this book), established in the 1630s. A wampum is a covenant that cannot be broken and is a hand-made beaded belt with deeply significant and symbolic representations of understandings. The Two-Row Wampum was established between Europeans[5] and the Haudenosaunee (Iroquois) Confederacy,[6] considered the original inhabitants of Turtle Island (now North America). The Two-Row Wampum is a permanent treaty about how they would treat each other and live in friendship; it is a treaty of noninterference and relationship, it is not a land ownership agreement.[7] The purple lines represent the respect for different ways of life and culture: European ways on one line, and the other purple line the ways of the Haudenosaunee. "Each will travel down the river of life side by side. Neither will attempt to steer the other's vessel," is the meaning of the two rows.[8] The Two-Row Wampum is critical to the story of Canada's Indigenous relations because it is the original covenant of a trustworthy and honoring relationship, intended to stand for all time and never be broken. In this way, the story of Canada's Indigenous relationships with governments is entwined with the histories of the United States.

Sometime in the 1600s, Indigenous inhabitants of the northern continent began the struggle to defend their lands and cultures from the claims of imperialism, the forces of colonization, and British Crown ownership. The settling of British North America did not take place in uninhabited lands, though the British and then Canadian governments enacted legislation as though it did. For most people, and especially for Canadians, it is the story of a hidden relationship characterized by disparity in power, violations of trust, and lingering, unresolved disputes, unknown to most nonIndigenous Canadians of settler and newcomer origins.[9] Historical developments in the relationship between the British (and subsequent Canadian governments) and Indigenous people, including the century-long national policy to erase language and culture through the Indian residential school policy, are critical to understanding the current need for reconciliation.

Much of what has happened that has been harmful has happened through government policy and its implementation. The difference between this story and many of the world's conflicts is the notable absence of armed conflict.[10] The reparations of those harms caused by our government actions (and inactions) are part of our current reconciliation journey. This chapter explores reconciliation through the window of government policy, and concludes with cautious hope that the long-standing need for reconciliation is evidencing a recognition of the "need to give time and place both to justice and peace, where redressing the wrong is held together with the envisioning of a common, connected future."[11]

THE FUR TRADE

By the early 1700s the land now called Canada and its wealth of natural resources were the object of the colonial interests of the French and British empires, and provide an early window into our reconciliation journey. The Hudson Bay Company (HBC) of England, established in 1670, and the North West Company, founded by the HBC and Simon Fraser in 1779, were engaged in the fur trade and Indigenous relations long before Canada's Confederation in 1867. After losing the war of 1755 in Europe, France ascribed its claims to some parts of the land to Britain. Shortly thereafter, as part of British King George III's *Royal Proclamation of 1763*, the entire continent of what is now North America was claimed for the British Empire, with statements of protection and preservation of the lands of Indigenous peoples. In 1764, the signing of the *Treaty of Niagara* established a framework for coexistence, included the reading of the *Royal Proclamation*, and established relationships of honor between Indigenous people, the British, and settlers who arrived to a harsh life of extreme weather and remoteness.[12] Our reconciliation conflict has its early roots in this period.

Canada was established as a Dominion in 1867 by the merging of French and British imperial interests through the Royal Assent granted to the *British North America Act*. For over a century to follow, all Canadian legislation was sent to Britain to undergo the processes of British Parliament before becoming law. In 1982, this process ceased when Queen Elizabeth II signed *The Constitution Act*. All treaties and agreements, including the *Royal Proclamation* and the Two-Row Wampum, and those among France, Britain, and Indigenous people remain the foundations beneath current Canadian law. Alternative interpretations of the meaning of honoring the terms of these agreements among government officials and their Indigenous cosignatories are evident in the actions of government as Canadian history unfolded.

Originally, the fur trade compelled good relations between Indigenous people and the Scots/Irish/French and British that populated the HBC and the North West Company from at least 1670 into the late 1700s. Both companies established forts as busy trade centers at the Forks of the Red River and the Assiniboine River in what is now Winnipeg, in central Canada. It would appear that economic motivations of colonialism to assure access to natural resources for the French and British empires were at the origins of the relationship.[13]

The Industrial Revolution changed the economic needs of England, causing a decline in the importance of the fur trade to Europe, and signaling the end of the need for cooperative relations between England, France, and the Indigenous people in North America, for the interests of Britain and France. With the new industrial economy, Britain began to aggressively pursue possession of North American land, and the relationship became a colonial one. Partly in response to his need for natural resources, and partly in formal response to protests of land encroachment by powerful Indigenous chiefs near modern day New York, King George III signed the *Royal Proclamation of 1763* and established a critical piece of relationship in Canada's reconciliation journey.[14]

In addition to seizing control of the land and claiming benevolent protection for the original inhabitants, this legislation also imposed British rule and exacted legal relationships that were eventually transferred to Canada under Section 25 of the *Canadian Charter of Rights and Freedoms* within the *Constitution Act, 1982*. Standing on the traditions of French civil law, British Westminster democracy, *The Royal Proclamation*,[15] and the regulations and legislation that flowed from these, the structural foundation for the official relationship between Canada and Indigenous people living within her boundaries is established. The Two-Row Wampum and the *Treaty of Niagara* are not, at time of writing, part of official Canadian government declarations of respected agreements.

Prior to 1830, Indigenous people in British North America (now Canada) were administered by a branch of the British military. Any alliances with First Nations were apparently solely for the purposes of military alliances, primarily against American continentalism.[16]

THE INDIAN ACT, 1876

Shortly after the formation of Canada in 1867, the *Indian Act* was established. Since its initial enactment, the *Indian Act* remains the primary law governing the relationship between Indigenous people as defined by the *Indian Act*, and the Canadian government. There is a list of who qualifies and how in the legislation. With its passage in 1876, the *Indian Act* consolidated the many pieces of legislation pertaining to the regulation and control of Indian people and Indian lands in Canada.[17] It is the only legislation in the world designed for a specific race of people. The document formally defines Indigenous people according to identity indicators established by the British government.[18] According to conflict scholar Stefan Wolff, "ethnicity, above all, means identity with one's own ethnic group" but the *Indian Act* removed collective identity to focus on individuals.[19] The *Indian Act* legislation, the 1857 *Gradual Enfranchisement for the Civilization of Indians Act*, and even the treaties established the legal and political identity "Indian" in Canada in terms that were virtually unrecognizable from the relationship accountabilities of the Two-Row Wampum, and the *Treaty of Niagara*. After 1876, traditional Indigenous ceremonies and practices like self-governance were forbidden or outlawed and Canadian legislation alone formally established the identity, governance, and even cultures of Indigenous people and nations, imposing a municipal-like Band Council elected leadership.[20] Nowhere in the *Indian Act* is a direct relationship between chiefs and the head of state (the Crown) and the head of government (prime minister) established.

There has been almost no meaningful change to the formal legislation since 1869. However, nearly a century and a half later, public awareness is slowly increasing regarding the gap in education levels, housing standards, and general health between Canadians and Indigenous people. Most Canadians did not know of these gaps, and many still are skeptical. Evidence of shocking and extreme poverty and other social ills in First Nations communities continue to emerge in media and in government reports,[21] with little meaningful government response.

OUTLAWING TRADITIONAL CEREMONIES AND SELF-GOVERNANCE

Traditional Indigenous cultures were self-defining and self-governing. Decisions were undertaken by the community as a whole through public gatherings and ceremonies. After Confederation, most Indigenous ceremonies were outlawed by the Canadian government. The assault on culture and customs focused on the Potlatch ceremony, recognized as the heart of Indigenous government, spiritual activity, and focal point of the community. A Methodist minister wrote to his annual conference in 1899, affirming the powerful role of the Potlatch as central to Indigenous life:

> No better description could be given of the Indian people than that supplied by the name they give themselves . . . truly they are a public people, for they have no private business, no private rights and no domestic privacy . . . . Every matter is regulated by a public manifestation of assent on the part of the united clans . . . Potlatch is a necessity from an Indian point of view in order to preserve the unity, distinctions and traditions of the race.[22]

For example, it was through the Potlatch ceremony that chiefs were chosen, decisions to relocate were made, and agreements or treaties with other

Indigenous nations were reviewed and accepted. Evidently, the deeply democratic and spiritual strengths of the Potlatch ceremonies were contrary to British interests in North America.[23] The Potlatch was outlawed from 1880 to 1951 under the prohibitions of the *Indian Act*.[24] Also in 1885, the prairie Sun Dance was outlawed, similarly important to prairie First Nations people as a form of self-governance, further dismantling Indigenous identity and damaging Indigenous relations with the Canadian government—and by extension—the Canadian people.

THE *NUMBERED TREATIES* OF THE WEST

As Canada expanded north and west into North America, government authorities established treaties with the leaders of the Indigenous First Nations. These treaties, especially Numbers 1-11 that cover the Canadian prairie, define land rights and distribution. Like wampum, these are covenants intended to stand "as long as the sun shines, the grass grows, and the rivers flow."[25] The treaties are stewardship agreements and are regarded as such today. In fact, the "Government of Canada and the courts understand treaties between the Crown and [Indigenous] people to be solemn agreements that set out promises, obligations, and benefits for both parties."[26] History suggests that Indigenous people did not perceive any threat to their identities or to their life upon the land, partly because imperial interests in land ownership were outside the philosophical paradigm of Indigenous people.[27] Also, since Indigenous people did not lose a war against the Europeans, nor consent to being governed by the French or the British, they did not recognize or experience loss of land rights through conquest—as international law prescribes necessary for the submission of one people group to another.[28] The treaties were and are very significant in the ongoing long conflict and Canada's reconciliation journey.

While Canadian legislation and some literature interpret the treaties as exchanges or ceding of land for other benefits provided by Canada, including ammunition and farm animals, this is not a universal acceptance. The meaning of the treaty relationship between Indigenous people and the rest of Canada and is a contested area of Canadian politics, despite current proclamations by government of the importance of the treaties to Canada's future. However, the signing of the treaties began a significant transition in First Nations identity, as people left a nomadic hunting lifestyle and moved to established land reserves to commence a primarily agriculture-based economy under the Band Council structure. Treaties and how they are interpreted remain important to understanding the Canadian conflict with Indigenous people and the challenges in our journey toward reconciliation.

During the late 1800s and early 1900s land was settled and eventually established Canada, but the relationship with Indigenous people seemed to diverge into one of false assumptions and failures from British and Canadian authorities. In 1920, prevailing assumptions were expressed by senior Canadian bureaucrat Duncan Campbell Scott before a special committee of Parliament: "Our objective is to continue until there is not a sing are long, complex, and multicau le Indian in Canada that has not been absorbed into the body politic and there is no Indian question, and no Indian Department."[29] This was consistent with ethnocentric attitudes and policies around the globe and across the British Empire promoting "displacement and assimilation, and new philosophies that trumpeted the superiority of 'civilized' Europeans over 'uncivilized', even 'savage', [Indigenous] people."[30] These words and their meanings are a departure from the covenant of the Two-Row Wampum of 1631 and the Niagara Treaty of 1874.

RESIDENTIAL SCHOOLS

In the 1880s, the Indian residential schools policy was enacted by the Canadian government. Although the policy was out-sourced to churches by government, its explicit intent was assimilation of Indigenous children into mainstream Canada. Over the years children were deliberately removed far from their families and communities, which disrupted the intergenerational socialization of families with the intention of integrating graduates into the nonIndigenous world.[31] The Royal Canadian Mounted Police routinely assisted in the forceful removal of children to the residential schools, and were also associated with the enforcement of curfews and cultural practice bans declared by government of the time. These traumas and negative associations have lingered trans-generationally in the consciences of many Indigenous people to the present day, embedding deep distrust in Canadian police services.

Residential schools were established in all but three Canadian provinces; the last school closed on the Canadian prairies in 1996. In total, approximately 150,000 First Nations students and nonIndigenous students attended the schools. This re-education of the young represents another core contribution to this conflict and to the complications of the contemporary Canadian political landscape for reconciliation. All Indigenous languages and practices were forbidden in the residential schools. The *Report of the RCAPs* is clear that the purpose of the residential school policy was to extinguish the language and culture of Canada's Indigenous population, a practice that continued in Canada for almost a century.[32] This policy direction was halted entirely in the 1980s, but it was not until 2007 that the *Truth and Reconciliation Commission of Canada,* (TRC) a recommendation of the 1996 *RCAP,* was established and began their investigation into the depth of pain and trauma caused to individual Indigenous people by the Indian residential schools policy.

EFFORTS TO ABOLISH THE *INDIAN ACT* IN 1969

The existence of the inequitable relationship between the Canadian government and Indigenous peoples potentially came to light for ordinary Canadians with the 1969 tabling of what has become known as *The White Paper.*[33] Five years earlier, the Hawthorne report to government had investigated the contemporary situation of the "Indians of Canada with a view to understanding the difficulties they faced in overcoming some pressing problems and their many ramifications."[34] *The White Paper* was based on the philosophical convictions of Prime Minister Pierre Trudeau that Canada must be a just society in which no people have a more privileged relationship with the Canadian government than others. Trudeau recommended and championed the repealing of the *Indian Act.* This would include the abolishment of all legal recognition of registered Indians (those with a special status, with the Canadian government), and the dissolution of all treaties. Trudeau's proposal was met with much controversy and remains a highly animated, though as yet unresolved, segment of Canadian political history. Responding with *Citizens Plus,*[35] also known as *The Red Paper,* in 1971 the chiefs of the Indian Association of Alberta explained the critical role of the treaties as relationship with Canada, and the need for a self-governance model that reflected Indigenous perspectives. Most importantly for Canada's reconciliation journey, the *Indian Act* was neither abolished nor significantly revised despite the careful articulations of Indigenous leaders at the time. Issues of self-governance and legal treaty recognition, central to the *Red Paper,* were ignored by the politicians leading the Canadian government for several more decades.

When Canadian federal governments want information, recommendations, and public recognition that they are undertaking action but are not necessarily committed to changes in policy, they will establish Royal Commissions. In 1996 Canada's government received a commissioned multithousand-page, five-volume report from the *RCAP,* which had been established five years earlier. The *Report* emphasized that Canadians know little about the conflict, or about the peaceful and cooperative relationship that grew up between Indigenous people and the first European visitors during the early years of contact in the seventeenth and eighteenth century. *The Report* also provided a graphic depiction of the difficult life circumstances of Canada's Indigenous people in the 1990s, and offered over sixty detailed recommendations toward a renewed and remedial relationship. These included profound Constitutional amendments and specific changes in areas that included health, education, mental health and healing, the family, and arts and heritage. *The Report* recommendations were basically ignored.

Writing in 2015, after five years of inquiry into the experiences and consequences of Indian residential schools policy, the TRC reported:

> In 1996, the *Report of the Royal Commission on Aboriginal Peoples* urged Canadians to begin a national process of reconciliation that would have set the country on a bold new path, fundamentally changing the very foundations of Canada's relationship with Aboriginal peoples. Much of what the Royal Commission had to say has been ignored by government; a majority of its recommendations were never implemented. But the report and its findings opened people's eyes and changed the conversation about the reality for Aboriginal people in this country.[36]

Though there was much passion and proclamation by government authorities within the Liberal government of the day and since, virtually no changes were implemented over the ten year period after the 1996 report, and government inertia further entrenched the need for authentic reconciliation.[37]

RECONCILING AN IDENTITY CONFLICT

Canada's current relationship with Indigenous Canada is recognized in peace and conflict studies literature as an identity conflict, and it is heartbreaking. This is a type of conflict that is particularly difficult to transform and to reconcile, and until what has happened in Canada's past and present is recognized as an identity conflict, it will be difficult to resolve, transform, or reconcile fully. Identity conflicts are not identity crises, but are unique and often difficult to identify until they are transforming, in part because they are long, complex, and multicausal.[38] Blame will not resolve the deep damages and harm of the people living in such identity conflicts; nor, frankly, will exposed "truth," though the opportunity to tell one's story to someone who actively listens has been proven to provide a path to authentic healing.[39] Individual and community healing is required, though broken hearts cannot be healed by government policy alone. Identity conflicts are deeply personal and communal. Scholar and widely respected peace practitioner Jay Rothman says "identity-driven conflicts are rooted in the articulation of, and the threats or frustrations to, people's collective need for dignity, recognition, safety, control, purpose, and efficacy,"[40] all of which have endured sustained attack by the policies of the federal governments of Canada since at least 1869.

Identity conflicts also remain within a structural framework that serves the purposes of one party, but not the other. In our case, the government has benefited while Indigenous people have suffered.[41] Identity conflict is also rooted in land. Conflict scholars have established the correlation between land and identity, especially for Indigenous people, though most land-owners would also concur that there is a correlation.[42] Often, land is closely tied to politics and identity and so becomes part of the conflict,[43] while helping us to understand why the interpretations of treaties and the potential abolition of the *Indian Act* continue to be contested.

Although some identity conflicts are not violent, lack of violent confrontation does not mean the conflict is not protracted or not to be acknowledged as serious, but only that it has not yet escalated to war. Canada has created an identity conflict. In our story, there has been foreign aggression, abuses of power, oppression, and unjust control, lack of autonomy, threats to self-rule and challenges to sovereignty, human rights abuses, and threats to identity or way of life, through the deliberate policy decisions of the Canadian government to act or not act. In these ways, it is evident that the historical relationship between Canada and Indigenous people is a protracted identity conflict. At the same time, in this analysis and acknowledgment are the kernels of hope.

Conflict transformation is about positive change, and although stubborn and very slow, identity conflicts have the potential to transform positively. The process includes periods of going backward, apparent stagnation, and going forward in relationships.[44] However, when change is thought of as a horizontal spiraling circle, there may be forward, desired movement, followed by an impasse, and may even include times when the change processes seem to be going backward, but importantly, "the circle recognizes that no point in time determines the broader pattern."[45] In this way, it may be recognized that Indigenous relations in Canada, despite potential setbacks, are transforming forward in a desired direction.

INDIGENOUS IDENTITY

At the core of our reconciliation journey is the matter of personal, communal, and national identity. Indigenous identity is land-based and spiritual. Prior to European contact, Indigenous societies were "self-reliant, socially coherent, healthy, and had a clear direction. They evidently thrived without welfare, without unemployment insurance, and without government transfer payments."[46] Other historical documents, including those recorded within the diaries of Europeans, reflect Indigenous nations as self-governing, sophisticated, and flourishing cultures with complex social structures.[47]

British colonial policies dismantled Indigenous culture and identity mostly by invalidating and outlawing social structures and institutions, and this continued after Canadian Confederation in 1867.[48] Democracy was used for control purposes.[49] Through the *Indian Act*, government imposed the Chief and Council, similar to municipal councils, and extremely different from the governance structures of the Potlatch and the Great Law of Peace. The democratic right to choose one's leadership was no longer undertaken by traditional processes of ceremony and full community participation by Indigenous people, but by electoral regulations outlined in the *Indian Act*.

A policy of relocating Indigenous people to land reserves distant from mainstream society and far from their original territories was also enacted under the authority of the *Indian Act*. Loss is also prevalent among one party in an identity conflict, and Indigenous culture and traditional ways began to submerge beneath the weight of so many losses. The establishment of reserves imposed the loss of home and belonging, loss of food sources, loss of spiritual places, loss of lifestyle, and loss of freedom.[50] During one period of Canadian history, in fact, Indigenous people could not leave their reserves without a form of "passport" issued by the Canadian government. The removal from the traditional lands and hunting grounds was devastating; "the most essential value, because it is the most meaningful, is first and foremost the land, which must provide bread and, naturally, dignity."[51] In these and many other ways, the colonization process established and entrenched identity conflict between the citizens and structures of Canadian democracy, and Indigenous people.

Government also maintained an implied threat of violence against settlers by displaced Indigenous people. Enemy-imaging of Indigenous people as "savages," as "uncivilized," and even as "warriors" throughout this period also served as a means of control and maintained inequality; Indigenous people were increasingly hidden from mainstream Canadians through legislation, policy, and geographical isolation.[52] For Indigenous people, traditional personal and cultural identity steadily eroded in the context of the evolving and increasingly regulated relationship with Canadian government structures.

The reserve structure, still in place today, attacks the foundations of Indigenous self-government. Only the chiefs communicate with government officials. This means that all power is centralized at the elite level, while community members remain voiceless and powerless.[53] There are no lines of accountability. There are still no checks and balances in the system today, and so the government structures on reserves are fair grounds for corruption, nepotism, and fiscal abuse.[54] At the same time, the establishment of chiefs and Band Councils as reserve leadership was deceptive; ultimate authority and permission really resided (and remains) in the nonpublicly accountable office of the Indian Agent (now a large bureaucracy headed by a cabinet minister appointed by the prime minister). In this way, entrenched structure maintained and still maintains a colonial relationship with Indigenous people, despite political promises, grandstanding by politicians, or public concern.[55]

POTENTIAL HARM

The *Report of RCAP* and the Kelowna Accord (formally *called First Ministers and National Aboriginal Leaders: Strengthening Relationships and Closing the Gap*) represent two initiatives by the Canadian government in the last twenty-five years that appeared to address the conflict and its attendant issues, but in reality, due to government inaction, did not shift power relations or provide concrete building blocks toward peace.[56] Although the *Royal Commission Report* provided Canadian Parliament with startling data, information, statistics, and recommendations, firm action was not forthcoming in policy directions.[57] Scholars suggest that another benign response to the Commission is evidence of the unwillingness of the Canadian governments of the day to genuinely reconcile the conflict, leading to more harm and a further entrenchment of the identity conflict.[58]

Ten years after the recommendations of the *RCAP*, in 2006, the Kelowna Accord was heralded by the Canadian government and media at the time as unique in its degree of involvement from national and Indigenous leaders. The goal of the collaborations, according to then Prime Minister Paul Martin, was to address five key areas: education, health, housing, drinking water, and economic development, and to "make a real difference."[59] Ironically applicable, peace and conflict studies scholar Ho-Won Jeong states that "strategies for transforming conflict dynamics cannot simply rely on the assumption that improved communication and changed perceptions [will] put parties on an equal basis,"[60] yet it seems that such arrogance were the strategies leveraged by the Canadian government.

Despite promises to allocate $5.1 billion toward carefully articulated and identified Indigenous issues, the potential for further mistrust, deeper identity conflict, and even violence emerged as it became apparent that there was no money allocated by government in the federal budget to fulfill these promises.[61] After many years of promises for change that did not come, the reign of the Liberal government ended in late 2006.[62] Although the consultations leading to the Accord have been heralded as "unique in Canadian history,"[63] in fact none of the structures or underlying conflicts presented in this paper were materially addressed during the tenure of the outgoing government that promised to address them. Research has evidenced that "the root causes of ethnic conflict cannot be wished away" and real action is required for reconciliation.[64] There are specific conditions and goals in order to address conflict adequately and appropriately.[65] When conditions do not converge, "the effort fails,"[66] and the conflict is entrenched more deeply by interpretations of disingenuousness.[67]

However, while they did not produce any real change for Indigenous people and communities, nor did they address the Canadian identity conflict, both the *Kelowna Accord* and the *Royal Commission* raised awareness across the country for the general population. The processes of the *Accord* and of the *Royal Commission* provided legitimate forums for constructive storytelling and community construction for Indigenous people, and were helpful and important to transformation.[68] According to scholars, these may be recognized as creating conditions that contribute toward conflict de-escalation.[69]

GOVERNMENT EFFORTS AND RECONCILIATION

In 2006 the new Government of Canada undertook deliberate action with public statements to acknowledge their responsibility in the conflict, tangible reparations for Indigenous people, and spoke the language of meaningful reconciliation. When voters elected a Conservative government in 2006, despite no precise statements toward Indigenous reconciliation during the election campaign deliberate, constructive transformation began to emerge quietly through public policy and through the leadership of the Canadian government under Prime Minister Stephen Harper. Interestingly, and with the astute observation of hindsight, this coincided with the efforts of similar leadership systems in other global efforts in former British colonies toward racial reconciliation, in particular New Zealand, Ghana, Botswana, and the United States.[70]

Under the leadership of Prime Minister Stephen Harper, Canada formally but quietly began to take action. This included three actions that, according to esteemed scholarship, are significant for reconciliation.[71] These actions were the Parliamentary approval of money to be released from the Canadian Treasury Board (budgeted and approved) as compensation for ills, a public apology, and genuinely inclusive consultations with Indigenous leaders for legislative change. These events, beginning in early 2007, began to transform the entrenched and seemingly intractable identity conflict toward peace and with justice. According to peace scholarship, the state is a logical form for addressing core causes of identity conflict and structural conflict.[72] That the Harper government undertook concrete action is important to understanding the transformation of this conflict. Historically and in recent decades, the Canadian government has only promised, not acted.

Although "there is no 'uniform' theory of reparations that fits all cultures, all nations, and all peoples,"[73] there is an emerging literature exploring reparation and redress for historical harms.[74] Significant for peace and conflict studies, the Apology was issued between two other postcolonial national apologies in three former British colonies. In addition to Canada's Apology, the New Zealand Apology to Vietnam veterans for postwar treatment was issued in May 2008, and the American House of Representatives Apology for US Slavery and Jim Crow Laws was issued in July 2008.

According to researcher and scholar Robert Weyeneth, there are two elements of an apology that are critical for reconciliation: apology and forgiveness.[75] The federal Apology meets both criteria. In Canada, on June 11, 2008, the prime minister, as the leader of Canada's government, and in many ways the many histories of Canada, rose in the House of Commons (Canada's center of government). Reading a speech he had allegedly written himself, the prime minister humbly asked forgiveness from the Indigenous people for the Canadian Indian residential schools policy. In part, he said,

> You have been working on recovering from this experience for a long time, and in a very real sense we are now joining you on this journey. The Government of Canada sincerely apologizes and asks the forgiveness of the aboriginal peoples of this country for failing them so profoundly.[76]

Evident in the Apology is a key element of reconciliation: the responsibility of the Canadian governments over time in the pain of identity loss. The full text of the Apology is reproduced at the end of this chapter as Appendix A.

The prime minister's Apology also contained Weyeneth's second crucial component: the recognition that one has been in the wrong. The prime minister did not justify or offer excuses for the actions of the Canadian government toward Indigenous people, he stated "we were wrong,"[77] and asked forgiveness. Also important to resolving identity conflict, the prime minister closed his Apology with "We are sorry" in five languages: Canada's two official languages (French and English) and in the dominant Indigenous languages of the land. The Apology was accepted on behalf of all Indian people by leaders of Canada's Indigenous groups.

Additionally, the payment of reparations is apology in material form.[78] Significantly, monetary reparations were sent to residential school survivors by the government before the national apology, lending significance and sincerity to the prime minister's statements while addressing some of the underlying consequences of the conflict. Apologies have been used historically to diffuse potentially volatile situations, and so in Canada's case the federal Apology might be seen as a tipping point in conflict management. The action has great potential toward reconciliation because of the involvement of leadership.[79] The Apology was offered by the country's national leader, and accepted by Indigenous leadership by the Grand Chief of the Assembly of First Nations (AFN) on behalf of all Indigenous people. One other notable distinctive of the Apology is that it accepted responsibility, which is also important toward reconciliation.[80] Although the actions were undertaken and accepted by officials and elites (and rejected by some nonleaders), according to scholars important criteria for reconciliation were met.

Another significant action of the Canadian government was the actual flow of dollars from the Canadian Treasury. Like the individual monetary settlement for former students of residential schools, the release of federal dollars for Indigenous communities also represents material apology. In the timeframe between his election and Harper's Apology, over $700 million was designated in the federal budget and released from the Treasury Board directly to Band governments for the restructuring of reserve institutions.[81] There was a notable absence of these releases in the Canadian media. Research regarding the role of the mass media in conflict perpetuation and the potential role for the media in conflict transformation remains a field of great potential for study on our reconciliation journey.

The payment of reparations in material form and the acknowledgment of responsibility mean that the delivery and acceptance of the Apology is a pivotal transformation point for this conflict and the first meaningful, tangible effort by government toward healing, restoration, and reconciliation.

THE TRUTH AND RECONCILIATION COMMISSION, 2015

One of the strong recommendations of the 1996 *RCAP* was the establishment of a Royal Commission to inquire into the experiences of people with the federal government *Indian residential school policy,* especially those who had been students. Those still alive are collectively recognized in Canada as "residential school survivors," or "survivors." A Statement of Reconciliation was established in 1998, but it was another eight years, a change of government, and a new Conservative prime minister in Canada before the Commission was actually established.

Established in June 2008, TRC was one of the mandated aspects of the 2006 *Indian Residential Schools Settlement Agreement* (IRSSA), with a $60 million budget over five years. The guiding principles were very clear, and determined collaboratively with Indigenous people:

> accessible; victim-centered; confidentiality (if required by the former student); do no harm; health and safety of participants; representative; public/transparent; accountable; open and honourable process; comprehensive; inclusive, educational, holistic, just and fair; respectful; voluntary; flexible; and forward looking

in terms of rebuilding and renewing Aboriginal relationships and the relationship between Aboriginal and non-Aboriginal Canadians.[82]

The Harper government established the TRC, but since it was led by nonIndigenous leaders, there was a great deal of controversy and eventually three Indigenous leaders were appointed as the Commissioners. These three led the Commission for five years and provided a compelling, six-volume *Final Report* to Canadian Parliament in 2015. The stories within the report are disturbing windows into deep personal and communal wrongs. In addition to the Report were ninety-four *Calls to Action* intended to guide the reconstruction of the relationship with Indigenous people.

Until the *Indian Act* is changed, overhauled, or repealed, the structural legislative foundations for the conflict remain largely intact. According to the tenets of democracy, any movement toward reconciliation remains at the mercy and political processes of the Canadian government as the country's leadership. However, First Nations leadership at the AFN seems to be emerging out of a colonized paradigm into a unified voice to positively articulate both basic and social needs for Indigenous people, also critical for conflict transformation.[83] The policy platform of the AFN is described as two main thrusts: "Reconciliation and recognition of First Nations governments affirming treaty and Aboriginal rights, consistent with Section 35, *Constitution Act, 1982*"; and "sustainability and structural change" which includes change in the fiscal relationship, nation-building support and "federal policy renewal . . . in the form of the elimination of the *Indian Act*" (AFN, 2014). This suggests that Indigenous people are building a new, transformed, and stronger identity apart from the structures of British North America.

Timing is critical in reconciliation, and active leadership of the AFN and of the Canadian government coincided to create a window of opportunity for transformation and reconciliation that both parties have found the courage to seize. According to ethnic conflict scholar Stefan Wolff, "the key is for individual leaders to recognize and use the opportunities that exist for settling their differences without recourse to violence."[84] This has been notable among First Nations leaders and in former Canadian prime minister Stephen Harper, as demonstrated in particular through the Apology and through monetary reparation and redress.

CONCLUSION

The story of Indigenous relations with Canada is a long story, now indicating evidence of potentially permanent transformation. There have been catalysts within the early years of the new millennium toward building respectful and responsible peace, as the core causes of identity conflict are patiently addressed through careful and purposeful leadership.[85] The next phase will require structural change. The *Indian Act* has been and continues to be the primary structural tool used to deconstruct Indigenous identity. As the last century and a half has passed, the relationship between Canadian government and Indigenous people was primarily framed to justify the policies of domination and assimilation; but the greatest challenge has been the determined unwillingness of government to pursue reconciliation, and its preference for meaningless, expensive government restructuring, and hollow rhetoric.

The processes that led to the *Report of the RCAP* and the *Kelowna Accord* are significant recent developments in the conflict. According to scholars, conflict could have escalated due to words without action on the part of the Liberal government. Instead, after a symbolic and material apology by the Conservative prime minister for the wrongness of the assimilation policies, there has been evidence that leaders in Canada and among people at all levels of Indigenous Canada are willing to engage in toward reconciliation.

But our future is still veiled. In 2015, Liberal prime minister Justin Trudeau made much fanfare of the costly changing the name of the federal department that manages Canada's Indigenous people. The department has an annual budget of close to $10 billion. Crown–Indigenous Relations and Northern Affairs is the new name (an apparent nod to the *Royal Proclamation*). Trudeau claimed that during his time in office that he would ensure all ninety-four Calls to Action of the *Truth and Reconciliation Final Report* would be implemented. We all felt hope.

To date, his record has been very poor and Indigenous reconciliation was not one of the political issues of his 2019 federal election campaign, from which he was reelected. Instead, Canada is deeply divided. This is discouraging. Although this chapter has explored the role of the federal government, reconciliation is at work at different levels of Canadian society, as presented in the following chapters of this book.

Canada's story stands in the context of a growing global climate toward reconciliation and redress of harm often related to imperialism, but some Canadian and Indigenous leaders over the past decade have decisively pursued the reparations of the past in Canada with courage and strength, and this must be recognized. We know that the process of change is circular, meaning that there may be setbacks, and at times, stagnation.[86] Reconciliation, according to scholars and practitioners, "must be proactive in seeking to create an encounter where people can focus on their relationship and share their perceptions, feeling, and experiences with one another, with the goal of creating new perceptions and a new shared future."[87]

But the actions undertaken this far in Canada, in particular the 2008 Apology and the efforts of the *Truth and Reconciliation* Commissioners to truly hear the stories of those who have suffered suggest that for the first time in recorded history, peace with justice may be taking its first fragile steps. We are witnessing some leaders of Canadian government attempting to undo the wrongs of the past as much as a government is able to heal broken hearts. Courage and strength for real reconciliation at all levels of Canadian society will provide hope, change, and transformation, and build a strong, shared future for all of us that call Canada home.

NOTES

1. "Aboriginal" is the contemporary conventional and *Constitutional* term for the collective recognition of approximately 1.1 million Indigenous people in Canada, and is used similarly to include First Nations, Inuit, Métis, and non-Status Indians. Although these are Indigenous people, they are not one people group. However, Canadian democracy has and does legally identify all these people as "Aboriginal," but only "First Nations" and now Métis people maintain a distinct relationship with the Canadian government and are legally what early legislation identifies as "Indians" as detailed in *The Indian Act*. For an extensive discussion of Canada's Indigenous people, cultures and traditions, and the relationships between the groups, see http://www.aadnc-aandc.gc.ca/eng/1100100013785/1304467449155

2. Royal Commission on Aboriginal Peoples, *Report of the Royal Commission on Aboriginal Peoples, Volume 1: Looking Forward Looking Back* (Ottawa, ON: Canada Communication, 1996) 7.

3. John Paul Lederach, *Building Peace: Sustainable Reconciliation in Divided Societies* (Washington, DC: United States Institute of Peace Press, 1997), 35.

4. David A. Price, *Love & Hate in Jamestown* (New York, NY: Vintage Books, 2003)

5. There are earlier records of ongoing contest with the Spanish, but the current claims to North America and relational conflict originated with the British and the settlement at Chesapeake Bay, Virginia, in approximately 1604. See for example, Price, *Love & Hate,* 8–29.

6. The five nations of the Haudenosaunee (Iroquois) Confederacy at that time are recognized as by their anglicized names: the Seneca, Oneida, Mohawk, Onondaga, and Cayuga.

7. John Borrows, "Wampum at Niagara: The Royal Proclamation, Canadian Legal History, and Self-Government," in *Aboriginal and Treaty Rights in Canada: Essays on Law, Equality, and Respect for Difference* (Vancouver: University of British Columbia Press, 1997), 155–172, https://www.sfu.ca/~palys/Borrows-WampumAtNiagara.pdf

8. Onandaga Nation, Two-Row Wampum-Guswenta, 2019, https://www.onondaganation.org/culture/wampum/two-row-wampum-belt-guswenta/

9. Indian and Northern Affairs Canada, 1996, Volume 1, Chapter 1, paragraph 17.

10. Stefan Wolff, *Ethnic Conflict: A Global Perspective* (New York, NY: Oxford University Press, 2006), 64.

11. Lederach, *Building Peace,* 31.

12. Borrows, "Wampum at Niagara," 155-172.

13. Calvin Helin, *Dances with Dependency: indigenous Success through Self-Reliance* (Vancouver, BC: Orca Spirit Publishing, 2006).

14. See *The Royal Proclamation, 1763.* English text available at https://www.aadnc-aandc.gc.ca/eng/1370355181092/1370355203645

15. *The Royal Proclamation* has been acknowledged as "a foundational document in the relationship between First Nations people and the Crown and laid the basis for Canada's territorial evolution." Indigenous and Northern Affairs Canada, https://www.aadnc-aandc.gc.ca/eng/1370355181092/1370355203645, line 1.

16. Stephen Brooks, *Canadian Democracy* (New York, NY: Oxford University Press, 2007), 25.

17. Helin, *Dances.*

18. Assembly of First Nations, 2014; Indian and Northern Affairs Canada, 1996.

19. Wolff, *Ethnic Conflict,* 31.

20. Harold Cardinal and Walter Hildebrandt, *Treaty Elders of Saskatchewan: Our Dream Is That Our Peoples Will One Day Be Clearly Recognized as Nations* (Calgary, AB: University of Calgary, 2000).

21. Indian and Northern Affairs Canada, 1996.

22. John McCullagh, "The Indian Potlatch: Substance of a Paper Read Before C.M.S. Annual Conference at Metlakatla, B.C." (Toronto, ON: Woman's Missionary Society of the Methodist Church, 1899): n.p. Accessed November 26, 2019, http://www.canadiana.org.

23. Homer Barnett, "The Nature of the Potlatch." *American Anthropologist* 40–3: 1938, 349–358.

24. Allan Cairns, "The Potlatch Papers: A Colonial Case History (Review)." *Journal of Interdisciplinary History* 30–2 (1999): 357–360.

25. Aboriginal Affairs and Northern Development Canada, *Treaty Guide to Treaty Number 8* (2010a), http://www.aadnc-aandc.gc.ca/; Aboriginal Affairs and Northern Development Canada. *Treaties with Aboriginal People* (2010b), http://www.aadnc-aandc.gc.ca/.

26. Aboriginal Affairs and Northern Development Canada, *Treaties with Aboriginal People.*

27. Helin, *Dances.*

28. Ibid.

29. Indian and Northern Affairs Canada, *Report of the Royal Commission on Aboriginal Peoples: Looking Forward, Looking Back* (Ottawa, ON: Canada Communication Group, Volume 5, Chapter 13, paragraph 1.

30. INAC, *Report of the Royal Commission on Aboriginal Peoples*, paragraph 8.

31. INAC, *Report of the Royal Commission on Aboriginal Peoples.*

32. INAC.

33. The Statement of the Government of Canada on Indian Policy (The White Paper). Accessed July 16, 2019, https://www.aadnc-aandc.gc.ca/eng/1100100010189/1100100010191

34. HB Hawthorn, Ed, *A Survey of the Contemporary Indians of Canada: A Report on Economic, Political and Educational Needs and Policies in Two Volumes* (Indian Affairs Branch, Ottawa: 1966), http://caid.ca/HawRep1a1966.pdf

35. See Aboriginal Policy Studies, https://journals.library.ualberta.ca/aps/index.php/aps/article/view/11690.

36. Truth and Reconciliation Commission, *Truth and Reconciliation Commission Final Report: Canadian Residential Schools,* Volume 6 (TRC.CA: 2015), 3.

37. Jay Rothman, *Resolving Identity-Based Conflict in Nations, Organizations, and Communities* (San Francisco, CA: Thousand Oaks, 1997), 11.

38. Peter Black, "Identities," in *Conflict: From Analysis to Intervention,* ed. Sandra Cheldelin, Daniel Druckman, and Larissa Fast (New York: Continuum, 2003); Celia Cook-Huffman, "The Role of Identity in Conflict," in *Handbook of Conflict Analysis and Resolution,* ed. Dennis Sandole, Sean Byrne, Ingrid Sandole-Staroste, and Jessica Senehi (London, UK, 2008): 17–29; Rothman, *Resolving Identity-based Conflicts in Nations, Organizations, and Communities,* 7; Taras and Ganguly, 2010; William W. Wilmot and Joyce Hocker, *Interpersonal Conflict*. 8th ed. (New York, NY: McGraw-Hill, 2007); Wolff, *Ethnic Conflict*.

39. Laura E. Reimer, "Transformative Research: Mindful Design for and as Conflict Resolution." *Peace Research: The Canadian Journal of Peace and Conflict Studies* 47, nos. 1–2 (2015): 85–108.

40. Rothman, *Resolving Identity-based Conflicts in Nations, Organizations, and Communities,* 7.

41. Ho-Won Jeong, *Peace and Conflict Studies: An Introduction* (Hants, UK: Ashgate Publishing. 2000).

42. Judy Carter, "Lessons to Ponder: Insights and Advice from the Front Lines," in *Regional and Ethnic Conflicts: Perspectives from the Front Lines,* ed. Judy Carter, George Irani, and Vamik Volkan. (Upper Saddle River, NJ: Pearson Prentice Hall, 2009).

43. Carter, "Lessons to Ponder," 304.

44. John Paul Lederach, *The Little Book of Conflict Transformation: Clear Articulation of the Guiding Principles by a Pioneer in the Field* (Intercourse, PA: Good Books, 2003), 2003.

45. Lederach, *Little Book of Conflict Transformation,* 43.

46. Helin, *Dances,* 66.

47. Helin, *Dances*; Paul W. Wallace, *The White Roots of Peace: Iroquois Book of Life* (Saranac Lake, NY: Chauncy Press, 1986).

48. Franz Fanon, *The Wretched of the Earth,* translated by R. Philcox (New York, NY: Grove Press, 2004) (Original work published in 1963).

49. Johan Galtung, "Structural Theory of Imperialism." *Journal of Peace Research* 8, no. 2 (1971): 81–117.

50. Darien Thira, "Beyond the Four Waves of Colonization." Accessed December 7, 2019, http://www.swaraj.org/fourwaves.htm.

51. Fanon, *Wretched of the Earth,* 9.

52. Beverly Crawford, "The Causes of Cultural Conflict: An Institutional Approach," in *The Myth of "Ethnic Conflict,"* ed. Beverly Crawford and Ronnie D

Lipschutz (Berkeley, CA: University of California at Berkeley, 1998), 1; Galtung, "Structural Theory"; Indigenous and Northern Affairs Canada, 1996.

53. Jean Allard, "Big Bear's Treaty: The Road to Freedom," *Inroads* 11(2002): 108–167.

54. Allard, "Big Bear's Treaty."

55. Wallace, *White Roots*.

56. Jeong, *Peace and Conflict,* 2000.

57. Indigenous and Northern Affairs Canada, 1996.

58. Ho-Won Jeong, "Peace Building in Identity Driven Ethnopolitical Conflicts," in *Reconcilable Differences: Turning points in Ethnopolitical Conflict*, ed. Sean Byrne and Cynthia Irvin, assoc. ed. P. Dixon, Brian Polkinghorn, and Jessica Senehi (West Hartford, CT: Kumarian Press); Wolff, *Ethnic Conflict*.

59. Lisa Patterson, *Aboriginal Roundtable to Kelowna Accord: Aboriginal Policy Negotiations 2004–2006* (Ottawa, ON: Library of Parliament, Parliamentary Information and Research Division, 2006). Accessed December 8, 2019, http://www.parl.gc.ca/information/library/PRBpubs/prb0604-e.htm

60. Jeong, *Peace and Conflict,* 37.

61. Patterson, "Roundtable."

62. Ibid.

63. Metro Coalition for a Non-Racist Society, "The Kelowna Accord: Closing the Gap?" Accessed November 26, 2008, http://www.chebucto.ns.ca/CommunitySupport/MCNRS/AboriginalRightsPanel/KelownaAccordBackgrounder_short.pdf

64. Metro Coalition, "Kelowna Accord," 206.

65. Louis Kriesberg, "Policy Continuity and Change." *Social Problems* 32–2 (1984): 89–102; Patrick G. Coy and Lynne M. Woehrle, *Social Conflicts and Collective Identities* (Lanham, MD: Rowman & Littlefield, 2000).

66. Kriesberg, "Policy Continuity," 97; Wolff, *Ethnic Conflict*; Carter, "Lessons to Ponder."

67. Carter, "Lessons to Ponder."

68. Sean Byrne and Cynthia Irvin, eds., *Reconcilable Differences: Turning Points in Ethnopolitical Conflict* (West Hartford, CT: Kumarian, 2000).

69. Jeong, *Peace and Conflict*; Kriesberg, "Policy Continuity."

70. Kwadu Osei-Hwedie and Morena J. Rankopo, "Indigenous Conflict in Africa: The Case of Ghana and Botswana," in *Cultural Bases of Conflict, Conflict Resolution and Peacebuilding in Africa*, ed. Kwaku Osei-Hwedie and Morena J. Rankopo (University of Botswana: Gabarone, BW, 2010); University of Waterloo, n.d.

71. Robert Weyeneth, "The Power of Apology and the Process of Historical Reconciliation." *The Public Historian* 23–3 (2001): 9–38.a.

72. Byrne and Irvin, *Reconcilable Differences,* 117; Carter, "Lessons to Ponder."

73. Rebecca Tsosie, "Acknowledging the Past to Heal the Future: The Role of Reparations for Native Nations." *Reparations: Interdisciplinary Inquiries* (2007): 43.

74. See for example Chris Cunneen, "Colonialism and Historical Injustice: Reparations for indigenous Peoples." *Social Semiotics* 15, no. 1 (2005): 59–80; Konstantin Petoukhov, "Recognition, Redistribution, and Representation: Assessing the Transformative Potential of Reparations for the Indian Residential Schools Experience."

McGill Sociological Review 3 (2013): 73–91; Margaret Urban Walker, "Truth Telling as Reparations." *Metaphilosophy* 41, no. 4 (2010): 525–545.

75. Weyeneth, "The Power of Apology."

76. Prime Minister Stephen Harper, *Statement of Apology*, 2008, Accessed December 8, 2019, https://www.thecanadianencyclopedia.ca/en/article/government-apology-to-former-students-of-indian-residential-schools

77. Harper, *Apology.*

78. Weyeneth, "The Power of Apology."

79. Byrne and Irvin, *Reconcilable Differences.*

80. Weyeneth, "The Power of Apology."

81. Indigenous and Northern Affairs Canada, 2009.

82. Working Group on Truth and Reconciliation and of the Exploratory Dialogues (1998–1999), *Statement of Reconciliation*, January 7, 1999, http://www.trc.ca/about-us/our-mandate.html

83. John Burton, "The Resolution of Conflict." *International Studies Quarterly* 16–1 (1972): 5–29.

84. Wolff, *Ethnic Conflict,* 40.

85. Terrance Northrup, "The Dynamic of Identity in Personal and Social Conflict," in *Intractable Conflicts and Their Transformation* (Syracuse, NY: Syracuse University Press, 1989), 55–82, 155; Rothman, *Resolving Identity-based Conflict,* 7; Wolff, *Ethnic Conflict,* 2.

86. Lederach, *Little Book.*

87. Lederach, *Building Peace,* 30.

BIBLIOGRAPHY

Aboriginal Affairs and Northern Development Canada. (2010a) *Treaty Guide to Treaty Number 8.* http://www.aadnc-aandc.gc.ca/

Aboriginal Affairs and Northern Development Canada. (2010b). *Treaties with Aboriginal People.* http://www.aadnc-aandc.gc.ca/

Allard, Jean. "Big Bear's Treaty: The Road to Freedom." *Inroads* 11 (2002): 108–167.

Assembly of First Nations. Accessed January 14, 2014, http://www.afn.ca/article.asp?id=3.

Barnett, H. "The Nature of the Potlatch." *American Anthropologist* 40–3 (1938): 349–358.

Black, Peter. "Identities." In *Conflict: From Analysis to Intervention.* Ed. Sandra Cheldelin, Daniel Druckman, and Larissa Fast (New York: Continuum, 2003).

Brooks, Stephen. *Canadian Democracy* (5th ed.). (Toronto, ON: Oxford, 2007).

Burton, John. "The Resolution of Conflict." *International Studies Quarterly* 16–1 (1972): 5–29.

Byrne, Sean and Cynthia Irvin. Eds., *Reconcilable Differences: Turning Points in Ethnopolitical Conflict* (West Hartford, CT: Kumarian, 2000).

Cairns, Allan. "The Potlatch Papers: A Colonial Case History (Review)." *Journal of Interdisciplinary History* 30–2 (1999): 357–360.

Canada. *The Indian Act*, 1880–1985. Justice Laws. Accessed December 8, 2019, https ://laws-lois.justice.gc.ca/eng/acts/i-5/.

Cardinal Harold and Walter Hildebrandt. *Treaty Elders of Saskatchewan: Our Dream Is That Our Peoples Will One Day Be Clearly Recognized as Nations* (Calgary, AB: University of Calgary, 2000).

Carter, Judy. "Lessons to Ponder: Insights and Advice from the Front Lines." In *Regional and Ethnic Conflicts: Perspectives from the Front Lines*. Ed. Judy Carter, George Irani, and Vamik Volkan (Upper Saddle River, NJ: Pearson Prentice Hall, 2009).

Carter, Judy, George Irani, and Vamik Volkan (Eds). *Regional and Ethnic Conflicts: Perspectives from the Front Lines* (Upper Saddle River, NJ: Pearson Prentice Hall, 2009).

Cook-Huffman, Celia. "The Role of Identity in Conflict." In *Handbook of Conflict Analysis and Resolution*. Ed. Dennis Sandole, Sean Byrne, Ingrid Sandole-Staroste, and Jessica Senehi (London, UK: 2008), 17–29.

Coy, Patrick G. and Lynne M. Woehrle. *Social Conflicts and Collective Identities* (Lanham, MD: Rowman & Littlefield, 2000).

Crawford, Beverly. "The Causes of Cultural Conflict: An Institutional Approach." In *The Myth of "Ethnic Conflict."* Ed. Beverly Crawford and Ronnie D Lipschutz (Berkeley, CA: University of California at Berkeley, 1998).

Crawford, Beverly. "The Causes of Cultural Conflict: Assessing the Evidence." In *The Myth of "Ethnic Conflict."* Ed. Beverly Crawford and Ronnie D. Lipschutz (Berkeley, CA: University of California at Berkeley, 1998).

Cunneen, Chris. "Colonialism and Historical Injustice: Reparations for indigenous Peoples." *Social Semiotics* 15, no. 1 (2005): 59–80.

Fanon, Franz. *The Wretched of the Earth*. Translated by R. Philcox (New York, NY: Grove Press, 2004). (Original work published in 1963).

Friesen, Rudy. "Reflections on Oka: The Mohawk Confrontation." *Conflict Resolution Notes* 8, no. 4 (1991): 36–38. Accessed December 8, 2019, https://www.beyondintractability.org/artsum/friesen-reflections

Galtung, Johan. "Structural Theory of Imperialism." *Journal of Peace Research* 8, no. 2 (1971): 81–117.

Harper, Stephen. Prime Minister of Canada. "Statement of Apology," June 10, 2008. Accessed December 8, 2019, https://www.thecanadianencyclopedia.ca/en/article/government-apology-to-former-students-of-indian-residential-schools

Helin, Calvin. *Dances with Dependency: indigenous Success Through Self-Reliance* (Vancouver, BC: Orca Spirit Publishing, 2006).

Indigenous and Northern Affairs Canada. *Report of the Royal Commission on Aboriginal Peoples: Looking Forward, Looking Back* (Ottawa, ON: Canada Communication Group, 1996).

Indigenous and Northern Affairs Canada. *Statement of Apology*. Accessed December 8, 2019, https://www.aadnc-aandc.gc.ca/eng/1100100015644/1100100015649.

Jeong, Ho-Won. *Peace and Conflict Studies: An Introduction* (Hants, UK: Ashgate Publishing, 2000).

Jeong, Ho-Won. "Peace Building in Identity Driven Ethnopolitical Conflicts." In *Reconcilable Differences: Turning Points in Ethnopolitical Conflict*. Ed. Sean

Byrne and Cynthia Irvin. Assoc. Ed. Peter Dixon, Brian Polkinghorn, and Jessica Senehi (West Hartford, CT: Kumarian Press, 2000).

Kriesberg, Louis. "Policy Continuity and Change." *Social Problems* 32–2 (1984): 89-102.

Lederach, John Paul. *Preparing for Peace: Conflict Transformation across Cultures* (Syracuse, NY: Syracuse University Press, 1995).

Lederach, John Paul. *Building Peace: Sustainable Reconciliation in Divided Societies* (Washington, DC: United States Institute of Peace, 1997).

Lederach, John Paul. *The Little Book of Conflict Transformation: Clear Articulation of the Guiding Principles by a Pioneer in the Field* (Intercourse, PA: Good Books, 2003).

Martin, Paul. House of Commons speech on the *Kelowna Accord Implementation Act*. 2006. Accessed May 4, 2013, http://www.paulmartin.ca/en/speeches-20060602-1.

McCullagh, John. "The Indian Potlatch. Substance of a Paper Read before C.M.S. Annual Conference at Metlakatla, B.C." (Toronto, ON: Woman's Missionary Society of the Methodist Church, 1899). Accessed November 26, 2019, http://www.canadiana.org.

Moore, Christopher and Peter J. Woodrow, "Collaborative Problem Solving within Organizations." In *The Consensus Building Handbook: A Comprehensive Guide to Reaching Agreement*, Ed. Lawrence Susskind, Sarah McKearnana, Jennifer Thomas-Larmer (Thousand Oaks, CA; Sage, 1999), 591–630.

Metro Coalition for a Non-Racist Society. The Kelowna Accord: Closing the Gap? 2006. Accessed November 26, 2008, http://www.chebucto.ns.ca/CommunitySupport/MCNRS/AboriginalRightsPanel/KelownaAccordBackgrounder_short.pdf.

National Aboriginal Database. 2009. Accessed December 29, 2010, http://epe.lacbac.gc.ca/100/205/301/ic/cdc/aboriginaldocs/m-stat.htm.

Northrup, Terrance A. "The Dynamic of Identity in Personal and Social Conflict." In *Intractable Conflicts and Their Transformation* (Syracuse, NY: Syracuse University Press, 1989), 55–82.

Osei-Hwedie, Kwaku and Morena J. Rankopo, M. "Indigenous Conflict in Africa: The Case of Ghana and Botswana." In *Cultural Bases of Conflict, Conflict Resolution and Peacebuilding in Africa*. Ed. Kwaku Osei-Hwedie and Morena J. Rankopo (University of Botswana: Gabarone, BW, 2010).

Patterson, Lisa. "Aboriginal Roundtable to Kelowna Accord: Aboriginal Policy Negotiations 2004–2006." (Ottawa, ON: Library of Parliament, Parliamentary Information and Research Division, 2006). Accessed December 8, 2019. http://www.parl.gc.ca/information/library/PRBpubs/prb0604-e.htm

Petoukhov, Konstantin. "Recognition, Redistribution, and Representation: Assessing the Transformative Potential of Reparations for the Indian Residential Schools Experience." *McGill Sociological Review* 3 (2013): 73–91.

Reimer, Laura E. "Transformative Research: Mindful Design for and as Conflict Resolution." *Peace Research: The Canadian Journal of Peace and Conflict Studies* 47, no. 1–2 (2015): 85–108.

Rothman, Jay. *Resolving Identity-based Conflicts in Nations, Organizations, and Communities* (San Francisco, CA: Jossey-Bass, 1997).

Taras and Ganguly, 2010; William W. Wilmot and Joyce Hocker, *Interpersonal Conflict*. 8th ed. (New York, NY: McGraw-Hill, 2007).

Thira, Darien. "Beyond the Four Waves of Colonization." Accessed December 7, 2019. http://www.swaraj.org/fourwaves.htm

Thomas, Murray R. "Can Money Undo the Past? A Canadian Example." *Comparative Education* 39–3 (2003): 331–343.

Tsosie, Rebecca. "Acknowledging the Past to Heal the Future: The Role of Reparations for Native Nations." *Reparations: Interdisciplinary Inquiries* (2007): 43–68.

University of Waterloo. *Public Apology Database* (CCM Lab: University of Waterloo, Waterloo, ON, n.d.).

Walker, Margaret Urban. "Truth Telling as Reparations." *Metaphilosophy* 41, no. 4 (2010): 525–545.

Wallace, Paul W. *The White Roots of Peace: Iroquois Book of Life* (Saranac Lake, NY: Chauncy Press, 1986).

Wilmot, William W. and Joyce Hocker. *Interpersonal Conflict*, 8th ed. (New York, NY: McGraw-Hill, 2007).

Wolff, Stefan. *Ethnic Conflict: A Global Perspective* (New York, NY: Oxford University Press, 2006).

Working Group on Truth and Reconciliation and of the Exploratory Dialogues (1998–1999), *Statement of Reconciliation*, January 7, 1999. Accessed December 8, 2019. http://www.trc.ca/about-us/our-mandate.html

Weyeneth, Robert. "The Power of Apology and the Process of Historical Reconciliation." *The Public Historian* 23–3 (2001): 9–38.

Chapter 2

Leadership, Reconciliation, and Friendship

Paul E. Vogt

The historic challenge of reconciliation in Canada is, among other things, a challenge of leadership. Murray Sinclair, the chair of the *Truth and Reconciliation Commission of Canada* (TRC), likens the transformation called for in the TRC Report to the scaling of a mountain, and has cautioned that "getting to the truth was hard; reconciliation will be harder."[1] As both the *Report* and the *Calls to Action* make clear, the issues are at once urgent, deeply rooted and multifaceted; addressing them will require dedicated efforts from all levels of government and from the nation as a whole.

The issue of leadership comes up frequently in assessments of the TRC process. Some commentators single out instances of exemplary leadership while others lament the lack of leadership demonstrated in response to the ninety-four *Calls to Action*. Taken together, these responses prompt a more general reflection. What does effective leadership mean in this context? What kinds of leaders and what leadership practices does the task of reconciliation require?

Recent writing on leadership in the context of public policy has reacted sharply against a paradigm (well represented in the business management sections of bookstores) that reduces leadership to a set of individual traits, presumed to be effective in any setting. The reaction against the traditional paradigm insists on the contextual nature of leadership. It counters the abstract quality of leadership manuals by foregrounding a consideration of the different settings in which leadership is practiced, and the question of ends—*leadership for what*?

The writers who pose these questions often draw a distinction between leadership that is transactional in nature, meaning that it accepts existing relationships, and leadership that aims at a transformation of relationships. In the latter case, they suggest that the key issue is not the leadership traits possessed by those at the top, but leadership understood as a collective process—a capacity for effective action that is developed across a group or network.[2]

Some of the ideas developed in this revised understanding of public leadership offer a starting point, I will suggest, for reflecting on the kind of leadership reconciliation requires. The aims of the TRC are indeed transformational, touching on virtually every aspect of public policy and inviting all Canadians, whether of Indigenous or Settler descent, to commit to building a future relationship very different from the one that exists today.

Network governance is one idea current in public administration theory that has particular relevance for the encompassing, multisided task of reconciliation. It is a term that describes an important feature of the twenty-first-century context, which is the way societies appear to be at once highly fragmented and highly interconnected: networks of interacting open systems. It also describes the imperative for government leaders to collaborate with groups outside of government to achieve public goals.

Complementary to the idea of network governance, and likewise a subject of growing interest for public administration theorists, is the idea of *wicked problems*.[3] Wickedness in this case is not a value judgment but a shorthand way of describing a policy challenge so complex and deeply rooted that it is impossible to specify a solution—or to imagine a point at which the need to generate solutions might stop. Challenges of this kind are becoming more prevalent in public affairs: climate change, growing inequality, diseases linked to lifestyle are high on the list of wicked problems; reconciliation as a national imperative could surely be added. They complicate the idea of leadership and how it is practiced. To address a wicked problem is to embark on a journey for which the paths and the destination are unclear, and solutions must be found along the way.

These ideas are helpful but they are starting points only. The idea of contextual leadership suggests that different goals require different leadership styles. Transformational leadership, especially, needs to model the changes it seeks. The task of reconciliation raises unique challenges, which are well captured in the TRC *Report* and reflected in themes that recur throughout the ninety-four *Calls to Action*. One is the idea that education policy, the means by which an historic wrong was done to Canada's Indigenous people, will also be the principal means by which a new chapter is begun. "Education got us into this mess" Murray Sinclair has said, "and education will get us out."[4] Another theme is the need for a fundamental "change in historical consciousness,"[5] going beyond an acknowledgment of what was done to children in the residential schools to address the cluster of attitudes—still prevalent in Canada—which brought that policy into being. A third theme is the reclamation of Indigenous identity, an objective that goes to the root of the reconciliation project and the efforts to eradicate Indigenous identities that prompted it. Recovering that essential asset is an emotional and untidy process, ongoing in the communities, organizations, and individuals engaged by the *Calls to Action*. It calls for a form of leadership that is consistently alert to the needs for healing and self-discovery.

In a way that is hard to state more precisely, leadership that aims to transform relationships, and to cultivate resilience, adaptability, and creativity across a network of actors, needs to keep connecting people to the *spirit* of what they are doing. Murray Sinclair has used the idea of friendship as a way to think about reconciliation and the form of leadership it requires.

PUBLIC LEADERSHIP RECONCEIVED

The literature on leadership is extensive and continually growing. In the past century it has given rise to a sizable industry, consisting of how-to manuals, consultants, and coaches. Dale Carnegie's 1936 classic, *How to Win Friends and Influence People*,[6] established a formula that subsequent authors have kept evergreen: a list of the personal traits that make for effective leadership and ways they can be cultivated.

The key traits promoted in the leadership manuals have remained more or less the same through the years: vision, integrity, focus, creativity, and perseverance. Most presentations employ a recipe card format ("the seven habits" or "the six styles" of leaders) that allows for easy memorization and suggests that the same insights and stratagems can be applied in any setting. That idea is reinforced by the tendency of writers to draw leadership lessons from strikingly different contexts.[7]

Although it is not always made explicit, most leadership manuals *do* assume a context in which the key responsibilities of a leader, such as setting goals and ensuring operational focus, will be carried out. It is what social theorists call a Weberian organization, which has a functional separation of duties and a clear hierarchy. Also, much of the leadership literature, from Carnegie's time to the present, is addressed to business leaders or those who aspire to success in business.[8]

There is, however, a separate literature addressing leadership in government and public administration, which has at times utilized paradigms and insights drawn from the business world and at other times insisted on the unique requirements for leaders operating in the public sphere. The trends seem to alternate. With the New Public Management (NPM) movement that began in the 1980s and the 1990s, the pendulum swung toward the idea that public sector managers could benefit from concepts prominent in business management courses, such as entrepreneurial leadership and accountability frameworks, tied to outcome measures. The approach influenced public sector reform efforts throughout the world, and its influence continues to be felt—although the claims of NPM proponents to be reinventing government are now thought to have been overstated.[9]

The past two decades have witnessed a reaction against the NPM model. The new approach, sometimes called New Public Service, accepts the ongoing challenge to innovate and do things differently but insists there are features of the current public policy context that require a different conception of leadership. Among the features practitioners and analysts highlight is the emergence, in our postindustrial society, of economic, political, and communication networks that are at once highly dispersed (beyond the control of any governing authority) and highly interdependent. In her 2011 book, *A New Synthesis of Public Administration*,[10] Canada's former top civil servant Jocelyne Bourgon argues that the key twenty-first-century leadership challenge is understanding these networks and acquiring the skills and relationships needed to operate within them.

Contextual intelligence is the leadership trait Bourgon and other writers identify as most essential to public servants addressing themselves to major challenges. Possessing contextual intelligence is not the same as possessing a strategic vision, because understanding of this kind is both acquired and demonstrated through collaborative practice. In an era of declining sovereignty, governments can no longer operate as closed systems, designing policies within departmental hierarchies before moving to a public implementation stage. Leaders need to participate directly

> in the expanding public space forged by the interaction of our networked society and multiple virtual communities. They must act with imperfect knowledge, while knowing that many events are beyond their control. Their role is to leverage the collective capacity to influence the course of events toward a better future and to help society adapt and prosper even in the face of unforeseen circumstances.[11]

The starting point for this form of leadership is an understanding of the organized interests and networks relevant to each policy domain and an ability to anticipate reactions, points of alignment, and potential obstacles. Collaborative leaders think in terms of the co-creation of value between governments, nongovernmental organizations, and citizens. They are able to see beyond institutional boundaries and to lead horizontally or from the middle of policy networks. Their broader aim, beyond the achievement of specific policy goals, is to build networks that are resilient, adaptable, and have the capacity to respond to new information and developments.

The idea of network governance summarizes this approach. Some writers have described the specific leadership practices needed to support it, such as adaptive management and social learning. Bourgon believes that the combination of global interconnection and social media has created a genuinely new situation for public policy, because seemingly small actions can have a cascading effect that rapidly heightens their impact—for good and for ill. A crisis in the US mortgage sector can trigger a global recession; a solitary act of protest in Tunisia can destabilize regimes throughout the Arab world; and one eloquent teenager may shift the international conversation around climate change. Examples like these underline the element of uncertainty networks introduce, and the importance for leaders to be alert to emergent solutions and the opportunities that can suddenly arise to "leverage collective capacity."[12] Another element of the public context for leadership is the rise to prominence of what policy analysts have come to call wicked problems. The adjective wicked in this case does not mean evil; it is used to describe a problem so large and complicated that there is no foreseeable solution set and efforts to resolve it have no clear stopping point. To address a wicked problem, therefore, is to set out on a journey for which both the pathways and the destination are uncertain.[13]

The set of problems commonly described as wicked includes environmental problems like climate change and the degradation of water systems; health problems like obesity and diabetes; and social problems like intergenerational poverty and gender- or race-based inequality. This is an abbreviated list but even so it brings home some key points: (1) the set of wicked problems includes many of the key public policy challenges of our time; (2) the intractability of these problems, either considered separately or as a whole, is due to the fact they are woven into the very fabric of our society—*the way we live now*; (3) wicked problems are frequently associated in the public mind with policy failure, and cited to explain a loss of trust in government or, more broadly, in the ability of contemporary societies to come to grips with their most fundamental challenges.

Another point about wicked problems ties back to the condition of interconnectedness that forms the backdrop for discussions of network governance. In our postindustrial society, which can be pictured as a network of interacting open systems, the biggest problems tend to overlap with and feed on one another. "[E]very wicked problem can be considered to be the symptom of another wicked problem," is the pithy formulation offered by the sociologists who first coined the term.[14] This is part of the explanation for why wicked problems are so intractable. There will always be controversy over where efforts to solve the problems should begin. What are the starting points, the most effective ways to leverage action and resources? An addition, the scale of the problems, fully realized, can trigger despair, cynicism, or (at the leadership level) attempts to shift the responsibility for finding solutions.

Wickedness in this special sense has become a major element of the twenty-first-century policy context. Addressing herself to those currently serving in public leadership roles, Bourgon suggests they are "the first generation" to

> face simultaneously difficult, complicated and an increasing number of complex public policy issues . . . (the first) to serve in a world where virtual communities contribute to shaping the issues and transforming the context in which public policy challenges must be met . . . (and the first) to serve in a context characterized by increasing uncertainty, volatility and unpredictability.[15]

The combination of these elements adds to the requirements for effective leadership. A broad understanding of the issues and actors in a given policy domain must be combined with a nuanced understanding of how the various domains interact. Leaders must learn to tolerate a wider margin of ambiguity, accepting that progress will often be gradual, murky and uneven. Yet they must also be prepared to seize on opportunities to find synergies between polices, or to amplify or propagate successful practices.

The *Truth and Reconciliation Report* is structured in a way that supports the practice of collaborative leadership. It recognizes the interconnection between policy domains and anticipates the requirement (and some of the challenges) of coordinating efforts across a broad range of institutions. The ninety-four *Calls to Action* are addressed to leaders at every level of government and to a range of nongovernmental institutions that includes schools, colleges, and universities; churches and faith-based groups; social agencies, professional societies, media, and sports organizations. Ultimately the leadership challenge is directed to all Canadians: reconciliation begins with each and everyone of us.[16] Murray Sinclair has urged all citizens to read the *Report* and commitment themselves to advancing at least one of the *Calls to Action*.

By broadening the challenge in this way, the TRC does not diminish the specific responsibility of elected leaders. In seventy-two of the ninety-four *Calls to Action,* the federal government is required to introduce legislative or policy changes. At least twenty-four require action on the part of provincial and territorial governments. The calls for government action are, in most cases, very specific, and it is clear the commissioners looked to government to make the first and most comprehensive moves to launch the process of reconciliation. It is equally clear that, from the outset, and over the long run, reconciliation will be an exercise in network governance. Indigenous peoples and their leaders will play a key role; numerous nonstate actors are looked to, to provide leadership; individual Canadians will need to do their part to make reconciliation an everyday practice. The *Calls to Action* include the establishment of several reporting bodies and a federally funded National Centre for Reconciliation to guide and track progress, but the array of actors and initiatives is horizontally rather than vertically oriented, and the Report anticipates the emergence of a leadership capacity that is dispersed rather than centralized.

LEADERSHIP TOWARD RECONCILIATION

The idea of contextual leadership (in contrast to the business manual idea of leadership-as-traits) points not just to the social context but to the goals that leadership serves. Where transformative change is sought, it is important that the style of leadership—the practices and words used by leaders—in some sense models those goals. Of course, the goals of the TRC are strikingly ambitious: first to establish the "truth" about the 150 years of residential schools in Canada; then to "transform Canadian society" through a comprehensive, sustained set of Actions, so that "our children and grandchildren can live together in dignity, peace, and prosperity."[17] But set within the broad scope of the *Report* are some thematic points of emphasis, recurring throughout the narrative and threaded into each section of the *Calls to Action*: education, historical consciousness and identity.

This is where some of the unique aspects of leadership toward reconciliation come in. One is a focus on education policy, reflecting a determination to reclaim one of the major instruments of individual and community self-empowerment from a dark historic legacy. At the heart of the TRC *Report* is a detailed, and often harrowing, account of the residential school experience and its lingering impacts. But as Murray Sinclair has written, "it is precisely because education was the primary tool of oppression of Aboriginal people, and miseducation of all Canadians, that we have concluded that education holds the key to reconciliation."[18] A full twenty-eight of the TRC's *Calls to Action* involve education reform. And as Sinclair's comment suggests, the Calls address not only the need to improve education, at all levels, for Indigenous Canadians, but also the need to educate non-Indigenous Canadians in ways that promote mutual understanding.

The direction of leadership efforts toward the education sector has proved to be one of the most encouraging aspects of the TRC process. Canadian schools and postsecondary institutions were the first institutions to respond, in a concerted way, to the *Calls to Action*, followed by a number of professional associations that introduced cultural training for their members. In Manitoba, schools, colleges, and institutions committed in 2016 to a joint Indigenous Education Blueprint addressing curriculum, student supports, and community engagement. The University of Manitoba became the home of the Archives

(Call 70) and, across the country, at least a dozen postsecondary institutions introduced specialized programs related to aspects of reconciliation.

These are first steps, of course, and it would be a gross understatement to say that there is still a long way to go. Call 7 focuses on the need to narrow the gap between Indigenous and non-Indigenous with respect to education and employment outcomes—which is surely the ultimate and overriding goal. Call 8 suggests an obvious starting point, which is to eliminate the discrepancies in funding between on- and off-reserve schools. That step has not yet been taken. Neither has the overwhelming evidence supporting the importance of early-years education led to consistent programming for Indigenous children (Call 12).

Another feature of the reconciliation movement is the need to reverse attitudes that have become entrenched in mainstream institutions. As the report points out, residential schools were one of many policy instruments used in pursuit of a single aim, which was (in the words of John A. MacDonald) to ensure that Canada's Indigenous peoples "acquire the habits and modes of thought of white men."[19] That aim in turn was bound up with a mindset encapsulated in the Doctrine of Discovery and its counterpart, the legal concept of *terra nullius*. The mindset, and the cluster of ideas supporting it, remains part of an enduring myth (reinforced by national acts of commemoration) that the founding of Canadian society begins at Contact and is traced through milestones marking the establishment of institutions by the growing Settler society.

For the purposes of this discussion the important point is that the historical narrative is reinforced by viewing Indigenous people primarily as objects of administration—or, to put the same point somewhat differently, as adjuncts to a narrative in which all the active roles are played by leaders of the Settler society. There are still vestiges of this mindset in the way Indigenous peoples and Indigenous communities are categorized by governments; the way Indigenous issues are discussed in the media and in our public conversation; and in the way the lands Indigenous peoples have used and inhabited are perceived by those who have other designs for them.

Of course, it is not possible, and not the intent of the TRC, to repudiate the historical record. The fates of Indigenous and non-Indigenous peoples in Canada are irrevocably entwined and there are important aspects of the historical relationship, such as the commitments made in the *Royal Proclamation of 1763* and the ensuing *treaties*, that will play a key role in reconciliation. Similarly, the importance of resource development as a potential path to prosperity raises questions about ownership and the distribution of benefits that must be posed and dealt with in the framework of current economic realities.

Yet the need to challenge this cluster of ideas—the Doctrine of Discovery, *terra nullius*, and Indigenous peoples as objects of governance—is an imperative that shapes the present leadership challenge of reconciliation. The TRC calls for a change in historical consciousness that must be supported by new ways of talking about Canada's history (Call 57), new public acknowledgements and commemorations (Calls 79–82), and changes in school curricula (Call 62). Although the subject lies beyond the scope of this paper, the extent to which First Nations and Métis self-government becomes a reality—in particular in the key areas of policing, family services, education, and economic development—is a mark of the progress made on reconciliation.

Another fundamental aspect of reconciliation is reclaiming Indigenous identity. The residential schools and related government policies did not succeed in their goal of extinguishing Indigenous culture but the damage they did to individuals, families, and communities by cutting off the transmission of culture and instilling a crippling sense of shame about Indigenous heritage was significant and lasting. The TRC *Calls to Action* include many measures to restore Indigenous languages and names (Calls 13–17), reestablish cultural practices (Calls 5, 12, 21, 22, 35), and promote artistic expression (Call 83).

There is another side to this imperative that is alluded to in parts of the *Report* and has been eloquently described in several of Murray Sinclair's speeches. The struggle to assert an identity, often against a lengthy background of disempowerment, intimidation, and repression, does not follow a prescribed path. Many organizations dedicated to advancing the goals of reconciliation have been driven by internal divisions centered around these struggles; many people seeking to contribute to the goals have been unprepared for the emotions they encounter. A critical aspect of leadership in this context is a measure of empathy going far beyond the idea of alliances formed around shared goals. As a practical matter, resources need to be found, and space needs to be given, for journeys of healing and self-discovery.

FRIENDSHIP FOR A START

"Finding the right words at the right moment" is Hannah Arendt's formula for the kind of public leadership known as statesmanship.[20] Canada's Truth and Reconciliation process, like the process launched in postapartheid South Africa, has summoned an eloquence rarely heard in our national conversation. It began with the *TRC Report* itself, which is a detailed account of the residential school policy and its impacts, written in a way that is accessible and often very moving. Since the *Report* was issued, many people have spoken and written powerfully about the significance of the historic reckoning and the task of reconciliation that lies ahead. I have paid particular attention to Murray Sinclair's speeches and writings in this essay because he has been the most prominent spokesperson for the Commission itself and has sought to frame the *Calls to Action* as a leadership challenge addressed to all Canadians.

A notable aspect of Sinclair's public presentations is a carefully balanced assessment of the progress that has been made in implementing the Calls, conveying his frustrations at the pace of progress but also cautioning against a dismissal of the process or falling into a despairing characterization of Canada's receptivity to change. Sinclair's precise message, it seems, is that much more should be done by governments and others in positions of responsibility to initiate the reconciliation process—efforts to date are slow and partial—yet it is gathering steam at the grassroots level and in particular among Indigenous youth. What is more, the movement carries with it a sense of inevitability: however long it takes, we have no option but to learn respect for one another.

Another notable aspect of Sinclair presentations is his frequent invocation of the idea of friendship to describe the spirit of reconciliation: I have your back you have mine. The simplicity of this idea is part of its appeal, helping to universalize the leadership challenge and provide a familiar staring point. But the simplicity is also somewhat deceptive. The suggestion that friendship is a political virtue (in a sense *the* political virtue) goes back to Aristotle and is bound up with the enduring idea that political associations are grounded in a shared sense of community. Aristotle distinguished between different kinds of friendship, some of which are instrumental in nature. The kind most relevant to political relationships is a friendship between equals, animated by some common idea of what it means to behave virtuously. But friendship also accepts the individuality of both parties—the goals and identity of friends as each defines them—and realizes a value that comes from difference. Friendship, in that sense, goes a step beyond tolerance and fair treatment, but also helps to convert those principles into unthinking practice. "Where there is friendship (talk of) justice is unnecessary. But even where there is justice, friendship is still necessary."[21]

To go back now to the initial question: what does leadership look like in the context of reconciliation? Reflections drawn from recent public administration suggest that it is a collaborative form of action, aimed at establishing a network in which a myriad of actors work across numerous policy domains toward one broad goal. Leadership is needed to maintain the connections between these actors, identifying points of convergence and ensuring that social resources are fully leveraged. At the same time, leadership must grasp the scale and complexity of the challenge, anticipate uneven progress, support processes of social learning, and remain open to emergent solutions.

In the context of reconciliation, the practice of leadership must also model the principles and themes invoked by the TRC. Education is a constant focus: a natural starting point in the movement to right historic wrongs; a means of empowerment for Indigenous people; and a means for both Indigenous and non-Indigenous people to come to terms with their shared past. Closely connected to this is the idea of establishing new historical consciousness. It is an essential element of leadership practice because common narratives have denied agency to Indigenous people and still perpetuate, in modern idioms, the mindset that led to the residential schools policy. Another distinctive feature of leadership toward reconciliation is allowing a central place for efforts to reclaim Indigenous identity. The TRC threads this dimension through every section of its *Calls to Action*, describing many concrete ways to support communities and individuals in their efforts to discover and confidently declare who they are. But that process must follow its course in all the organizations contributing to reconciliation, in ways that are often inspiring and sometimes discomfiting. It requires a measure of empathy that is constantly modelled by leadership and demonstrated through practical supports.

NOTES

1. Murray Sinclair, "The Truth is Hard: Reconciliation is Harder." CCPA-BC Gala Speech, 2017.

2. Paul G. Thomas, "Leading the Public Sector into the Future." Address to the National Conference of Public Administration in Canada, August 26, 2008, 5.

3. Gille, Paquet, *Tackling Wicked Problems* (Ottawa: Invenire Books, 2013).

4. Murray Sinclair, "Education: Cause & Solution." *The Manitoba Teacher*, December 2014.

5. Murray Sinclair, "Murray Sinclair Shares Why He's Still Hopeful about Reconciliation." *CBC*, 2017, https://www.cbc.ca

6. Dale Carnegie, *How to Win Friends and Influence People* (New York, NY: Simon and Schuster, 1936).

7. Consider for example, Sun Tzu; Winston Churchill; Steven Jobs.

8. Paul G. Thomas, "Democracy and the Public Service in the 21st Century," 2007, 2.

9. Ricardo Morse, "Developing Public Leaders in an Age of Collaborative Governance, 2017."

10. Jocelyne Bourgon, *A New Synthesis of Public Administration: Serving in the 21st Century.* (Montreal: Queen's University School of Policy Studies, 2009).

11. Bourgon, *A New Synthesis,* 19.

12. Ibid., 27.

13. Horst W. Rittel and Melvin Weber, "Dilemmas in a General Theory of Planning." *Policy Sciences,* 1973: 19.

14. Rittel and Weber, "Dilemmas," 165.

15. Bourgon, *A New Synthesis,* 19.

16. Truth and Reconciliation Commission of Canada, *Calls to Action.* Accessed December 13, 2019. http://trc.ca/assets/pdf/Calls_to_Action_English2.pdf

17. TRC, *Calls.*
18. Murray Sinclair, "Education: Cause & Solution." *The Manitoba Teacher*, December 2014.
19. Truth and Reconciliation Commission, *Final Report*, 2015: 2. Accessed December 13, 2019. http://nctr.ca/reports.php
20. Hannah Arendt, *The Human Condition* (Chicago: The University of Chicago Press, 1958), 27.
21. Aristotle, *The Nicomachean Ethics*, trans. Terrence Irwin. (Indianapolis: Hackett, 1985), 208.

BIBLIOGRAPHY

Arendt, Hannah. *The Human Condition* (Chicago: The University of Chicago Press, 1958).
Aristotle. *The Nicomachean Ethics,* trans. Terrence Irwin (Indianapolis: Hackett, 1985).
Australian Public Service Commission (APSC). *Tackling Wicked Problems: A Public Policy Perspective.* 2007. Accessed December 12, 2019, https://www.apsc.gov.au/tackling-wicked-problems-public-policy-perspective.
Bourgon, Jocelyne. *A New Synthesis of Public Administration: Serving in the 21st Century* (Montreal: Queen's University School of Policy Studies, 2009).
Carnegie, Dale. *How to Win Friends and Influence People* (New York, NY: Simon and Schuster, 1936).
Morse, Ricardo S. 2017. "Developing Public Leaders in an Age of Collaborative Governance."
Paquet, Gilles. *Tackling Wicked Problems* (Ottawa: Invenire Books, 2103).
Rittel, Horst W, and Melvin Weber. "Dilemmas in a General Theory of Planning." *Policy Sciences* 4 (1973): 155–169.
Sinclair, Murray. "Education: Cause & Solution." *The Manitoba Teacher*, December 2014.
Sinclair, Murray. "For the Record: Justice Murray Sinclair on Residential Schools." *Macleans*, June 2, 2015, https: www.macleans.ca
Sinclair, Murray. "Murray Sinclair Shares Why He's Still Hopeful about Reconciliation." *CBC*, 2017, https://www.cbc.ca
Sinclair, Murray. "The Truth is Hard. Reconciliation is Harder." CCPA-BC Gala Speech, 2017.
Thomas, Paul. "Democracy and the Public Service in the 21st Century." Manitoba Public Service, 2007.
Thomas, Paul. "Leading the Public Sector into the Future." Address to the National Conference of Public Administration in Canada, August 26, 2008.
Truth and Reconciliation Commission of Canada. *Final Report of the Truth and Reconciliation Commission of Canada: Summary*. Winnipeg: Truth and Reconciliation Commission of Canada, 2015.

Chapter 3

Walking in the Footsteps of the Peacemaker

A KENIENKĒ: HAKA *Personal Odyssey of Reconciliation*

Brian Rice

This chapter is based on one facet of a methodology that I created and used to write my dissertation *The Rotinonshonni: A Traditional Iroquoian History for Modern Times*[1] in 1998. I realized that it is, in itself, a vital form of personal reconciliation that in many ways must be part of the larger reconciliation narrative. I decided that in order to validate the writing of my dissertation I would need to utilize a different approach than the conventional forms of research and that would allow me to earn the right to write my dissertation. In order to do that, I decided to embark on a walking journey of discovery. I wanted to find out what had happened to the lands of *Kenienkē:haka* (Mohawk) people in the traditional territories of what is now Central New York State, since the thirteen arrows (Americans) had taken over their lands.[2] Due to space limits, this chapter will concentrate on my people, the *Kenienkē:haka*, and the conversations and dialogues I had on my walking journey across the land, rather than the historical aspects because we all bring our biases into our conversations; however, it is only through dialogue with one another that we can truly find reconciliation. Reconnection with the land and with all of Creation is at the base of all reconciliation; and this chapter tells the story of how I made that reconnection.

It had been more than 200 years since the thirteen, now fifty, arrows had ethnically cleansed the traditional lands of the *Kenienkē:haka* of its original people. As part of reconciliation, I want to tell the story through the lens of the twins in Creation, *Sawiskera* and *Teharonhia:wako*. They have been commonly referred to as the left-handed twin and right-handed twin, or bad and good twin among contemporary *Kenienkē:haka*. Today, they have become less known among contemporary *Kenienkē:haka*. *Sawiskera* is viewed today as a disrupter while ***Teharonhia:wako* is referred to as *Sonkwiatison*, the one who makes our bodies.

In the Creation story of the twins, Turtle Island (North America) is divided into two islands with each twin having more control of one than the other. *Sawiskera's* island is thought of as being on the other side of the ocean—or the place the colonizers came from. In the Creation story, *Teharonhia:wako* and *Sawiskera* had battled over control of Turtle Island. This chapter is based on the premise that *Sawiskera* won control of Turtle Island, with most *Kenienkē:haka* forced to live outside of their traditional territory. The territory itself represents the area of Turtle Island gifted to the *Kenienkē:haka* by *Teharonhia:wako*. I wanted to better understand why this had happened from a land-based perspective? The only way I could do it was to walk on the land and meet some of the people who now resided there.

I had been encouraged to make my journey by a woman who was also interested in finding out more about her *onkwe:honwe*, which is a generic name for Iroquoians, including the *Kenienkē:haka*. I had heard that she had a doctoral program where people could work within their traditions and where they would find validation for them.

One day, I decided to call her and find out how if it could be done? When she answered, I told her, "My name is Brian Rice, and I have heard that you have a doctoral program where I can work on learning about the *onkwe:honwe* culture and philosophy. I am told that I can also get a PhD if I work hard enough."

She replied, "I am trying my best to find a way to do it; however, it is difficult. There are many opposed, who don't want us to know our original traditions any longer. This is the way it is throughout the world for traditional people. It is important that you get your PhD because this is what is recognized. You will be able to reinforce what you believe in by having this and then maybe help others."

I said, "I am interested in joining your program so that I can go out and learn more about the culture and get a PhD. I hope I am worthy of it?"

Upon hearing my story and what I was seeking, she replied, "I can make you only one promise; that is, the experiences that you will receive here will be so profound in our learning community that you will never find them anywhere else."

I answered, "Then I will join your traditional knowledge doctoral program and come and learn with you and the others. Maybe, one day I can get a PhD."

I knew that there were *onkwe:honwe* who were much more knowledgeable about the culture than I was. However, I wanted to be a small part of those who contributed to keeping the teachings alive.

At the doctoral center of traditional learning, students came to study among trees that stood 200 feet high in the Red Woods of Marin County California.

I thought to myself, "We are like the shoots that are growing. We will never be as great in size as the trees before us; however, we can still be large and beautiful in what we have to learn and offer."

While there, I met others like myself. They came from every corner of Turtle Island (North America). There were even some non-*onkwe:honwe* who would join. They were also tired of *Sawiskera's* world of control. They had remembered that their ancestors also had the life spirit of *Teharonhia:wako* blown into them during the time of Creation, although they had manifested him in a different way. Their ancestors had also lived in balance with the Creation at one time.

I thought to myself, "It is too bad that there are not more like them. However, it is good that they are here and want to make changes."

In fact, I knew it was their people who were the first to be affected by *Sawiskera's* power and influence. They had been the first to suffer from disease and were the first to lose their connection to the rest of the Creation and, in some cases, their lands as well. Although they now seemed to be in control of Turtle Island and the island across the sea, there were some who were becoming afraid of *Sawiskera's* power. They wanted to find a way to live with the Creation and not against it.

PREPARING FOR THE JOURNEY

During my doctoral research, I had traveled to listen to the traditional stories from an *onkwe:honwe* royan:er (Good Minded chief), who held the *Kaokwa:haka* title, *Teiohonwe:thon* (Two Equal Things). He was better known by his Canadian government name Jacob Thomas; however, his traditional name was *Hadagihgrentha* (He Looks to the Sky).

Hadagihgrentha was the most knowledgeable person about the *onkwe:honwe* culture that I had ever known. From him, I had learned the stories about the *onkwe:honwe*, such as Creation, the Great Law of Peace, and the Good Message of *Skaniatar: io*. *Hadagihgrentha* was a *royan:er* who did not live in the place of his ancestors, *Kaokwa:haka* territory. In fact, like the *Kenienkē:haka*, there were almost no *Kaokwa:haka* living in their homelands any longer. Instead, he lived in the place where the *onkwe:honwe* had sheltered under the Great Elm Trees to escape the thirteen arrows, in Six Nations Ontario.

Over time many of the *onkwe:honwe* would be destroyed by disease, the mind-changer (alcohol), and warfare. Others in their grief would forget who

Teharonhia:wako was and what he had taught them, and become Christian. *Onkwe:honwe* children would be taken away and be abused by the Christian spiritual leaders from *Sawiskera's* island. My grandfather was one of those children taken away.

The place that my *Kenienkē:haka* grandfather Peter Rice was sent was close to the place of the Great Elms (Six Nations Ontario). This was the place where children, such as my grandfather, were taught to forget about the things *Teharonhia:wako* had taught the *onkwe:honwe*.

Hadagihgrentha used to say, "The thirteen arrows took the teachings of unity from the *Kayeneren:kowa* and then united and created their country.[3] However, they forgot the two most important things. They forgot that the laws within the *Kayeneren:kowa* came from the Creator, and, for them to work, women have to be paramount in leadership and men must remain at peace."[4]

The thirteen arrows made small parcels of land called reservations and they moved the *onkwe:honwe* there. Many of the reservations or reserves were far removed from the places where the *onkwe:honwe* and the other Turtle Islanders (First Peoples) resided. They were told that their lands were forfeited in exchange for bringing Christianity to them. Like the *onkwe honwe* who live where the Great Elm Trees stand, many *onkwe:honwe* were now Christian themselves.

Even on the reservations, there were institutions and monuments to the Christians. For those who continued the *onkwe:honwe* teachings, they were tolerated as a part of *onkwe:honwe* present-day reality. For the Christians, they were a sign of their victory over what they deemed as paganism and the devil's work. The *onkwe:honwe* had been warned long ago by *Teharonhia:wako* that *Sawiskera* would find a way to control their beliefs, and it seemed like he had achieved his purpose.

Hadagihgrentha had said to me one day, "It seems like everything is really getting mixed up today. The people are so confused about who they are. Everything that *Skaniatar:io* (Handsome Lake) said would happen seems to be coming true. That one day he would control the Creation."

Long ago when he brought his Good Message, *Skaniatar:io* had warned that this would happen. There were those who were *onkwe:honwe* who did not believe in *Teharonhia:wako* and what he had taught them. They had accepted the teachings of Christianity. There were some from *Sawiskera's* island, who were believers in the ways of *Teharonhia:wako*. Others still were confused and no longer believed in anything.

I decided, one day, that I would embark on a journey to find out what had happened since the thirteen arrows had taken over the *onkwe:honwe* lands in the land of the Longhouse of One Family and to the *onkwe:honwe* who had remained behind.

The opportunity came when I attended an assembly at the place of the Great Elms where many of the believers in *Teharonhia:wako* had come together to discuss how the knowledge could be adapted into the educational systems of those who now controlled all of Turtle Island.

I had not seen *Hadagihgrentha* for quite a while, and it was great to be reacquainted with him. When the assembly had finished, I and a few of my friends gathered for a ceremony to commemorate the rising of the Elder Brother the Sun. *Hadagihgrentha* was the one who conducted the ceremony that morning, and everyone felt content and happy.

That evening a friend named Bill had an idea. He said to *Hadagihgrentha*, "Brian is about to make a long journey. He will follow the trail of the Peacemaker to see what has happened to the *onkwe:honwe* who lived in the territory of the Longhouse of One Family. He wants to replicate the journey that the Peacemaker took and visit many of the sacred sites. Is there anything that we can do to see him off in a safe way? Is there a ceremony that you could perform for him?"

Hadagihgrentha replied, "I am bringing back one of the ancient ceremonies that is now forgotten by our people. Come in the morning, and we will do it together."

I thought to myself, "This is fantastic. I wanted to find a way to begin my journey in a ceremonial manner, and now it will be fulfilled."

That night Bill and I slept, and in the morning we went to *Hadagihgrentha's* place. At the place of the ceremony, there was Brian, Bill, *Hadagihgrentha* and his wife and daughter.

Hadagihgrentha said, "Last night, I cooked up some medicine. We will use it in this sweat lodge where we will be cleansed. When we are finished, do not wipe the sweat for a full day. It takes that long for the medicine to work."

That morning he burned tobacco. We then went into the sweat lodge. So hot was it that *Hadagihgrentha* did not stay too long, for he was old. However, everyone was cleansed and felt purified.

That day, he said to me, "My wife has asked me to give you something to protect you on your journey."

He then went into his pocket and said, "Here are three wampum beads. Carry them with you on your journey. They will give you protection if you believe in them."

Bill also said, "I want to give you something as well. Here is a medicine pouch and some *onkwe:honwe*, Real Tobacco, to burn on your journey."

I thought to myself, "Now I am ready to begin my journey."

It was decided that Bill and I would travel together the next morning to a place where I could better begin my walk. That day we took a bus to Peterborough, Ontario. I was allowed to sleep over at the Native Friendship Centre and the next morning proceeded to head to the *Kenienkē:haka* community of Tyendinaga, the birth place of the Peacemaker.

On my way, I met a young man who was a follower of the system that seemed to want to control all other belief systems, a Christian. I could see from his complexion that he was a young man of integrity for his age nonetheless.

I greeted the young man, "How are you?"

"I am fine," the young man answered.

I asked the young man, "What is your name?"

The young man answered, "Chad is my name."

I asked Chad, "Where are you going?"

Chad answered, "I am a Christian, and I am going to a meeting of young Christians in Kingston."

"Where are you going?" Chad asked me.

I answered, "I am going to follow the path of the Peacemaker who brought the great way of peace to the *onkwe:honwe* of Turtle Island long ago."

The young man was interested; he asked me, "Are the teachings like the teachings of Christ?"

I answered, "They are like the teachings of Christ in a way, although the Peacemaker never said he wanted to save everybody for the spirit world. He was more concerned about saving them in the Earth World."

The young man answered, "That is where our teachings differ. One day I want to go to other lands and teach the message of Christ to others so that they can be saved by him before they depart from the earth."

I told him, "Your intentions are good, but don't be misled. Often what happens is that Christians go into places, and they destroy the sacred teachings that have been given to the people by the Creator. They then end up controlling those people as well as their lands."

The young man answered, "I have heard there were abuses. I only want to save the people by bringing them the message of Christ."

I asked the young man, "Why do you think they need to be saved?"

The young man answered, "They should be saved from sin."

I told the young man, "You have to be careful in what you are doing. There are many well-intentioned people like yourself that have done much harm to others. You must show the people respect by allowing them to teach you as well."

The young man understood, but was not completely convinced,

"It is more important that they be saved," he replied.

I knew that this young man Chad was a good person who had a lot of integrity for his age. He also knew that this is how *Sawiskera* had gained control over the beliefs of many of the *onkwe:honwe*. Few of them were better off for it. In fact, the divisions that occurred among them over their changing beliefs had resulted in warfare and eventually the loss of their homelands.

Today, it was *onkwe:honwe* themselves living on *Teharonhia:wako's* island that were trying to change the beliefs of their own people so they did not have a connection to their lands any longer. I knew the harm that would come when the *onkwe:honwe* no longer believed in *Teharonhia:wako's* teachings.

Nonetheless, I was amazed at the young man's strong convictions. The young man named Chad and I parted in a cordial manner as I had reached my stop at *Tyendinaga* reserve.

In spite of our differences in beliefs, Chad said to me as I left, "I will always remember what you have told me for the rest of my life."

I thought to myself, "I hope you use what you have learned so as not to make the same mistakes as others."

JOURNEY TO EAGLE HILL, BIRTHPLACE OF THE PEACEMAKER, THE FIRST SACRED SITE

Before we departed, I had made plans to meet *Hadagihgrentha* somewhere in the land of the *Rotinonshonni*. Bill would be taking *Hadagihgrentha* back to his people's homeland, perhaps for the last time. They had hopes that by bringing some friends to see the beauty of the culture and the land, that they would help preserve his knowledge.

Tyendinaga was another place like the place of the Elms, a reserve that was set up by those from *Sawiskera's* island to control the *onkwe:honwe*. It was also at the Bay of Quintē where the Peacemaker was born and where I would officially begin my walking journey.

I had been here once before with *Hadagihgrentha* and his wife. They had brought a group to visit many of the *onkwe:honwe* cultural places. Still, I was not sure exactly where I was. In order to carry my provisions, I had borrowed my son's baby stroller. Long before I began my journey, I had searched for something that could help me carry my equipment. For a long time, I could not find anything. One day, while I was slowly jogging with my son, I noticed that the stroller was about the perfect fit for my tent and pack sack. My son, Jacob Thomas, named after *Hadagihgrentha*, had shown me the way I could make the walk.

I knew that trying to carry all the equipment I would need for 700 miles would be impossible. I was aware that there was a prophecy that said that one day a little boy would lead the *onkwe:honwe* back to the territory of the Longhouse of One Family. I thought about the prophecy as I walked that day.

As I was walking, I stopped at a restaurant where I met a former band council chief named Hill. The chief told me, "Near the bridge down the road is a maple tree that has grown, and it is said that this is a sacred spot." The chief was a Christian; however, he knew some of the stories of the Peacemaker. The chief continued, "If you follow the road where the bridge is, you will come to Eagle Hill by the airport, the place where the Peacemaker was born." I replied to the chief, "Nia wen kowa." This meant thank you in the *Kenienké:haka* language.

As I turned to walk toward Eagle Hill where the Peacemaker was born, I approached a Christian televangelist bible college. I could see a sole figure walking toward me in the distance. It looked like a spirit approaching, as there was a haze from the dew surrounding him.

I thought to myself, "Wouldn't it be funny if it were the *Kenienké:haka* television evangelist Russ." As the man came closer, I could see that it was him. We stopped and looked at one another and shook hands.

I said to the evangelist, "She: kon! My name is Brian. I am on a journey which will begin at Eagle Hill and take me through our lands in New York."

The evangelist answered, "That is interesting. My name is Russ, and I am the head of Spirit Alive ministries."

Neither I nor the evangelist mentioned anything about belief. The Christian evangelist simply said, "If you are looking for Eagle Hill, it is straight ahead, just past the airport hangers."

Russ then said, "Good luck with your journey."

We then parted from each other.

I thought to myself, "What an interesting meeting? Here are two people on opposing ends of the spectrum. Should I consider him an adversary and is that how he views me?"

I wondered to myself, "What an interesting coincidence, to meet Russ my first day out." As I walked toward the airfield and Eagle Hill, I noticed that the sky was getting darker.

"It will soon rain, and I had better get to Eagle Hill quickly," I told myself.

I then walked further until I passed the airport bunker. To my left, I noticed a small road that led up a hill. I left my equipment about half way up the hill until I came to an opening.

"This must be Eagle Hill, birthplace of the Peacemaker" I thought to myself.

I then took out some of the tobacco that Bill had given me at the sweat, and I lit a small fire. Then, I said some words to the Creator. I gave thanks the best that I could to the rest of Creation. Just at that moment a bird sailed overhead, circling as I gave thanks.

"I wonder if it is an eagle," I asked myself. It was not long after, that the clouds became dark, and it began to rain. "This isn't the best way to begin my journey," I thought to myself. After a few moments of deliberation, I decided,

"I have a long journey to go, perhaps it is better that I begin now rather than wait here to be soaking wet overnight."

Journey to Cohoe Falls; Where the Peacemaker Was Tested by the *Kenienké:haka* Resulting in the *Kenienkē:haka* Accepting the Message of the Great Peace, The Second Sacred Site

Before I left, I looked over my surroundings. I could see the Bay of Quintē in the distance. I imagined that, from Eagle Hill, the view had probably remained much the same as when the Peacemaker was born.

I then continued on my journey, passing several historical marks. One was the place where the *Kenienké:haka* had landed on the shore of their new homeland by the river. This had happened after the American Revolutionary War that had resulted in their dispersal. These *Kenienké:haka* were from a place called Fort Hunter near Schoharie Creek, just where the valley of the *Kenienké:haka* came to an end. They had been known as the lower Mohawks.

After a night's rest, I resumed my journey. As I began to walk that morning, my legs felt great. So good did I feel that I thought to myself, "I will run and see how far my legs will take me." That day I ran for six miles. As I ran, I thought, "If I keep this up, I will only get stronger. Perhaps I will get strong enough to run a marathon again."

As I arrived in Kingston Ontraio, I thought to myself, "The British and thirteen arrows had fought over lands that did not belong to them. Like the others that had arrived from *Sawiskera's* island, they believed they had the right to other people's land because they were Christian. They then fought each other over who had rightful ownership.

I wondered to myself, "What would have happened if the *Rotinonshonni* had remained neutral? I am sure they would have still lost much of their land."

With the victory of the thirteen arrows over the British, most of the *Kenienkē:haka* were sent into exile, along with most of the other *onkwe:honwe*. This was one of the reasons that I wanted to make his journey. I had asked myself, "Can the thirteen arrows really call it their own homeland when they don't even know the cultural places of the Peacemaker that are there?"

I had decided that I wanted to connect the stories *Hadagihgrentha* had told me about those cultural places. In fact, I believed, by doing this, in some way, I was reclaiming the land back for the *onkwe:honwe*.

After spending the night in Kingston, and burning my tobacco that morning, I walked to the docks where I was to catch the ferry to Wolf Island. As the ferry left the docks, I felt that I was walking into another world. In fact, I felt like I was in some way going home. Not only because I was part of *onkwe:honwe*, but because I was born in the land that I was entering into. My family had left many years before. Upon arriving at Wolf Island, I decided to myself, "I will run the seven miles across to the other side and then catch the ferry to our homeland."

As I ran and walked, I thought to myself, "After the coming of the *Sawiskera's* islanders and war commenced on Turtle Island, the *Rotinonshonni* did not take slaves; instead, prisoners were adopted to live among them. Most never wanted to return once they became members of the society." That was the case with my family. In 1703 a raiding party of Catholic *Kenienkē:haka* from *Kahnawakē* across from present-day Montreal captured two English boys from Worcester Massachusetts: my two ancestors Timothy and Silas Rice, along with their cousins. Although they were given opportunities to return home, they chose not to return even after visiting. One wonders why? Once adopted in they had become community leaders, and they never wanted to leave. They were adopted by a Catholic *Kenienke* family and so the blending of the two different islanders began in my family. Therefore, reconciliation for myself was more complicated than simply us versus them.

As I walked, I thought about my father who was decorated in World War II. My father had fought in another Whiteman's war where *onkwe:honwe* went away to fight for the Whiteman's freedom on Sawiskera's island. They did this so that they could feel equal to the Whiteman who had taken away their lands. The war had destroyed my father and almost his family. In fact when my father got a job as a welder, they referred to him as the savage. The war had killed his mind, but the peace had killed his spirit inside.

I remembered what *Hadagihgrentha* had told me about what the Peacemaker had said. "The Peacemaker had said that war is like a ball of snow; once the killing begins it never stops, and as it rolls, it keeps growing and growing."

I remembered being told by *Hadagihgrentha*, "It was with the help of the *onkwe:honwe* soldiers who had fought in the Whiteman's wars that the last governing council, based on the teachings of the Peacemaker of the confederacy, was deposed in 1924 by the Canadian government."

I also thought of my friend Bill who had been drafted to go to the Vietnam War. Long before he knew the culture from *Hadagihgrentha*, he had said no to going to war and had fled to Canada from the United States.

As I walked that day, I weighed these ideas in my mind. The country that surrounded me was beautiful.

First one and then two deer crossed the road.

I already had several dreams referring to my journey, but could not remember them. That night I dreamed that the door to my room had been busted open and that I had tried to close it with my foot, but was not strong enough. It seemed that spirits had gotten in and surrounded me, and I felt their presence. I clapped my hand three times to ward off any evil that might have entered, and at that moment I saw a white dot which quickly disappeared. I hoped that they would let me sleep as I knew I had a lot of work to do the next day. A good feeling prevailed over me, and I slept well.

After burning my tobacco, I left the next morning. I had to make a decision as to whether I would make my turn toward Cohoes Falls at Port Ontario or go as far as Oswego some twenty miles further. That morning I attempted to run. However, my legs would barely move. I proceeded at a slow jog. This country was beautiful. I saw four large fish in a stream and a deer.

As I approached a large hill going down, I could see a nuclear power plant in the distance. This was like the place where they made bombs that could destroy all the Creation. A *Kenienkē:haka* traditionalist from *Kahnawakē* had once said, "The uranium that they take from the ground are the hot snakes that *Sawiskera* had created that would one day appear again and try to destroy *Teharonhia:wako's* Creation."

Finally, quite exhausted, I reached Port Ontario where I decided to make my turn. Oswego was another twenty miles. This is where oral tradition had said that the *Kenienke haka* made their final escape from the *Atirontok* when they lived by the mountain between two rivers, now known as Montreal. I decided to turn at Port Ontario because it would lead me directly to a few historical places I wanted to visit. Port Ontario was where Samuel de Champlain had landed with some *Wendat* and *Atirontok* and attacked an *Oneota:haka* village in 1615.

As I entered the town of Polaski, a strange man greeted me.

He said, "Hello! I am a school teacher. I see you are walking somewhere."

I could tell that the man was tall and thin but in good shape. I answered politely, "It is true; I am walking to Albany." I thought to myself that maybe this is too much information given already.

The man replied, "Why don't you come with me? We can have supper together at my house and talk."

I remembered the young girl in the Sky World story who was led astray by other creatures. I thought to myself, "When we are on our spiritual journeys, we must not allow ourselves to be distracted or we can be thrown from our purpose."

I said to the man, "You are kind, but no thank you. I have to be on my way."

I knew that I did not have time to be caught in an uncomfortable situation. The man then moved on.

I thought amusingly, "I wonder if he turned into a wolf, a bear or a turtle." I knew there are more truths than not in what I was thinking.

The next day as usual, I burned my tobacco and said my greeting of thanks. There were some other good reasons to be away besides the walk. It was nice to be free of any troubles that were left back at his home.

The country was becoming more beautiful. I was at the head of the *Onontaka:haka* country and about to enter the upper part of *Oneota:haka* country. As I walked, a woman stopped her car in the middle of the road.

"What you got there?" she asked pointing to the stroller?

I answered politely, "Just my equipment." I then showed her the insides of my stroller, not wanting to alarm her.

The woman said, "I thought there was a baby under there."

I thought to myself as she drove off, "What a brave or stupid woman. I could have been anybody on the road."

Next, a man stopped his car. He asked me, "Where are you going?"

This time I decided to be honest with him. "I am following an ancient Indian trail, one that a Peacemaker took long ago. He united the many nations that once lived here in a confederacy of peace."

The man replied, "I live in the mountains here with my wife. I think what you are doing is great. God bless you on your journey."

As I kept walking. I passed by an old cemetery where soldiers of the Revolutionary War were buried. I thought to myself, "Our people fought in this war against each other; a war that was not of their own making. Now these soldiers' ancestors control the *onkwe:honwe* lands."

That night I stayed by Fort Stanwix. While there, I noticed a sign by the road that said, "The Oneida Carrying Place at Woods Creek."

My spirits lifted because I knew I was at the place that I had read about in many of the journals of the first explorers who had come from *Sawiskera's* island. This was the place that separated the *Oneota:haka* territory from the *Kenienkē;haka* territory. It led right to the Mohawk River, the English name for the *Kenienkē:haka*.

The next morning like so many before me, I took the path that led to Woods Creek and the Mohawk River. I also had to make a personal decision. That morning I said to myself, "I have to put away my anger if my journey is to be a success. It is important that I carry a good heart."

That day I walked to Oriskeny. If ever there was a place that needed healing, it was Oriskeny. It had become a monument to a thirteen arrows victory, even though they had been almost wiped out by *Kenienkē:haka* war chief Joseph Brant's forces. Unfortunately, in that battle there were *Oneota:haka* who were scouting on behalf of the thirteen arrows. It became a battle of brother against brother. Each was fighting in a war which was not of their making. The divisions among the *onkwe:honwe* that occurred that day would persist into the present. This was where the foundations of the *Kayeneren:kowa* had been shattered.

As I looked on, I thought, "For some of the *Oneota:haka*, it was the time when they became Americans. For the *Kenienkē:haka*, it was a time where they would begin to be forced out of their valley. They had both broken the covenant on *Rotinonshonni* territory against fighting one another, and it was all for the Whiteman who would steal their lands."

I thought about what *Hadgihgrentha* had said about the truth of the Peacemaker's message. "Once the killing begins, the consequences are never ending." In fact, one *Oneota:haka*, who had joined the British side, would meet in later years his brother who had been taken captive by the *Sonontowa:haka*. When asked what should be done with him, the brother answered, "Kill him!"[5]

As I continued to walk, everywhere I went I saw signs with the name Mohawk written on them. They were like signs made for ghosts. There were no *Kenienkē:haka* anywhere to be seen. There were even streets written in the *Kenienkē:haka* language. Almost all the *Kenienkē:haka* lived in Canada now.

That evening I met some people who were very interested in my journey. One of them was a historian of the area. The first thing she asked me after been introduced was, "What would you like to know?"

I answered, "I am not really sure what you can tell me." I continued, "I have come from the Bay of Quintē, and I am following the path of the Peacemaker who confederated the nations who once lived here."

The historian answered, "The Indians used to tell stories long ago in the oral tradition, but it is too bad that the knowledge is lost."

I thought to myself, "If it is all lost, how come I am following the trail of one of those stories." I did not want to argue with this person about history or create a bad atmosphere when people were trying to be kind. Instead, we departed from each other in a cordial manner. I knew that although this woman was a historian, I knew the older history of the two, thanks to elders like *Hadijihgrentha*.

The next morning, I burned my tobacco and began my walk again. My legs were still very sore from the day before. I decided that I needed a bit of a rest, so I stopped at Little Falls.

That day in Little Falls, as I was walking down the street, a young man stopped his car and called me over. "Do you want a lift?" he asked?

I replied, "I can't; I am on a walk."

The young man then said, "I recognize the accent from Canada. In fact, there is a part-Native American woman from Canada who lives in the mountains not far from here. You should go and visit her."

I replied, "If I get the time, I will try to do so."

After resting for an hour, I decided I would make the trip to the mountain to see the woman. There I met the young man once again who said to me, "I will show you where to go."

As we climbed the hill, I could hear barking in the background. Finally, I came to an old dilapidated trailer that was the home of the woman and others. "Hello!" I yelled out.

"Hello!" said her boyfriend. "We heard you might be coming."

The boyfriend then introduced me to the owner of the land.

After being introduced, she said to me, "Please come into our trailer."

I entered the trailer, and I noticed right away the many artifacts that were laying around.

The woman said, "These are everywhere around here. There is everything from Spanish swords to Mohawk burial sites in this mountain. Many strange things occur here, if you stay long enough."

She then asked, "If you decide to stay for a while, would you like to go to the sites?"

I answered, "That sounds great."

She then led me down a trail, where she pointed out certain rock formations. She then tried to explain what they represented, but they were hard to make out.

Then they went further into the woods. She pointed to several mounds that had been covered with rocks. She said to me, "Here are the burial mounds."

I asked, "Could I offer some tobacco?"

She replied, "No problem."

I then took out some of Bill's tobacco and placed it by the mounds. We then went to a freshwater stream. This was the most refreshing water that I had ever tasted. *Hadagihgrentha* had told Bill and me once, "The spring waters that you find in the mountains are medicine water."

I could sense the spirituality that was in this place. After I left, I walked along a trail back to the village. It had the same feeling as Eagle Hill.

The next morning after burning my tobacco, I knew it was time to leave. As I was walking down the road, the young man I had first met drove by and stopped. "How are you doing?" he asked.

I answered, "I am fine."

The young man said, "Do you know that my two great grandfathers were Generals Schuyler and Herkimer."

"That is interesting, since my grandfather was a Mohawk," I answered.

He then went into his pocket and took out a finely cut diamond. He said, "They aren't worth much, but everyone comes to the mountains searching for them anyway."

The young man said, "Have this for good luck."

I replied, "Thank you."

Continuing my walk, I finally arrived at Palatine Bridge. Across the river was the town of Canajoharie. Canajoharie was the village that the *Kenienkē:haka* of Six Nations Ontario were from.

After making arrangements to stay the night, I decided that I would visit the village of Canajoharie. I was told that if I wanted some historical information I should try the library.

I asked the librarian, "Do you know anything about the Mohawk people who used to live here?"

The Librarian answered, "I don't think any Mohawk ever lived here in the village. I think they lived some three miles up the road on top of the mountain. In fact, there have been archeological digs back in the 1950s which showed the foundations of Longhouses."

I believed the man to a certain extent. I thought to myself, "There probably was an old village sight up there."

However, I also knew that before the Revolutionary War, the *Kenienkē:haka* had lived in houses in Canajoharie village that were better equipped than any of the houses that the settlers had. These houses even included glass windows.

That day, I decided I would take the Canajoharie side of the river when I left in the morning. Perhaps, I would visit that old *Kenienkē:haka* village sight the librarian mentioned. I knew that *Sakokwenionkwas* (Tom Porter's[6]) place was only five miles away on the other side of the river, but instead I decided that I would visit him on my return from Cohoes Falls.

Sakokwenionkwas is a *Kenienkē:haka* elder who had decided to leave the *Akwesasnē Kenienkē:haka* community because of the violence that had begun as a result of a warrior society asserting their power and dominance over the community. Ironically, had it not been for peaceful *Sawiskera* Islanders who wanted to help him, *Sakokwenionkwas* could never have returned.

I said to myself, "It would be wrong to visit *Sakokwenionkwas* unless I make it to Cohoes Falls first. But, how can I visit a *Kenienkē:haka* traditionalist before Cohoes, if I am following the Peacemaker's trail? That wouldn't make sense."

"This is tough country to walk." I told myself after walking up a large hill.

As I continued on, I noticed a road that veered to the left. Once I was on it, I started heading downhill. On the side of the road was a clearing. This was a perfect sight for a village. From this point, I had the best view of the Mohawk valley as of yet. "How many *Kenienkē:haka* had looked over this sight before me," I thought to myself?

I then walked down the hill and once again came to the old highway. I walked for about an hour until I came to a shrine. The sign said, "The village of Ossesseron, the place where two priests Rene Gobiel and Isaac Jogues were martyred." I looked and all around there were statues to the martyrs.

I thought to myself, "This was a *Kenienkē:haka* village, not a Jesuit Catholic village. Why is there no shrine to the *Kenienke:haka* that lived here?"

I continued walking that day, reflecting upon the things I had seen. Finally, I came to a bridge that crossed the Schoharie River.

I thought to myself, "Here is the place where the *Kenienkē:haka* who live at the Bay of Quintē originally came from."

Nearby was a woman who was getting on her bike.

I asked her, "Excuse me, are you from here?"

She nodded, "I am."

I continued, "Do you know if there is anything here that is a reminder that this was a Mohawk village at one time? Is there a museum or something?"

She answered, "We know that this was a Mohawk village a long time ago, but there is nothing here any longer. I think they lived along the river bank. Perhaps, if you ask one of the farmers they may help you. They are always finding artifacts laying around."

"Thank you," I answered.

As she spoke I thought to myself, "The only reason I am here is because *Hadjihgrentha* was willing to teach anyone who was willing to learn about the culture. Otherwise, the journey would have no purpose for me." I decided that there was no point going further into the village. There would be no *Kenienkē:haka* living there. I decided to walk onto Amsterdam, New York and stay overnight.

The next morning, I could feel that I was getting close to one of my destinations. I burned my tobacco and moved on toward Schenectady. I then met a man on the road who had seen me walking the day before. "Hello! I saw you walking the other day. Where are you going?" he asked.

I answered, "I am going to Cohoes Falls."

The man said, "There is a better way for you to get there if you follow my instructions. Go up the road about a mile and you will find a bicycle path. The path will take you right to Cohoes Falls. In fact, it follows the Mohawk River and is probably about twenty miles or so away."

I replied, "Thank you." I then followed the man's directions and found the path.

I wondered to myself, "If I reach Cohoes Falls maybe that will be enough."

I then thought some more about it, and told myself, "I have to go on. I have to try and finish this journey no matter what happens."

The next morning after burning my tobacco, I began to follow the bicycle path. This was the best road that I had been on yet. I could hear the birds singing in the woods. The scenery was pleasant as well, with mostly woods on each side of me. After walking for around ten miles, I noticed the Mohawk River next to me.

I then walked for a few more miles and thought to myself, "What better route than this to take! Young *Kenienkē:haka* should have a chance to walk this path. Maybe one day, I will bring some back with me." I succeeded in doing this eighteen years later.

All around I was surrounded by beautiful trees and the river. Finally, I was on the last stretch to Cohoes Falls. By this time, the nicely paved bicycle path had turned to dirt. Suddenly the path came to a road that opened onto a residential street. I saw a young man walking up the street.

I asked him, "Do you know where Cohoes Falls is?"

The young man pointed down the road and said, "It is right down this hill."

I looked around and thought to myself, "Here was the place where the Peacemaker met the *Kenienkē:haka* war chiefs and where the sun entered the eastern door, shining its light of peace into the confederacy territory. So much had begun and ended here."

I knew that as long as you had the stories, the traditions would live on "Nothing ever has to die, if you want to keep it alive," I told myself.

I had probably walked close to 300 miles to reach this place. I thought to myself, "In a sense, from this point on, I will be walking *Ayenwatha's trail*, as well as that of the Peacemaker."

I then walked to the lower part of the village. There was a road that led to a bridge that went to the other side of the river. There was a sign on the side of the road that said, "Here is an ancient trail that the Mohawks and *Mahican* used to travel upon." In fact, this was the road that divided the *Rotinonshonni* territory from the territory of the Algonquian peoples, such as the *Mahican*.

I decided that I had enough that day. I thought to myself, "I will cross to the other side of the Mohawk River and stay there overnight. That will give me time to do some exploring before I start my journey back west."

I was really exhausted at this point, and the bridge was further than I thought. I wanted to find some place to rest but was told the closest place was three miles away in Troy, New York. I decided that Troy was where I would head for, even though it was in the opposite direction to where I was going.

The neighborhood I was walking through seemed pretty rough. I thought, "There is a lot more poverty in the land of the thirteen arrows than I expected. The people seem to be just existing. There is no sense of them having any spiritual connection to this place." Finally, I found a place to spend the night.

WEST INTO *KENIENKĒ:HAKA* TERRITORY

The next day after burning my tobacco, I finally headed west. "This is great," I thought. "I am finally on my way back home."

I noticed that the flow of the land was changing. It seemed like I was more against the wind and walking against the grain of Mother Earth. After walking about a mile toward the bridge, I noticed a path in the mountains heading in the same direction as I was going. In fact, there was even another bridge I could cross on, much further up the Mohawk River.

I decided, "I will take that path and come down towards the far bridge. This will put me near the cliffs, where the Peacemaker was forced into the gorge by the *Kenienkē:haka*." He would reappear to them the next day with his message of peace.

As I walked, I kept getting higher up into the mountains. When I felt I was at the right place, I took out some tobacco and burned it.

After descending the hill and crossing the river, I found the bicycle path and headed back toward Schenectady. Unfortunately, it was extremely hot that day, and I was running out of water. As I kept walking, I became more and more tired. Then I came to a huge hill, and knew that this was going to be tough. Exhausted, I climbed to the top, only to come to a small baseball field. There I met a young man who seemed a little slow-witted, and we walked together for the last five miles. The young man said to me, "I am six foot five and want to play professional football."

I looked at him and noticed he was no taller than five feet nine. The young man seemed to be confused, as if he had no self-esteem and had to make up stories to feel good about himself.

I thought to myself, "It is sad that this society turns out young people like this who are completely out of touch with themselves." It seemed whenever I got close to a large town, there were people like this young man. Perhaps, he reminded me of myself, when I was in my teenage years, a young man totally out of touch with reality. Even in the days when I used to go to bars, it seemed like everyone wanted to try to be something other than who they really were.

Finally, I made it to Schenectady. That evening I spoke to another young man who worked at the hotel I was staying at. When the young man heard what I was doing, he asked, "My grandmother Angela Hall was Mohawk. Could you help me find out where she was from? I am searching my roots and would like to know my ancestors."

I answered, "I know some people who might be able to help you. The only thing I can promise is to try."

The young man left a number with an address, in case I ever found out where Angela Hall was from.

I woke up that morning, and after burning my tobacco, headed for *Sakokwenionkwas* place.

As I climbed down a hill, I came to the road that would take me west to *Sokwenionkwas* place. I did not walk far when I arrived at the old *Kahnawakē Keniienkē:haka* village sight. This was the place my ancestors had come from. It had become famous because of a Roman Catholic convert named *Kateri Tekakwitha*.

This time I thought to myself, "I have to accept both my Christian and traditional ancestors that belonged to this village. They have both made me what I am today."

That day I moved on. After walking for around five more miles, I reached *Sokokwenionkwas* place, exhausted. In front was a young man doing some work.

"How are you? " I asked.

"Not too bad," answered the young man.

"My family is originally from *Kahnawakē*, and I have been walking a long time," I said.

"Come on in and meet my family, you can eat with us," said the young man.

"Thanks a lot," I replied.

I felt shy but honored. As far as I was concerned *Sokwenionkwas* was holding the eastern door open for other *onkwe:honwe* to reenter. He had opened up his home to any *onkwe:honwe* who chose to come through *Kenienkē:haka* territory. In all the miles I had walked, *Sakokwnionwas* was the first *onkwe:honwe* and *Kenienkē:haka* I had met who lived in the territory of the *Kenienkē:haka*. More importantly, like myself on my journey, he had been helped by what were once *Sawiskera* Islanders, but now belonged to *Teharonhia:wako's* Turtle Island.

"What better way for reconciliation to begin," I told myself.

NOTES

1. Now published as Brian Rice, *The Rotinonshonni: A Traditional Iroquoian History through the Eyes of Teharonhia:wako and Sawiskera (The Iroquois and Their Neighbors)* (Syracuse, NY: Syracuse University Press, 2013).

2. The dissertation itself is a much broader study including the whole territory of all of the Iroquois Five Nations known collectively as *Rotinonshonni* (Longhouse of One Family). I graduated with a doctorate in Traditional Aboriginal Knowledge from the Division of Transformative Learning at the California Institute of Integral Studies.

3. There is evidence that both Thomas Jefferson and Benjamin Franklin observed the workings of the Great Law among the Iroquois Confederacy and wrote some of them into the American Constitution, including the Speaker, and the Committee structures.

4. Jacob Thomas, *Great Law Recitals* (Oshwegan, ON: Jacob Thomas Learning Centre, 1992, 1994, 1996), 1.

5. Barbara Graymont, *The Iroquois in the American Revolutionary War* (Syracus, NY: Syracuse University Press, 1972), 2.

6. This refers to Dr Thomas Porter. See http://www.mohawkcommunity.com/toms corner.html

BIBLIOGRAPHY

Graymont, Barbara, *The Iroquois In the American Revolutionary War* (Syracuse, NY: Syracuse University Press, 1972).

Rice, Brian. *The Rotinonshonni: A Traditional Iroquoian History through the Eyes of Teharonhia:wako and Sawiskera (The Iroquois and Their Neighbors)* (Syracuse, NY: Syracuse University Press, 2013).

Thomas, Jacob. *Great Law Recitals* (Oshwegan, ON: Jacob Thomas Learning Centre, 1992, 1994, 1996).

Chapter 4

Beyond Apology
Decolonizing the Jesuits

Peter Bisson, S.J.

The spiritual is political,[1] because reconciliation is both spiritual and political. In this essay, I would like to offer my own reading of the spiritual aspects of reconciliation as experienced by one Christian Settler church group of which I am a member: what it has felt like to have our circles expanded, to grow from feeling indignant toward the notion of supporting Indigenous people in their self-determination, including Indigenous spiritual self-determination and, in the process, learning new things about what it means to be spiritual.

LOCATING MYSELF AND THE JESUITS IN RECONCILIATION PROCESSES

The group whose reactions and responses to processes of reconciliation I will discuss is the Jesuits,[2] more formally called the Society of Jesus, of which I am a member, and indeed, where I am a Roman Catholic priest. I will not discuss how Indigenous people may have experienced the same processes, for that is their story to tell. The Jesuits are a religious order of priests and brothers in the Roman Catholic Church, founded in 1540 in Rome by St Ignatius of Loyola (1491–1556).[3] We are a large religious order, organized in regional administrative units called "provinces," and we are active around the world. We understand our mission as the service of faith, of which the promotion of justice is an absolute requirement or—to express it in another common formulation—promoting reconciliation and right relations with God, between human beings and with the rest of creation.[4] We are especially known for work in spirituality, education and research, missionary activity, and more recently in social justice. We have a special corporate relationship with the Pope, who can send us wherever he feels the needs are greatest.

Jesuits first came to Canada in 1611, shortly after the beginnings of European colonization, as missionaries both to the Mi'kmaw and the French colonists in what is now Nova Scotia, a mission that lasted for about two years. A few years later the base of Jesuit activity shifted to Quebec and reached out to First Nations along the St Lawrence River and the shores of the Great Lakes. After an absence from Canada from 1800 to 1842, the Jesuits returned at the request of various Catholic bishops to work with Indigenous people and European Catholic immigrants. In the English-speaking parts of the country, Jesuit work among Indigenous people concentrated on pastoral and missionary activity among the Indigenous Anishinaabe people along the north shores of Lake Huron and Lake Superior, including Manitoulin Island in Lake Huron's Georgian Bay.

The Jesuit participation in Indian residential schooling began in 1913 and continued to 1958 in one school, St Peter Claver School for Boys. In 1947, the school became St Charles Garnier College, in Spanish, Ontario. This was preceded by a day school in Wikwemikong First Nations on Manitoulin Island, which began in 1841 and the Jesuits took responsibility for it in 1845.[5] The school was added to the Canadian government residential school system in 1894, then relocated to Spanish in 1913.[6] Across the road was St Joseph's School for Girls, a residential school run by the Daughters of the Heart of Mary, which operated from 1913 to 1962. Even though they were run by two different groups, because of their physical proximity and because of their shared beginnings in the Jesuit-run coeducational school in Wikwemikong, these two schools together are called the Spanish Indian residential schools. Today, many of the Indigenous women and men with whom Jesuits are partners in ministry are themselves former students of residential schools, and in particular of the Spanish residential schools.

There is a long history between Jesuits and Indigenous people in many parts of Canada,[7] but I will focus on our more recent experiences of relationship from the late 1980s, when Indigenous people started complaining to us of physical and sexual abuse by Jesuits, both in parishes where we worked and in our residential school. During this period, when these complaints were being made, we no longer ran any schools in the Anishinaabe areas of Manitoulin Island and the north shore of Lake Huron. In 1983 we started a new institution, the Anishinabe Spiritual Centre, also called Wasseandimikaning, in Espanola, Ontario, to train and support Indigenous men and women for ministry in the Catholic Church. Its governance is now shared among a board of trustees with Anishinaabe stakeholders. The Jesuits are associated with a similar center in Thunder Bay, Anemki-Wadj, in the Fort William First Nations. The Catholic worship services or rituals in these contexts regularly use Indigenous ceremonies like the smudge and the drum, with prayers and songs in Ojibwe language, and have been doing so for decades. Our contacts with the *Truth and Reconciliation Commission of Canada* (TRC)[8] and its work exposed us to a broader range of Indigenous people, a variety of nations and a greater variety of Indigenous intellectuals and politicians.

The nature of my location in the Jesuits is important for the reader to understand. From 2008 to 2012, I was the assistant[9] to the leader of the Jesuits for the English-speaking parts of Canada, whose title is Provincial. Then from 2012 to 2018, I served as Jesuit Provincial.[10] In both capacities, I represented the Jesuits at meetings of the parties to the IRSSA[11] with the Commissioners of the TRC. The period of TRC activity and the follow-up in subsequent years has been crucial in the collective Jesuit experience of growing reconciliation with Indigenous people.

Almost all of the stories I tell here are in one way or another autobiographical, and I tell them as a participant-observer, a religious leader, and a practitioner of reconciliation. This will be a story of both personal and collective (Jesuit) transformation. Many of the experiences I discuss were collective Jesuit experiences, but the point of view is my own, especially in virtue of the leadership role I played, which meant I not only had a more general view of things than most of my Jesuit companions, but I also had a hand in shaping some of these experiences. While acts of individual listening, apology, and compensation were part of my personal experience of leadership and affected me greatly, I will attend primarily to more communal experiences that affected my point of view as a leader, such as TRC meetings, Jesuit meetings, and other experiences that affected the points of view of many other Jesuits and colleagues in our ministries.

I do not write as a dispassionate neutral observer but instead as a participant very much committed to working for mutually respectful relations. I write as a Christian and a Settler with a collective past that is colonizing and missionary, at least in part. I also write as someone whose Christian identity has been very much unsettled by the processes of reconciliation in general, and by the work of the TRC in particular. My now unsettled religious identity is searching and waiting for the new heart and new spirit, and for the freedom that comes with receiving and telling the truth.

Some of the experiences of reconciliation that I share were informal processes and others were formal.[12] Informal processes of reconciliation involved interactions with Indigenous people where we live and work, and meetings of Jesuits and Indigenous colleagues for the sake of discussing and improving our relations and cooperation. I helped to initiate and organize many of the informal events. Formal processes of reconciliation involved official institutions such as the courts, the TRC, or the parties to the IRSSA.

What myth (in the good sense of a foundational story that gives meaning) and theory have guided my practice of reconciliation? First has been my relationship with Jesus Christ and his example of nonviolent welcoming love for all. In second place I acknowledge inspiration by profound changes in the Catholic Church and the Jesuits since the mid-twentieth century. With regard to the Catholic Church, I have been strongly affected by the spirit of the reforms of the Second Vatican Council (Vatican II, Rome, 1961–1965) whereby the modern world, which had been seen as a threat, came to be seen instead as a place where the Spirit of God is already at work and has things to teach us there. With regard to the Jesuits, I have been inspired, guided and challenged by the systematic commitment to social justice made in 1974–1975, where social justice had to be part of all of our work done in the service of faith.[13] This commitment has often placed Jesuits with marginalized communities and sometimes made us advocates with them, often with colleagues of very different value systems than our own Christian ones. Without these changes and commitments, the story I tell here might never have happened. With regard to theory that helped me to reflect more analytically and critically on my experience, the more I have become involved in reconciliation work the more I have found myself remembering the ideas about dialogue and the positive and challenging views of the Other, where God is also Other, in the work of the Jewish philosopher Emmanuel Levinas (1905–1995).[14] My own struggles to reconcile interiorly my family backgrounds of French Canadian and English Canadian identities, with their own differences and colonial relations, has perhaps also predisposed me positively to the far greater transformations demanded by Indigenous-Settler reconciliation.

I write this essay for three reasons: to understand better how I and the Jesuits have been affected by reconciliation and decolonization processes; to recognize patterns in our experience that might be applicable to other Settler groups, especially church ones, and that might help us engage more intentionally and responsibly in reconciliation; to encourage faith groups—including my own Roman Catholic Church—not to be afraid of reconciliation and decolonization.

PERSONAL JESUIT EXPERIENCES OF RECONCILIATION PROCESSES

My personal story of reconciliation with survivors started on my very first day as Provincial, when I began my role as a religious leader. It was May 31, 2012, the first day of a TRC event in Toronto. I went. I had been alerted that the official Catholic Church would be sparsely represented at this gathering, so it would be important that I attend, especially in my capacity as Jesuit Provincial. I asked other Jesuits to go too, and many did. I had also been advised by someone whose wisdom I trusted that it would be helpful if I were clearly identifiable as a priest, and so I should wear clerical garb to show that the church was interested, concerned and in solidarity with survivors. So I did. I wore a clerical shirt with a Roman collar and a grey suit.

When I arrived at the gathering venue in downtown Toronto dressed as a priest, I quickly realized that I had made a terrible mistake. Instead of being a symbol of peace, communion and solidarity I began to wonder if I was a trigger for traumatic memories of physical and sexual abuse, of loss of culture, language, territory, and spirituality. I could see people looking at me sideways, hesitating, flinching. Did I symbolize residential schools, and the dark connections between evangelization and colonization? I tried to dress down by taking off my jacket, rolling up my sleeves and taking out the tab from my Roman collar, but it was still obvious that I was a priest. While no one was rude to me, Indigenous people still seemed uncomfortable.

Inside myself I felt shame and vulnerability. I wanted to hide by seeking out the company of other church people. I resisted this desire with only modest success and tried to mix with the survivors and other attendees, but I felt like an outsider. I was the "other," and a visible other too. It got worse. At the end of the gathering there was a banquet. I went in, found a table with some people and a few empty chairs and sat down. I was the only non-Indigenous person at the table. I made small talk and received polite and brief replies. There was also silence. After about fifteen or twenty minutes, I noticed a small sign in the middle of the table that read, "Reserved for Survivors." I was in the wrong place. I felt too confused and self-conscious to draw further attention to myself by saying sorry and asking if I should move elsewhere. It also felt too late for that, so I stayed and squirmed.

I supposed that my shame was far less than the pain that survivors had experienced as children and young people, and far from the lingering harms that they, their families, and communities continue to suffer today. I also realized it was important that as a church person I experience the guilt, shame, grief, and responsibility for the pain that we as an institution had helped to cause, and that I not run away from these feelings and their meaning. Guilt, shame, grief, and responsibility were important parts of the truth I needed to feel not only as information and ideas in my head but also as emotions and values in my heart and in my body.[15] This was especially challenging to me as a church person, because I like to see myself as "nice," "kind," "generous," "good," and I like others to perceive me in this way. I like to be needed and helpful, and to receive gratitude for this. It was hard to feel uncomfortable for being what I thought I was called to be. But my heart needed to sink lower still.

Over the course of the gathering, I gradually noticed that while many felt uncomfortable around me, no one was rude or insulting or even condescending. Indeed, many were polite and respectful, and some even tried to make me feel welcome. Here I was a symbol of traumatic memories and oppression, and I was being made welcome by at least some survivors of the same oppression. This melted my heart. Both vulnerability and hospitality were at the beginning of my experience of religious leadership and reconciliation and marked my leadership from then on. Another aspect of my personal transformation came from ongoing contact with the TRC Commissioners, both formally in meetings with representatives of the parties to the IRSSA and informally outside of these meetings. While the commissioners were occasionally firm and critical of the church representatives, they were always courteous and respectful. Over time I came to realize that they never treated us as though we were defendants in an adversarial process, which I would have understood. Instead they treated us like potential partners in the long-term project of reconciliation and healing between Indigenous and non-Indigenous Canadians. Similarly, on Manitoulin Island and the north shore of Lake Huron and in Thunder Bay, despite the pain and damage that we Jesuits had helped to cause, Indigenous Catholics did not ask us to leave. On the Jesuit side, despite the humiliation of well-founded accusations and the painful realization that in many ways we had been a fundamental part of their problems, we stuck around too.

COLLECTIVE JESUIT EXPERIENCES OF RECONCILIATION PROCESSES

My willingness to enter into experiences of shame and vulnerability in the context of reconciliation has its roots in an older Jesuit story. The first hints of allegations of abuse in our residential school appeared in 1988 during preparations for the first reunion of former students of the Spanish residential schools. But the older alumni persuaded the younger ones to be quiet and to respect the priests. They did, yet the reunion was tense.[16] Within three to four years, the first allegations of sexual abuse appeared. More came from our Indigenous parishes than from the school, but allegations came from both. We did not want to believe the claims. Our refusal to listen led, reasonably, to lawsuits. We reacted defensively and used the law and legal process as weapons. We were angry.

We put our own financial and reputational interests before those of the victims and did not really listen to what they had to say. We were judging them negatively in order to defend our view of ourselves and our Jesuit history, and probably also to defend what we saw as our position of dominance. After a while, however, we began to realize that we were treating old friends like they were enemies. Because of this realization, we started listening attentively to the stories of the survivors, and designating certain Jesuits to be the listeners, and eventually non-Jesuit professionals, in order to be more objective. Noticing consistent patterns in the stories, we started to investigate the reports, and found disturbing truths that confirmed many of the allegations. Admitting the truths led us to admit responsibility for the harmful actions of our brothers, and to seek to heal the damage if the victims wished.

I describe this development briefly, but the transition to putting the victims first and Jesuit interests second took time and was not always smooth. Furthermore, admitting guilt and responsibility was a risk because it could have invited more lawsuits, and the payments we had made had already put our Canadian Jesuit group in financial distress. The greater risk however, involved changing our attitude toward ourselves and our past. The humiliation and the risk of apology were the narrow door that we had to pass through in order to continue our relationships with the Anishinaabe people and communities that we had known for generations. Perhaps unexpectedly, admitting guilt and taking responsibility did not lead to more lawsuits but instead led slowly to deeper and new relationships—relationships that were more of partnership than of superiority and inferiority, than of helper and receiver. Eventually we also worked up the courage and humility to say we had participated in cultural genocide, even if we had not intended to.

In 2013, at the TRC's Quebec National Event in Montréal, the Jesuits publicly read out our apology and Statement of Reconciliation.[17] It was delivered by Fr Winston Rye, S.J., who was at the time part of the Jesuits' leadership team for English Canada, and who was himself a Métis from Winnipeg. He helped to draft the statement. He became emotional as he read it. Afterward he deposited it in the Commission's bentwood box reserved for artifacts of reconciliation.

In 2014, there was a gathering of Jesuits, Anishinaabe people and others involved in Jesuit Indigenous ministries. Participants came from Regina, Thunder Bay, Manitoulin Island and the north shore of Lake Huron, Sudbury, Toronto, and Ottawa. We met for a few days at Wasseandimikaning, the Anishinabe Spiritual Centre. The sessions were chaired by a Jesuit priest and a Catholic Indigenous Elder. As the days unfolded, the sessions turned into something like mutual confession. The Anishinaabe people shared their pain and frustrations from the legacy of residential schools, colonialism, and being patronized, and the Jesuits shared their struggles with the stress of being the "bad white colonizer," guilt, shame, overwork, loneliness and alcohol. Then an Elder said something like: "Yes, that's all true. But I can see in the dark, and I see Jesus there too." I gasped internally when I heard this, for it was a repeat of my first days as Provincial, but in a stronger way: fully knowing our guilt and responsibility, we were welcomed by those who knew our guilt and responsibility, even if that welcome included a challenge and an invitation to a new attitude of partnership. The experience of mutual confession of pain and frustration was cathartic. It bound us together and moved us forward.

When the Jesuits left the gathering, we felt that we were no longer "serving" the Anishinaabe people, but that we were being helped by them and that we were becoming partners in building the common good and the Reign of God. While only a small number had this experience, it was nevertheless a pivotal one that served as a reference point and preparation for later experiences.

The Indigenous ministries meeting of 2014 paved the way for a similarly transformative meeting the following summer, one that was much broader in scope. Jesuits and colleagues from all our ministries across the country, who all had leadership responsibilities, gathered for a "communal apostolic discernment" exercise to interpret how the Spirit of God was calling us to prioritize our collective energies.[18] Using a spiritual method that we call spiritual conversation, which is very similar to Indigenous sharing circles, we listened to each other carefully, trying to feel in our exchanges how God was at work among us as we expressed our memories, hopes, desires, fears and anxieties about the world, about our work, about ourselves and about how we worked together. The first priority that emerged from this exercise was to promote spirituality, especially by using the Spiritual Exercises of St Ignatius of Loyola, the founder of the Jesuits. This was not a surprise.

The second priority to emerge, however, was a surprise. It was Indigenous relations. We did not mean Indigenous ministry, which already existed. Indigenous ministry meant pastoral work in Anishinaabe parishes, and training women and men there for leadership roles in the church. Indigenous relations included these activities but meant something much bigger. It meant that all our ministries should cultivate relations with Indigenous people and communities, learn what Canada looks like from Indigenous perspectives, and grasp what it means to be partners and friends—in short, it meant making Indigenous relations part of how we do things in Canada. Cultivating respectful Indigenous relations was no longer the responsibility of one sector of our ministries but had become the interest and responsibility of all. At the end of this exercise, an Elder announced, "Now I finally feel like a friend, an equal, a partner. Finally, I feel recognized." And this observation came after almost forty years of working together!

This new commitment was a significant change in Jesuit attitudes and priorities, which at first provoked some controversy among us. Some Jesuits reacted against the claim that we had participated in cultural genocide, even if unwittingly. Some Jesuits objected to the idea of taking a more critical view of aspects of our missionary past. In the years since then the commitment has settled and seems to be confirmed as more and more Jesuit ministries develop connections with Indigenous people and organizations. A number of factors allowed us to embrace this new priority: the earlier decision to listen nonjudgmentally to Indigenous accusations of abuse, the cathartic mutual confession of our Indigenous ministries gathering during the previous year and being stimulated by regular news about the TRC.[19]

An important feature of this new commitment is that it was arrived at collectively. It was not simply driven by a leader who would be replaced in three years' time. While it was part of my role as Provincial to express the commitment in concrete decisions and actions, I did have a broad base of support for doing so and could invoke the communal discernment exercise as a spiritual authority for following up on the commitment. We still have much progress to make in implementing it, but we have begun.

I have shared some of the things that have pushed and provoked the Jesuits forward on paths of reconciliation and, hopefully, decolonization. Now I would like to say a word about what has supported us along the way. This journey of transformation would not have been possible without scholarly research and the Archive of the Jesuits in Canada, in Montréal. Much that we have learned from our records was not comforting, but we shared them with the TRC anyway, for the sake of preserving and healing the memories of residential schools and of colonization. As the TRC maintained and our experience has confirmed, there can be no reconciliation without learning the truth, even if it makes us miserable for a time. Even more important for support through this journey has been ongoing relationships, through thick and thin, in ordinary life and in conflict, with Anishinaabe communities on Manitoulin Island, along the north shore of Lake Huron, and in the region of Thunder Bay. Listening to persons has helped us to hear the truth and to be affected by it. Staying in relationship despite the conflict, and being allowed to stay in relationship, has helped us bear our truth in a safe space. It is through relations that the Jesuits are being healed and maybe even decolonized, along with a good intellectual and reflective kick from the TRC.

ONGOING RECONCILIATION: NEW RELATIONS

In recent years, and especially since the 2015 commitment and contact with the TRC, the influence of Indigenous people on the Jesuits in Canada has grown in extent and depth. Here are some examples.

Jesuit relations in the urban Indigenous neighborhoods of Regina, Saskatchewan and Winnipeg, Manitoba have grown through our support of two middle schools (grades 6-8) there. They are Mother Teresa Middle School in Regina (started in 2011),[20] and Gonzaga Middle School in Winnipeg (started in 2016).[21] Both schools give a lot of attention to each pupil and their families, and teach Indigenous cultural and spiritual traditions. The schools are also committed to supporting their pupils after graduation, through secondary and postsecondary education, until full-time employment. The Jesuits do not run these schools, but we helped to start them, and the schools participate fully in the networks of Jesuit schools in Canada and the US (and around the world), which enables them to share in these networks' resources for curriculum development, pedagogy, and leadership training, among other things.

In 2016 we began to entrust part of the training of young Jesuits to the teaching and guidance of Elders in summer experiences of six to eight weeks. As this training gets repeated with new Jesuits over the years, we hope that more and more Jesuits in Canada will have had some experience of Indigenous life as interpreted by Indigenous people, so that this may in turn shape our perspectives on Canada, on the church, and on Christian faith.

The Jesuits have recently joined two new groups that promote reconciliation. Firstly, in direct response to the TRC's Calls to Action, some Indigenous and non-Indigenous Catholic leaders worked with the leadership of the Canadian Conference of Catholic Bishops to launch in 2016 the Our Lady of Guadalupe Circle.[22] It is dedicated to improving relations between Indigenous people and the Catholic Church, as well as between Indigenous and Catholic spiritualties. Secondly, in 2018, at the request of a former Moderator of the United Church of Canada and himself an Indigenous man, a number of representatives from various Christian backgrounds, including the Jesuits, began to explore how to decolonize the practice of Christian faith and mission.

Finally, did our commitment to Indigenous relations continue through the Jesuit leadership transition of July 2018? Probably the strongest sign of continuity is that, starting in September 2019, the new Provincial assigned me to work full time on promoting our 2015 commitment, that is, promoting decolonization among Jesuits in a more systematic way by encouraging our ministries to develop relations with Indigenous people, communities, and organizations. Now I would like to step back from storytelling to look at some patterns in the Jesuit experience of reconciliation.

DISCUSSION

In the stories I recounted above, the growth from unself-conscious paternalism toward reciprocally respectful relationship seems to have a pattern. I see five distinct phases in it: naïveté, resistance, transformative listening, first reconciliation, second reconciliation. While I will explain them one after another, the process in real life is neither linear nor steady. It can stall, regress, progress slowly, stumble forward accidentally, or move forward with some intent. The whole pattern probably needs to repeat itself again and again, and in different contexts, in order to deepen. Because the process is based on relationships, it can also be unpredictable. I see this pattern applying both to individuals and to organizations, like the Jesuits or the Roman Catholic Church.

Phase 1: Naïveté

The TRC understood reconciliation as: "an ongoing process of establishing and maintaining respectful relationships. A critical part of this process involves repairing damaged trust by making apologies, providing individual and collective reparations and following through with concrete actions that demonstrate real societal change."[23] Respectful relationship, that is, one of peers and maybe even partners, sounds simple. But as I have recounted above, getting to that "ongoing process" of mutually respectful relationship is not simple. Why? Because of its pre-starting points.

The pre-starting points or first phase came before the reconciliation processes began. It was naïve because there was little or no critical awareness that the policies of our ancestors and governments caused Indigenous people to suffer. There was therefore no critical self-awareness of a need to apologize whether for residential schools or for colonization and its impacts, nor was there self-critical awareness of the difference in power between Indigenous people and Settlers. We Jesuits saw ourselves as good people, well-intentioned, with something good to offer, and with some understanding of what Indigenous people need. Unsettling this naïve position and making it not only self-aware but also self-critical took energy and education. When Anishinaabe people first approached us with complaints, they did so by means of informal, interpersonal processes of reconciliation. These did not succeed in getting us to listen seriously. Instead it took the very formal processes of litigation to get our attention and to make us question ourselves.

In addition to colonizing attitudes there is another, related attitude to which church folk are especially prone. Historian David Shanahan explains it well when he observes about the Jesuits in his study of the Spanish residential school:

> It is an unfortunate habit of people trying to do the right thing for others that they often fail to ask of those they seek to help exactly what is the right thing to do. With a certain arrogance, the missionaries always seemed to assume that they knew what was the right thing to do. More importantly, they seemed to assume that the people agreed with them. The Jesuits came with a package deal for the Wikwemikong people: salvation, education, civilisation, etc.[24]

I once heard Dr Marie Wilson, the TRC Commissioner in charge of liaison with the Christian Churches and herself a Christian, say a similar thing, that church people seemed to have a harder time with reconciliation than others.[25] The attitude described by Shanahan is fundamental to maintaining a power differential between colonizer and colonized because the attitude masks the power difference from the colonizer. The surprise and shock at the lack of gratitude or even resistance with which these "acts of service" can be met is a sign of a lack of critical self-awareness.

I would further specify the problematic nonself-critical church attitude as being based on our view of ourselves as spiritually nonviolent and benevolent. Being accused of spiritual violence challenges not only our actions but also our spiritual identity, as it means being untrue to our foundational inspiration, Jesus Christ and his example.

The TRC itself discusses spiritual violence. It happens when one is not allowed to follow one's preferred spiritual tradition; when a different religious or spiritual path is forced on one; when one's spiritual or religious traditions, beliefs, or practices are demeaned or belittled; when one is made to feel ashamed of practicing their traditional or family beliefs.[26] Attitudes of superiority and spiritual violence, covered by naïve uncritical self-awareness, prevented informal processes of reconciliation from taking hold. A more formal approach was needed.

Phase 2: Resistance

Under the pressure of criticism, accusations, and finally, litigation, naïve self-awareness was challenged, shaken, and exposed. This is the true starting point for processes of reconciliation. The accusations, and the challenge to naïveté were resisted with anger and indignation—the beginnings of a troubled and unsettled conscience. After all, Christian leaders have seen ourselves as moral and spiritual guides, teachers, and judges for over four centuries on Turtle Island;[27] it is shocking to have the roles suddenly reversed and to be on the receiving end of moral and spiritual guidance, teaching, and even judgment.

The Jesuits were hearing but not listening. We were judging what and who we heard. We saw our accusers as ungrateful for the good we did or at least tried to do, and for the self-sacrifice of many of our members. Our self-identity as good, spiritually nonviolent people was challenged and shaken. We became defensive and acted this out in an adversarial manner in court. On the Indigenous side, this phase was the courage to speak out. On the Settler church side, this phase represented shock that the power differential was being revealed to us and challenged. It was not, however, as though criticism of the residential schools was new. Indeed, there were many instances of Indigenous people as well as government and church officials criticizing the system since the nineteenth century,[28] but it is only recently that such criticism has reached a groundswell.

In the 1970s and the 1980s, the Churches had come to see ourselves as social justice allies of Indigenous people. Before then, the mainline Christian Churches and the government of Canada shared similar attitudes toward Indigenous people.[29] In the Catholic Church in the 1960s a reforming spirit was nurtured by the Second Vatican Council (Vatican II, 1961–1964). This four-year gathering of all the Catholic bishops of the world greatly opened up the church's attitudes toward the modern world, updating everything from ritual to acknowledging social justice as a fundamental part of living out Christian faith. At the same time, the postwar period around the world saw movements for decolonization, liberation and human rights. In this international atmosphere, the Christian Churches in Canada in the 1970s and the 1980s frequently sided with Indigenous people against the federal government on social justice issues,[30] especially about natural resources—for example: the James Bay hydroelectric project in Quebec and the Mackenzie Valley Pipeline issue in the Northwest Territories.[31] In the early 1990s, Indigenous challenges about residential schools seemed to marginalize these newfound alliances, which changed the relationship with the Churches and caught us by surprise.[32] At the same time, starting in the 1960s and gaining momentum in the 1970s and the 1980s, Indigenous people in Canada were starting to assert themselves in new ways that many scholars in Canada now call Indigenous resurgence.[33]

Phase 3: Transformative Listening

This is where the Jesuits started to recognize the truthfulness of many of the allegations, as well as of the persons making them. This began when listening became nonjudgmental and non-defensive—we switched from merely "hearing" to listening with attention, to really receiving what was being said, and attending not only to the information but also the emotions and values being communicated and experienced by both the speakers and the listeners.[34]

This kind of listening is transformative because it is the beginning of critical self-awareness. Transformative listening allows feelings and experiences to become part of the data that is taken seriously. Transformative listening begins the revision of one's "received" story. This is when responsibility for past harm done to survivors starts to be accepted. Humility makes its bloody entry here. While this phase is transformative for the better, the loss of naïveté and innocence and the unmasking of spiritual violence are painful, and one must turn inward to begin the difficult process of examining oneself and one's collective history critically.

Phase 3 in processes of reconciliation is also liminal, where the process crosses an important threshold from naïveté to the beginnings of critical self-awareness of one's past. The passage to transformative listening is crucial because if Indigenous-Settler relationship does not make this transition, then it stays stuck in the second phase where it can solidify, perhaps into willful blindness, and then the process does not lead to reconciliation. It was in Phase 3 that informal processes of reconciliation started to work, and when the formal ones became less adversarial. This was the atmosphere in which the IRSSA was negotiated, and where the parties agreed to submit themselves to the five areas of reconciliation set out in the agreement: the Common Experience Payment, the Independent Assessment Process, Commemoration, Healing, the TRC. This was also where the Jesuit attention, which had been captured by litigation and by seeing Indigenous people in a more positive light, was further refined by contact with vibrant contemporary Indigenous intellectual and political life represented by the TRC.

Phase 4: First Reconciliation

This phase focused on the abuses committed in the residential schools; the corporate responsibility both of the Canadian government that mandated and supervised the schools and the Christian church bodies that ran them; on apology for the abuses; and on trying to heal the harm that was done. The government of Canada as well as most of the Christian church groups that ran residential schools have made apologies.[35] In Phase 4 the parties to the IRSSA intentionally submitted to the processes of reconciliation to which they had committed themselves in the agreement. Because they did so together, the agreement kept the parties interacting with each other since negotiations to set it up began in 2005.[36] Such sustained interaction gave time for the parties to the agreement to be affected by the rich intellectual and spiritual life that Indigenous people draw on and was manifested in the TRC—at least this was the case for the Jesuits. The first reconciliation phase was also where both formal and informal processes of reconciliation started to become public through the work of the TRC.

First reconciliation is another place where reconciliation processes can get stuck. Apologies can be sincerely made, and restitution offered, but if the underlying relations of domination and marginalization are not changed then the Indigenous-Settler relationship remains colonizing. For apology and restitution truly to transform the perpetrators and the situations of the survivors, it must lead beyond the residential schools to the underlying relationships of colonization, domination, and control that led to the residential schools in the first place. These attitudes and relationships continue today, represented in institutions like the *Indian Act* that governs relationships between the Canadian state and Indigenous people and greatly constrains Indigenous people.

Phase 5: Second Reconciliation

In this phase, attention shifts from concrete instances and institutions of colonization and assimilation to the relationships and attitudes that underlie them, and the focus shifts therefore from past to present. For the first reconciliation to be authentic and to start changing the Settlers' agency, it must move toward the second one. Scholars John Borrows and James Tully call this phase "transformative reconciliation."[37] I believe this is where decolonization and transformation begin. This is the beginning of relations of mutual respect, and possibly partnership. This, I think, is where hope takes root.

Phase 5 is where the Settler Churches face our own shadows and accept the more complete stories of our pasts, stories now made fuller by the Indigenous stories of how they experienced our actions and attitudes. This is where we accept our no-longer-naïve and newly critical self-awareness of having committed spiritual violence. The need to repent and make amends now comes from within as well as from without. This is also where Indigenous intellectual life starts to have a more consistent impact on the Churches. New power relations arise. The Churches are decentered both in the story of Indigenous-Settler relations and in the power dynamics of the relationship. The Churches still have agency in the relationship, but so do Indigenous people. I do not know, however, if second reconciliation can become a new resettled identity, and if a second "postreconciliation" naïveté could be possible.[38] If one remains alert and self-critical, that is, vigilant, then maybe one must also remain unsettled, and perhaps this is what a post-first-reconciliation identity looks like.

In the Jesuit case, the communal discernment exercise where we gave a high priority to Indigenous relations was in effect a collective commitment to decolonization, even if we did not have the language to express it. Without a notion of developing stages of reconciliation, we chose to move toward decolonization rather than let momentum, chance, or outside forces carry us there. Furthermore, the new Jesuit Provincial's decision to assign me the task of cultivating the attitudes to which we had committed in the 2015 discernment basically commits me to promoting decolonization among the Jesuits and our ministries.

Like Phase 3, transformative listening, second reconciliation is an important transitional or liminal phase, as this is where reconciliation becomes ongoing and begins to decolonize the underlying relations. If there is no passage from first to second reconciliation, to transformative reconciliation, then the process stays focused on past events and may stop there, without transforming the relationships. If there is no passage to second reconciliation, then there may be apologies and restitution, but the colonial relations of domination and subordination remain. In other words, if the processes of reconciliation are to be authentic, then they must be guided forward by an ideal of decolonization, a hope of mutually respectful relationships that respect our diversities.

The drama of reconciliation lies in Phases 1 to 4, when emotions are strong and sometimes dominant, but it is the quieter Phase 5 that is key to the transformation of Church Settler agency. Without it there is no lasting transformation, and therefore no ongoing reconciliation. Nevertheless, reaching Phase 5 is no guarantee that transformation will be ongoing, for decolonization must be intentional and constantly cultivated, with critical self-reflection and undertaken within partnership with Indigenous people. There are no shortcuts to Phase 5. Finally, Phase 5 is not a point of arrival where the journey of reconciliation is complete. Rather, this is where the ongoing journey begins. Hopefully, this is the space where the Churches will face the general challenges of decolonization, as well as the more specific ongoing needs of intergenerational survivors, that is, the families, descendants, and communities of residential school survivors, as well as the recommendations of the Report of the National Inquiry into Murdered and Missing Indigenous Women and Girls (2019).[39]

THE DYNAMISM

I have spoken about moving from one phase of reconciliation to another. But what makes the processes of reconciliation move forward? An ideal of decolonization, while salutary, feels abstract. The fuel that drives the whole process ahead, especially the passage into transformative listening and into second reconciliation, is ongoing relationship with Indigenous people, especially today, with Indigenous people experiencing resurgence.[40] It is this aspect of Indigenous life that constantly challenges the Settlers to act like honest peers and partners. It was resurgent Indigenous people who first challenged the Jesuits to listen by suing us. They were and still are the ones who call us to respectful relations. They are the ones who call us to go beyond apology and restitution for past concrete wrongs to the building of right relations for a shared future. Since decolonization and right relations with Indigenous people involve so many of the patterns of structural injustice in Canada, right relations with Indigenous people will be good for all of Canada.

I have developed Figure 4.1, which I hope visualizes the phases of reconciliation described above.[41]

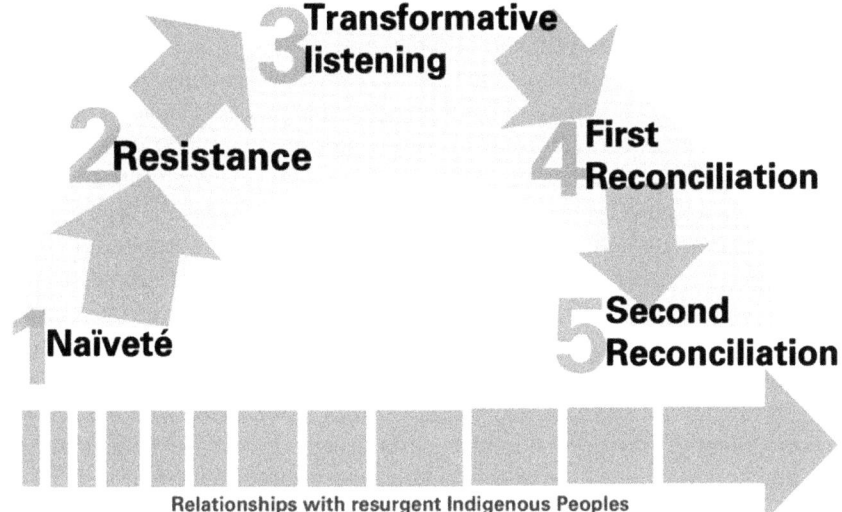

Figure 4.1 Phases of Reconciliation. *Source*: Author.

CONCLUSIONS

Having provoked us, is the truth setting the Jesuits free? In response to challenges to reconciliation and decolonization from Indigenous people, I see three important changes emerging in Jesuit spiritual agency, or our use of spiritual power, which I think also apply to spiritual agency in general: acting with a new kind of spiritual agency; treating nature/ecology with far greater spiritual seriousness; and seeing the spiritual as political. Before discussing these changes, I want to indicate from the outset that the challenge to reconcile and decolonize is a challenge to be transformed that is at its heart spiritual. It comes from Indigenous people who see themselves as spiritual agents (among other things) and is made to the Churches who also see themselves as spiritual agents. Because it is a spiritual challenge issued to "fellow" spiritual agents—the Churches—it cuts very close to the quick of our spiritual identities, and so feels like a challenge. But the spiritual nature of the challenge also means that there is considerable common ground between Indigenous people and the Churches, in which case the challenge feels more like an invitation. I believe that we in the Churches have not yet fully recognized this common ground, at least I think this is the case in my own Roman Catholic Church.

Firstly, what does a reconciling and decolonizing spiritual agency look like on the church side of Indigenous-Settler relations? Reconciliation and decolonization processes are slowly separating religion and Christian mission on the one hand from dominating and colonizing power on the other hand,[42] power with which we have been associated for centuries.[43] Being separated from this power is liberating our agency to become more truly spiritual. A crucial part of reconciliation and decolonization for the Christian Churches is embracing our confusion and vulnerability in all phases of the process. Treating feelings and experiences as serious forms of data is part of vulnerability and part of a spiritual process. Embracing one's confusion and vulnerability does not destroy our agency, but rather changes it. When this happens, then church spiritual agents are no longer at the center of the Indigenous-Settler story nor at the center of the power dynamics of these relationships. Decenteredness and vulnerability are the bases for transformative listening. We are also being challenged to replace attitudes of spiritual violence with spiritual nonviolence or spiritual "peaceableness," to express the idea positively. This change will help us to embrace our loss of innocence and to move ahead with our "new" history. Finally, this new, humbler spiritual agency will be helped by an appropriate goal. For this goal to support a more spiritual form of agency, it must be other-centered. This means supporting an Indigenous goal, likely that of Indigenous self-determination and Indigenous spiritual self-determination. Thus vulnerability, decenteredness, and spiritual peaceableness need to be at the heart of our transformed spiritual agency as Churches, which will give us the ability to support someone else's goals and accept someone else's leadership. This means letting our spiritual agency and identity in Canada be shaped in some key ways by Indigenous people. This is indeed an expansion of the circle[44] of belonging and identity, even if the Catholic Churches are now on its circumference instead of at its center.

Secondly, the challenge to reconcile and decolonize is also a challenge to assign high spiritual value not only to our human minds, freedom and spirits, but also to nature, which includes our bodies, emotions, imaginations, as well as the land and its gifts. Not only is nature part of our human life, but desacralizing it makes it easier to treat as a source of "natural resources" to be exploited, sold and even taken, which Settler economic interests have done with spurious justifications, like the doctrine of discovery.[45] Interestingly, Pope Francis is calling Catholics to change our notions of nature in very similar ways. In his 2015 encyclical letter, *Laudato Sí*, he invites all people of goodwill to include our relationships with nature in our relationships with each other and with God, in other words to be reconciled with nature as well was with each other and God, and to treat nature with very high spiritual value in its own right and as an important revelation of God.[46] While this integration is not new in the Christian tradition, it has been de-emphasized in modern, secularized cultural contexts. To include nature in our spiritual identities is an expansion of the circle of what it means to be spiritual, a call that is coming both from Indigenous people and from the Pope.

Finally, Indigenous people understand reconciliation as a fundamentally spiritual process and seem to be inviting the rest of us to do the same. Reconciliation certainly has important political, economic, social, and cultural dimensions, but it is also spiritual. Meetings about reconciliation begin with prayer and maybe a smudge, and often end with prayer. While Indigenous political leaders play key roles in the processes of reconciliation, the spiritual leaders—the Elders—shape the processes in important ways. The hope expressed in the TRC Calls to Action that the Pope will come to Canada to apologize for the Catholic Church's roles in residential schools and colonization is a hope for a spiritual act from a spiritual leader.[47] The spiritual dimension of reconciliation processes helps to make a safe space for truths to be shared and for healing and transformation to begin. The spiritual dimension is a direct appeal to the heart of the Christian Churches, an appeal from one spiritual agent to another. In our secularized and modernized cultures, it is remarkable that processes as public, political and challenging as reconciliation and decolonization should be so publicly spiritual. What Churches would call faith-based social justice work, what religious studies scholars would call engaged religion, and what Christian theologians would call liberation theology are all based on Christian teaching. Perhaps Indigenous resurgence is part of the resurgence of religion that is happening around the world. Indigenous people are inviting the Churches to join in, in a good way.

In our secularized cultures, the Christian Churches do not always have the courage to be so publicly spiritual. In the call to reconcile and to decolonize, Indigenous people are inviting the Churches to become more fully ourselves. This is another expansion of the circle, making the spiritual public and political. The spiritual dimension of reconciliation and decolonization makes for a lot of lived common ground between Indigenous people and the Churches.

NOTES

1. This expression is inspired by the slogan, "The personal is political" of second wave feminism in the United States in the 1960s and the 1970s. See Linda Napikoski. *The Personal Is Political: Where Did This Women's Movement Slogan Come From? What Does It Mean?* (2019), https://www.thoughtco.com/the-personal-is-political-slogan-origin-3528952 (accessed June 28, 2019).

2. This essay has its origins in the November 16, 2017 Jesuit Lecture at St Paul's College at the University of Manitoba, Winnipeg, in Treaty One Territory. It was entitled *All My Relations: The Healing of the Jesuits.* I especially acknowledge Dr Daniel MacLeod, director of the Jesuit Centre for Catholic Studies, and Dr Chris Adams, rector of St Paul's College for the invitation and for the opportunity to begin this reflection.

3. The acronym "S.J." after a person's name stands for the Latin *Societatis Iesu*, or "Society of Jesus" in English, and indicates that the person is a Jesuit.

4. The former formulation comes from the 32nd General Congregation of the Society of Jesus (a general congregation is a Jesuit legislative body of elected, *ex officio* and appointed members, and meets at need), 1974–1975, Decree 4, "Our Mission Today," paragraph 2; the latter comes from the 36th General Congregation of the Society of Jesus, 2016, Decree 1, "Companions of Jesus in a Mission of Reconciliation and Justice," paragraph 21. The latter formulation tries to say the same thing as the former, but in more relational language, and includes reconciliation with creation (ecological justice, broadly understood) as part of just relations among humans and with God. The former formulation, from 1975–1976, was a major transformation for the Jesuits, for it meant that work for social justice was no longer to be one ministry among others but meant to be part of our way of doing anything at all.

5. David Shanahan, *The Jesuit Residential School At Spanish: "More Than Mere Talent."* (Canadian Jesuit Historical Institute, Toronto, 2004), 15–17. The language of instruction in this school was Anishinaabemowin.

6. Shanahan, *The Jesuit Residential School at Spanish*, 30, 66. There were various reasons for the move. Spanish was close to the railroad, so this meant easier access for more Indigenous communities; there had also been tensions between the Jesuits and the community in Wikwemikong (including a strike by Indigenous construction workers) because of the Jesuits' attitude that they knew what was best for the people without consulting them—Shanahan, *The Jesuit Residential School at Spanish*, 50–54.

7. For example, see Michael J. Stogre, S.J., "The Jesuits' Ministry to the Native People of Canada," in Jacques Monet, S.J., *Builders of a Nation: Jesuits in English Canada 1842–2013*, Volume 2 in the *Jesuit History Series* (Toronto: Novalis, 2015), 27–72.

8. The Truth and Reconciliation Commission of Canada, or TRC, worked from 2008 to 2015. Its Final Report, issued in December 2015, included six volumes, a summary entitled *Honouring the Truth, Reconciling the Future*, and ninety-four Calls to Action. The Commissioners were: Justice Murray Sinclair (Chair), Grand Chief Wilton Littlechild, Dr Marie Wilson. The TRC was one of the key components of the IRSSA (see note 11).

9. In Jesuit terminology this role is called the "socius," which is Latin for "companion." In secular terms, the socius's role would be like that of a vice president.

10. The leader of a territorial Jesuit unit, called a "province," is called a "Provincial superior" or "Provincial," which is common usage in Catholic religious orders. A Jesuit Provincial is responsible for all the Jesuits and the ministries in his area. Under my charge, the area was the English-speaking parts of Canada, which included approximately 140 Jesuits, as well as well as many more colleagues in ministries from coast to coast, which included parishes, retreat and spirituality centers, schools, higher education institutions, social justice NGOs. From 1924 until 2018 the Jesuits in Canada were organized in two groups, French Canada, working mainly in Quebec, and English Canada, working in the rest of the country and in anglophone parts of Montréal. As of July 31, 2018, we are now one province, the Jesuits of Canada.

11. The IRSSA was finalized in 2006 and began to be implemented in 2007. The parties to the agreement were representatives of the survivors, the AFN, the Inuit Tapiriit Kanatami (ITK), the Anglican Church of Canada, the Presbyterian Church of Canada, the United Church of Canada, and the Corporation of Catholic Entities Party to the Indian Residential Schools Settlement. The IRSSA had five main components: financial compensation in two parts, the Common Experience Payment and the Independent Assessment Process; Commemoration; Health and Healing Services; and the Truth and Reconciliation Commission of Canada (TRC), which became the most well-known part of the agreement. At the time of writing, the implementation of the IRSSA is ongoing.

12. James Tully, "Reconciliation Here on Earth," in *Resurgence and Reconciliation: Indigenous-Settler Relations and Earth Teachings* (Toronto, Buffalo, London: University of Toronto Press, 2018), 83.

13. Society of Jesus, 32nd General Congregation; Decree 4, *Our Mission Today: The Service of Faith and the Promotion of Justice* (St Louis: Institute of Jesuit Sources: 1977), paragraph 2.

14. See especially his *Totalité et Infini: essai sur l'extériorité* (The Hague: Martinus Nijhoff, 1961).

15. On the insight that feelings are indicators of values at play, see Bernard Lonergan, *Method in Theology* (Toronto: University of Toronto Press, for the Lonergan Research Institute, first edition 1971), 37–38, 64–67.

16. Shanahan, *The Jesuit Residential School at Spanish*, 258. The most recent reunion was in 2016, in Spanish, Ontario.

17. S.J. Winston Rye and S.J. Peter Bisson, "Statement of Reconciliation – Jesuits in English Canada," 2013. See http://www.anishinabespiritualcentre.ca/statement-of-reconciliation-the-jesuits-in-english-canada/, accessed May 22, 2019.

18. The results of this meeting and of its preparations are expressed in S.J. Peter Bisson, *The State of the Province* (Toronto: Jesuits in English Canada, 2015).

19. Jesuit communities and ministries heard regular news of the TRC mainly in two ways: from the media and from the Provincial's annual visits to our communities and ministries where I would talk about what was going on with us across the country.

20. "Mother Teresa Middle School," (2019), http://mtmschoolregina.com, accessed June 5, 2019.

21. "Gonzaga Middle School," (2019), https://www.gonzagamiddleschool.ca/about-us/, accessed June 5, 2019.

22. "Our Lady of Guadalupe Circles Launches Inaugural Website," (2019), https://www.crc-canada.org/en/our-lady-of-guadalupe-circle-launches-inaugural-website, accessed June 4, 2019.

23. Truth and Reconciliation Commission of Canada, *Canada's Residential Schools, The Final Report of the Truth and Reconciliation Commission of Canada, Volume 6, Reconciliation* (Montréal, Kingston, London, Chicago: McGill-Queen's Press, 2015), 11.

24. Shanahan, *The Jesuit Residential School at Spanish*, 2004, 52.

25. Commissioner Dr. Marie Wilson, personal communication, June 2016.

26. Truth and Reconciliation Commission of Canada, *Canada's Residential Schools*, 96.

27. Indigenous people in Canada and the United States often use the name Turtle Island for North America.

28. J. R. Miller, *Residential Schools and Reconciliation: Canada Confronts Its History* (Toronto, Buffalo, London: University of Toronto Press: 2017), 14–18.

29. Miller, *Residential Schools and Reconciliation*, 13.

30. Ibid., 23.

31. Ibid., 27–29. The James Bay and Northern Quebec Agreement, between the James Bay Cree and the government of Canada was signed in 1975. Justice Thomas Berger released his report on the Mackenzie pipeline controversy, *Northern Frontier, Northern Homeland*, in 1977 which recommended a 10-year pause on energy development in the North until better regulation could be worked out and Indigenous land claims could be settled.

32. This insight about the sudden restriction in Indigenous-Church relations comes from Gerry Kelly in Ottawa who has long worked on promoting good relations between Indigenous people and the Catholic Church.

33. See John Borrows and James Tully, "Introduction: Reconciliation and Resurgence in Practice and in Question," in *Resurgence and Reconciliation; Indigenous-Settler Relations and Earth Teachings*, ed. Michael Asch, John Borrows, and James Tully (Toronto: University of Toronto Press, 2018), 3–12.

34. On the idea that feelings are signs of values in play, see Lonergan, *Method in Theology*, 37–38, 64–67.

35. The first apology specifically for residential schools, in 1991, was by the Catholic religious order, the Oblates of Mary Immaculate, or "Oblates" for short. The various groups of Oblates ran more schools than anyone else. Prime Minister Stephen Harper apologized on behalf of Canada in the House of Commons in 2008. All of the major Protestant and Anglican Churches that ran residential schools have apologized. Most Catholic religious orders and dioceses that ran schools have also apologized. (I do not know if all have.)

36. Miller, *Residential Schools and Reconciliation*, 139–140. Paulette Regan, *Unsettling the Settler Within: Indian Residential Schools, Truth-Telling, and Reconciliation in Canada* (Vancouver, Toronto: UBC Press, 2010), 141.

37. Borrows and Tully, "Introduction," 5–8, 15–16. They distinguish between nontransformative and transformative reconciliation. I try to express the same difference here with first and second reconciliation.

38. The French Christian philosopher Paul Ricoeur spoke of first and second naïvetés with respect to religion in secular contexts, where first naïveté was religion—Christianity—before secularization and modernization, and second naïveté was a new post-secular and postmodern form of religion that had appropriated in its own ways the uses of reason in secularized culture. See Ricoeur's *Symbolism of Evil* (Boston: Beacon Press, 1969), 349–357.

39. See National Inquiry into Murdered and Missing Indigenous Women and Girls, *Reclaiming Power and Place: The Final Report of the National Inquiry into Murdered and Mission Indigenous Women and Girls* (2019), http://www.mmiwg-ffada.ca, accessed June 28, 2019.

40. Borrows and Tully, "Introduction," 5.

41. After presenting an earlier version of these phases to a group of trustees of Catholic schools of Ontario, on January 17, 2019, a teacher encouraged me to visualize this in a graphic. This I did in a joint presentation with Sister Priscilla Solomon, CSJ, to members of the Institute for Catholic Education on April 10, 2019 in Toronto. I acknowledge Camille Legaspi of the Jesuits of Canada communications office for turning the graphic into a digital image.

42. Graham Ward, *True Religion* (Malden, Oxford, Victoria, Berlin: Blackwell Publishing, 2003); viii.

43. Other things, not only decolonization, are challenging and changing the Churches' agency. Similar changes are happening with the recognition of clergy sexual abuse and cover-up, with external and internal challenges to clericalism, and with the seeking of gender equity in the exercise of decision-making power in the Churches.

44. The TRC *Final Report* uses this expression, "Expanding the Circle" as the subtitle of the closing section of its chapter "Canada and the Churches" in its Volume 6, *Reconciliation*, 112.

45. One of the most important and powerful of these justifications has been the "doctrine of discovery", an idea in European international law, endorsed by some Renaissance popes and rejected by many modern ones, which allowed lands not governed by Christian rulers to be taken. In Canada this seems to be the historical and legal basis for the prior right of the Crown to land.

46. An important implementation of *Laudato Sí* happened in October 6–27, 2019, in Rome. The Catholic Church held a gathering of bishops (a 'synod') and Indigenous leaders from the Amazon basin in order to discuss how to live together responsibly and sustainably in an important biome, the Amazon basin. Indigenous leaders addressed other leaders from across the Catholic Church.

47. See TRC Call to Action Number 58.

BIBLIOGRAPHY

Andraos, Michel, Ed. *The Church and Indigenous People in the Americas: Between Reconciliation and Decolonization.* Studies in World Catholicism. Vol. 7 (Eugene, (Oregon: Cascade Books, 2019).

Asch, Michael, John Borrows, and James Tully, Eds. *Resurgence and Reconciliation: Indigenous-Settler Relations and Earth Teachings* (Toronto: University of Toronto Press, 2018).

Bisson, Peter, S.J. *All My Relations: The Healing of the Jesuits.* Transcript of The Annual Jesuit Lecture at St. Paul's College at the University of Manitoba (Winnipeg: St. Paul's College at the University of Manitoba, 2017).

Bisson, Peter, S.J. *State of the Province* (Toronto: Jesuits in English Canada, 2015).

Capitaine, Brieg, and Karine Vanthuye, Eds. *Power through Testimony: Reframing Residential Schools in the Age of Reconciliation* (Vancouver, Toronto: UBC Press, 2017).

Coulthard, Glen Sean. *Red Skin, White Masks: Rejecting the Colonial Politics of Recognition* (Minneapolis, London: University of Minnesota Press, 2014).

"Gonzaga Middle School". Accessed July 23, 2019. https://www.gonzagamiddle school.ca/about-us/

Levinas, Emmanuel. *Totalité et Infini: Essai sur l'extériorité* (The Hague: Martinus Nijhoff, 1961).

Lonergan, Bernard J. F. *Method in Theology* (Toronto: University of Toronto Press, for the Lonergan Research Institute of Regis College, Toronto, 1971).

Miller, J. R. *Residential Schools and Reconciliation: Canada Confronts Its History* (Toronto, Buffalo, London: University of Toronto Press, 2017).

"Mother Teresa Middle School." Accessed June 24, 2019. http://mtmschoolregina.com.

Napikoski, Linda. *The Personal is Political: Where Did this Women's Movement Slogan Come From? What Does it Mean?* Accessed June 24, 2019. https://www.tho ughtco.com/the-personal-is-political-slogan-origin-3528952.

National Inquiry into Murdered and Missing Indigenous Women and Girls. *Reclaiming Power and Place: The Final Report of the National Inquiry into Murdered and Mission Indigenous Women and Girls.* Accessed July 22, 2019. http://www.mmiwg-ffada.ca.

Niezen, Ronald. *Public Justice and the Anthropology of Law* (Cambridge: University of Cambridge Press, 2010).

Niezen, Ronald. *Truth and Indignation: Canada's Truth and Reconciliation Commission on Indian Residential Schools* (Toronto: University of Toronto Press, 2013).

"Our Lady of Guadalupe Circles Launches Inaugural Website." Accessed June 26, 2019. https://www.crc-canada.org/en/our-lady-of-guadalupe-circle-launches-in augural-website

Regan, Paulette. *Unsettling the Settler Within: Indian Residential Schools, Truth Telling, and Reconciliation in Canada* (Vancouver, Toronto: UBC Press, 2010).

Ricoeur, Paul (trans. Emerson Buchanan; original 1967). *Symbolism of Evil* (Boston: Beacon Press, 1969).

Ross, Rupert. *Dancing with a Ghost: Exploring Indian Reality* (Markham, ON: Octopus Publishing Group, 1992).

Rye, Winston, S.J., and Bisson, Peter, S.J. *Statement of Reconciliation – Jesuits in English Canada* (Toronto: Jesuits in English Canada, 2013).

Shanahan, David. *The Residential School at Spanish: "More than Mere Talent"* (Toronto: Canadian Institute of Jesuit Studies, 2004).

Society of Jesus. *Documents of the 31st and 32nd General Congregations of the Society of Jesus.* (Saint Louis: The Institute of Jesuit Sources, 1977).

Stogre, Michael, S.J. "The Jesuits' Ministry to the Native People of Canada." In *Builders of a Nation: Jesuits in English Canada 1842-2013*, Vol 2 in the *Jesuit History Series*. Edited by Jacques Monet, S.J. 27–72. (Toronto: Novalis, 2015).

The Truth and Reconciliation Commission of Canada. *Calls to Action.* (Truth and Reconciliation Commission of Canada, 2015.

The Truth and Reconciliation Commission of Canada. *Canada's Residential Schools: Reconciliation. The Final Report of the Truth and Reconciliation Commission.* (Montreal, Kingston, London, Chicago: McGill-Queen's Press, 2015).

The Truth and Reconciliation Commission of Canada. *Honouring the Truth, Reconciling for the Future. Summary of the Final Report of the Truth and Reconciliation Commission of Canada.* (The Truth and Reconciliation Commission of Canada, 2015).

The Truth and Reconciliation Commission of Canada. *What We Have Learned: Principles of Truth and Reconciliation.* (Truth and Reconciliation Commission of Canada, 2015).

Ward, Graham. *True Religion* (Malden, Oxford, Victoria, Berlin: Blackwell Publishing, 2003).

Young, Robert J. C. *Postcolonialism: A Very Short Introduction* (Oxford: Oxford University Press, 2003).

Chapter 5

Reconciliation and Indigenous Adult Learners

Reshaping Education through a Trauma-Informed Lens

Christa Yeates with Laura E. Reimer

Each day over the past decade, I have traveled into the heart of our Canadian prairie city where I teach in a unique learning environment designed especially for Indigenous adult learners[1] who are seeking to complete their secondary education. In this chapter, we call this school Maskawatisiwin (a pseudonym meaning strength of character). I am one of two teachers for the sixty students who are enrolled annually. All of the students are Indigenous[2] and over the age of eighteen. Over the years, some of our students have been over sixty years of age; many have earned their high school equivalency diplomas from us (specifically recognized as a mature student diploma), but the journey is a particularly challenging one for many. Trauma has had a profound impact on the way our students learn and perceive their identity as learners, and it takes a similar toll on us as teachers; yet, this seems to be a little-researched topic. The school and the school district administration have been able to offer little guidance to either of us as to how to recognize, acknowledge, or implement trauma-informed education for such learners, but we are realizing that it is critical to reconciliation. Trauma-informed strategies and models shape the approaches my colleague and I are taking as educators of traumatized students. Without doubt, a shared and healthy future for our larger society must include this recognition, and some practical changes in the classroom as part of the reconciliation process. This chapter establishes the recognition, confirmation, and understanding of how trauma manifests and must inform teaching in order to facilitate learning and improved educational outcomes not just for the students themselves, but for their families and future generations, and for the educators working in environments like ours.

TRAUMA-INFORMED EDUCATION

Our perspective of trauma-informed teaching contains hope and compassion, and does not look for blame or cause. We acknowledge that people are hurting and in our school we are striving to find ways to help them move forward. Our ability to suspend judgment and criticism of most behaviors is critical because for our students, trust and respect are crucial to the foundations of learning and living. The definition of trauma-informed care that guides us comes from the work of Harris and Fallot,[3] which refers to acknowledging the role of violence and victimization in people's lives and creating services that strive to not retraumatize them, while providing strategies to maintain the health of service providers—like us. This is a highly relevant topic that requires specific and accurate understanding and knowledge, and buy-in on all levels of education delivery—from the classroom to administration. Teachers left without administrative support and knowledge in this area can feel unsupported and admonished, and are at a risk of experiencing vicarious trauma. Through our years in the field we have felt and experienced those things but until recently did not recognize it as part of our work with traumatized people.

The ultimate goal of trauma-informed practice in education is "to create a physically and psychologically safe learning community that allows trauma victims to let down their guard and enables them to focus on learning."[4] Within the context of this chapter, trauma is defined as a natural, human response to a person's subjective interpretation of severe, overwhelming stress.[5] We have seen this frequently in our classrooms over the past ten years and learned to recognize that those behaviors that may be interpreted by the unaware as defiance or disrespect are actually the expressions of trauma emerging at school.

According to Harris and Fallot,[6] trauma should be viewed as a "defining and organizing experience that forms the core of an individual's identity." If this is true, as teachers we must acknowledge that trauma disrupts a person's life, influences their view of the world, and may negatively affect daily functioning and human development—which includes life inside our classroom.[7] Education is an acknowledged solution to many problems,[8] and educational attainment has been positively correlated with every single important positive life outcome. Some of the traumas experienced by students at our school provide real barriers to educational attainment. Research has confirmed that many students have historically endured shocking levels of loss, bullying, and the absence of a caring adult. Many have also experienced the impact of humiliating education laws that progressed students through the grades without ensuring they had grasped fundamental concepts for success.[9] In addition, our students experience everyday types of trauma such as jail time, housing issues, abuse, and poverty. For our students, the existence of trauma means that learning and teaching cannot occur as it does for most students.

Trauma-informed in the context of teaching is derived from Harris and Fallot's focus on service systems. To be trauma-informed is to acknowledge the "roles that violence and victimization play" in the lives of those who access our services, to then use this understanding to create systems that are welcoming and "accommodate the vulnerabilities of trauma survivors," and to create a role for the participant to feel as though they have input.[10] Trauma-informed practice in education has "the ultimate goal to create a physically and psychologically safe learning community that allows trauma victims to let down their guard and focus on learning."[11] This requires that teachers and the administrators who support them have a specialized set of skills, knowledge, and understanding which must also extend into an acknowledgment of vicarious trauma and support for the teachers in such classrooms. Based on our experiences and the trauma literature, this chapter explores our suggestions for extending this knowledge into the classroom.

While a growing body of literature identifies a number of sources for the learning challenges of Canada's Indigenous people, some scholarship asserts that assigning and defining the correct blame will bring healing. We have not found this to be helpful. The reasons may vary but regardless of who is at fault, it cannot be denied that the impacts of trauma are evident and prominent when one recognizes it especially in the Indigenous adult learners at our school. Importantly to discussions of healing, reconciliation, and a hopeful shared future, an economist James Heckman was awarded a Nobel Peace Prize for demonstrating that early intervention has produced more high school graduations, less criminal activity, increased employment, and decreased family and community violence in the long run.[12] This means that the cycle can indeed be broken. For us, knowing that these potential outcomes are possible also reshapes the way we respond to adult students. Our conduct is critical to the delivery of effective andragogy for those suffering from trauma.

THE ORIGINS OF TRANS-GENERATIONAL TRAUMA AMONG INDIGENOUS ADULTS

Trauma among Canada's Indigenous people began several hundred years ago. The culmination of many imperial policies for assimilation and nation building by French, British, and later Canadian governments[13] resulted in what we now recognize as trauma in the form of an erosion of cultural identity and a loss of self-worth.[14] The implementation of these assimilation policies across multiple generations has been identified as the primary origin of high rates of mental health and social issues for Indigenous peoples in Canada,[15] but all of the reasons for trauma do not lie in the distant past.

Between the 1870s and 1996, the British and then Canadian governments implemented an *Indian residential schools policy*. Approximately 150,000 children attended these boarding schools and the experience had a traumatic impact on most Indigenous people and their families; an impact that manifests in our classroom at Maskawatisiwin today. While residential schools were established in British North America at least as early as 1830 for Indigenous children, an 1884 amendment to the federal *Indian Act* implemented the *Indian residential schools policy* as mandatory and a critical part of an assimilation strategy. Based on the British boarding school model, the schools (referred to hereafter as residential schools) intentionally separated Indigenous children from the influences of their families and communities. This facilitated assimilation into the settler culture while separating the children from their Indigenous cultural heritage.[16] Shame and identity loss have been well established in literature as outcomes of this policy,[17] which was in force until the last school closed its doors in 1998.

Research has determined that those who attended residential schools experience(d) a profound sense of bereavement throughout their lives.[18] Many Indigenous adults exhibit symptoms of childhood trauma, including generalized anxiety, hypervigilance, guardedness, difficulty in establishing and sustaining intimate relationships, low self-esteem, alienation, and mistrustfulness.[19] We have witnessed all of these in our classrooms and we have found trauma-informed teaching to be very helpful for us as we work to extend kindness, compassion, and often extra time so that they feel safe in our learning environment.

Survival strategies are an outcome of trauma that is often evident in our adult learning environment. These include learned helplessness, passive-aggressive behavior, dissociation, substance use, denial, and in extreme cases, suicide.[20] As with most behavioral responses to trauma, these behaviors are often passed on from and to subsequent generations.[21] Consequently, many of the challenges inherent in Indigenous communities today, such as alcoholism, child abuse, domestic violence, lack of formal education, marginalization, unemployment, and suicide, have their roots attributed to residential schools.[22] Significantly, many of the children and grandchildren of people who attended residential schools and also those who did not attend demonstrate these traits, and we see this every day.

IMPACT OF TRAUMA ON LEARNING

The countless impacts of trauma on individuals have been well-documented and it is critical that we, as teachers are aware of them.[23] We are aware of the deep struggles that underlie the efforts of our students to learn. While the effects of trauma may be short-lived and can be unique to each person, often, the effects of trauma fundamentally modify the ways in which an individual perceives themselves and the world around them over a long period of time.[24] Trauma can have lasting effects on mental health, physical health, social connectedness, and personal characteristics.[25] Interestingly, despite the findings and recommendations of the Canadian *Royal Commission on Aboriginal People* in 1996, and the identification of the negative impact of role of residential schools in the *Truth and Reconciliation Commission Final Report*, there is almost no research about the impact of trauma on formal school learning among Indigenous students. Importantly, we could find no evidence that student teachers in Canadian universities are being trained to recognize trauma in their students—Indigenous or otherwise.

OUR SCHOOL

Maskawatisiwin is located in a city of close to a million people in Central Canada. Our province has legislation that is unique in Canada and provides a legal framework for educating adults in nonconventional learning centers; this created the space for the establishment of our school. The *Adult Learning Centres Act* was passed on July 1, 2003,[26] and we opened within several years of that legislation.

The school is not traditional. The building is a community center that sits in a gang-contested neighborhood of racialized poverty. It is one of Canada's poorest communities, and the site of murders and other gang activities like violence, the drug trade, alcohol abuse, and prostitution. The majority of the residents self-identify as Indigenous, a statistic that has grown significantly since the school opened.[27] Over 80% of the residents have not completed high school.[28] In addition to the legacy of residential schools, life is very difficult each and every day.

A student at Maskawatisiwin described the neighborhood history in one of her English class assignments and wrote, "While living in the developments twenty years ago there was auto theft, break and enters, murder, drinking, drugs and fighting. Today, younger people are more violent; they are stealing cars, fighting, killing one another, robbing stores and people for their clothing, money, etc. Younger children are involved in disturbing acts of violence, versus twenty years ago."[29]

We are learning to merge the required sensitivities of trauma-informed teaching with provincial curricular requirements for high school completion. In other words, before school learning can begin, and as their learning journey progresses, our students must work through layers of individual and group traumas. The neighborhood is characterized as "a web of poverty, racism, drugs, gangs, and violence" where residents are "caught in a cycle of interrelated problems,"[30] and we are recognizing that in their daily lives, many of our students are retraumatized. In addition to their personal traumas, the students face many barriers, including transportation issues, childcare for their preschool children, family resistance to further education, and general social opposition. Ensuring that we are trauma-informed is one of the key requirements for working with our students for their success in education and ultimately to improve the quality of their lives.

All adult residents of the city are eligible to attend our school if they meet mathematics and English requirements. The school has been intentionally structured to minimize and eliminate traditional barriers to further adult education and is part of a larger education network that includes job creation, and flows from community study and feedback. During the day, there are in-class tutors. Our administration was briefly able to fund a social worker for half a day a week to help us support our students. This addition was not only a great support to the students but also supported the staff by alleviating some of the strain they faced. One could only imagine the benefits a full-time social worker could provide: someone to work alongside us, also dedicated to helping the students move forward in positive and healthy ways. This would also have the beneficial spin-off of helping the staff to know the students were being cared for, and reduce the stress of feeling that we have to be everything for the students.

There are volunteer tutors at our school, trained by Frontier College, a century-old Canadian literacy organization. Originally, our tutors were students from a nearby university, but the transience of their student status was difficult for us and many of the Maskawatisiwin students; now we have older people as tutors who have been committed to our school and our students for multiple years. There is a strong need for one-on-one learning opportunities in at-risk populations, and the tutors provide this for students who can then work at their own pace.[31] The tutors are also integral in helping the students adjust to school at the beginning of the term and each day, and provide them with feel a sense of welcome and belonging. They are able to establish a close personal connection with many students, which is what is so needed in these types of schools and student populations. An advantage with Frontier College is the supply of appropriately trained tutors not contingent on funding.

Our Students

Nearly 100 students have graduated since our school opened, though the average daily attendance is low. While this may flag concerns by most administrative standards, life is very difficult for most of the students, and we recognize this reality. As teachers, we are usually confidentially aware of the reasons for student absences, through our close working relationships and trust with our students.

It is not uncommon for the adult students to be absent for weeks at a time and unable to attend classes until circumstances are safe or more settled. For other students, health concerns, family crises, housing issues, court, or even new babies can take them away from classes for extended periods. When these matters are resolved, the students return to the school (usually unannounced) and resume their studies. Often they do not phone to explain or say they are going to miss a few days or several months. It is nearly impossible to phone them because phone numbers are ever changing and sometimes they disappear for many months or a year or more. Due to these realities, students' experiences when they return cannot be minimized or ignored by placing them within the traditional evaluative categories of poor attendance and high dropout rates, nor by simply blaming history and residential schools.

For example, Claire (not her real name) has had two children, aged 1 and 3, with David (also a pseudonym). Both parents were students at Maskawatisiwin. David has stated repeatedly that he wants to complete his high school to set a good example for the children. The children, however, were taken from Claire and David at their births and placed into care by Child and Family Services. The children have been adopted by two other families. Claire dropped out of our program officially stating that she wanted to be a hairdresser, and insisted that earning her high school diploma would not help her achieve that. Two months later, David announced that they were expecting another child.

Another student left the school for an extended period because of lung and bronchial diseases resulting from wearing inappropriate winter clothing and footwear all season. She steadfastly continued to attend classes until the weather reached −40°C and her sickness became severe as no appropriately sized jackets were available in the clothing depot at the neighborhood resource center located next door. She stopped attending school.

A third student, expelled from the public school system in our province, enrolled in Maskawatisiwin and was absent the next day and for weeks following due to gall stones. Despite the young age of this student, and the severity of his pain, the doctors at the attending downtown hospital insisted that he take the public transit back to our school (a 35-minute ride on two buses) to get a note from us as his teachers, verifying his abdominal pain. Life is very difficult for the Maskawatisiwin adult students, and their difficulties are compounded and complicated by extreme poverty, racism, and often overwhelming and unfair bureaucracy of life inside Canada's social welfare system.

The Administration

Leaders are key in sustaining the momentum and development of a school such as Maskawatisiwin. Our first principal was engaged and actively involved and provided a particularly strong start for us. He was a seasoned administrator with much experience and he had been the leader of five adult learning centers (ALCs) before being assigned to us. He was appointed to the administrative position at Maskawatisiwin by the school division partly because the school is a satellite of the other ALCs, but he was also personally enthusiastic about the project. He also demonstrated extraordinarily high levels of commitment, capacity, and time—especially in light of his responsibilities with five other adult schools. The influence and presence of that principal at the school was crucial to its ongoing momentum and sustainability. He was frequently on-site and knew student names, he greeted them individually, and they were receptive to him and to his presence in the building. As with most schools, regular but not frequent visits from the school district occur, and the support provided through these interactions is helpful to us as teachers, and of course, for our students. These visits feel like support to all of us. According to Coleman's social capital theory and relevant to trauma-informed teaching, strong relationships can have positive effects on student learning because they constitute a form of trust, and traumatized people, whether vicarious trauma or actual, need to know trust.[32] Furthermore, Coleman's theory suggests that the actions of someone in a significant position, like a principal, can impact both individuals and the development of an ALC as a community.

Generally, teachers and administrators are student focused. This is reflected in how we grant credits in an environment where student attendance drastically fluctuates from one week—and sometimes one day—to the next. In contrast with the mainstream school system, Maskawatisiwin keeps track of each unit completed within a course. This way, students do not have to repeat an entire course if they did not complete all the units in a given school year (as is the situation in regular secondary institutions), though this sometimes changes with new administrations. One of our challenges is that outcome measurements important to school systems, such as number of graduates and number of credit obtained, may not be meaningful in this context, and so the divisional visits can provide helpful guidance as we work to balance what we encounter daily in the context of trauma and learning with the realities of our professional responsibilities.

Much has changed in the time that Maskawatisiwin has been open, which we are now recognizing has been particularly challenging for us as we work with a population suffering from various levels of trauma. Our first principal retired after our first year. Now, principals are assigned to us from schools all over our large and diverse district. Often times, working with adult students especially ones suffering from trauma experiences like ours, requires an adjustment in thinking and procedures for administrators as well as for us. Our senior administrative staff is located off-site, but the day-to-day oversight of our center has been assigned to a vice principal, an office that is also off-site. This means that we are trying to carefully and respectfully navigate between two levels of administration, but since our school is unusual in operation, with a somewhat complicated governance model compared to most, it is understandable that we all encounter additional administrative challenges. The realities of our students' lives and learning experiences can be very foreign to those who are not engaged as we are and who do not see the students in their daily contexts. For example, the trauma-informed lens means that as educators, we must take the time to truly understand the unique lives, experiences, and needs of our students, and how the school must operate unconventionally as a means to student success. Our connections with our administrators are important to us as educators in order to feel supported and that our work is valued, especially in an environment of traumatized learners. We also recognize that this is a unique place to be and to need and to work, and that the usual expectations of us as teachers do not neatly align with the unique demands of our roles, and the demands on our administrators, at Maskawatisiwin.

The Teachers

After the first year, one teacher (me) remained, and the other was replaced by a female Indigenous teacher named Rose (also a pseudonym). We have worked together ever since and at time of writing will do so again next term. We are both seasoned educators with much experience in adult learning and in challenging learning environments. In addition to our formal education and training, our partnership has been crucial to the success of the school because our complementary skills and knowledge bases bring credibility. We have a strong working relationship and expend a lot of energy reading and thinking about our work. Rose and I spend a lot of time discussing and initiating changes to our daily activities and school operations that will better address the needs of the students. One of my greatest challenges has been translating these informed conversations about what our students need in response to what they live and struggle with to the administrators. As teachers, we navigate the requirements of a traditional school system while striving to translate our deeply difficult work into language and expectations that others can relate to, understand, and resource. Rose respectfully incorporates Indigenous cultural aspects in our work. Many students have left our school saying that this is where they first learned about their culture, its history, and strength. Rose has given me the knowledge and confidence to also able to include these aspects in my lessons and in the school community. The students have often expressed that we helped them initially feel acceptance and comfort in the school. We both feel that our partnership and respect for each other's contributions has been an important part of our school's success, especially of our students' success.

The Classroom

The structure of Maskawatisiwin originally reflected a typical semestered school with two subjects in the morning, two subjects in the afternoon each day Monday through Friday. But each year for the first five years, the timetable and the course offerings evolved to find the best fit of time and subject matter to meet the learning needs of our students. This was not a simple process, and the changes and initiatives conceptualized and initiated by us that ensure maximized opportunities for our traumatized learners often required a lot of effort. Candidly, this kind of advocacy has a perceived personal risk (to our reputations or credibility) as we struggle to convince the administration to understand and then to authorize and support our proposed changes.

Currently, our school is restructured and does not operate like a typical high school—because we are responding to our student body. While we offer three trimesters, we also offer a continuous intake for some courses. This is an important arrangement that means our students can get credit for the work they have done. We intentionally structure our year so that trimesters end before major breaks in the mainstream academic year, when we have learned that many students may return home or get derailed from classes by the holidays. The continuous intake means that we can welcome and accept students as soon as they arrive and are ready to start (or restart) their learning, meeting them where they are at.

Some of our less typical adaptations include the absence of a firm deadline for submission of materials, that students enroll in a maximum of one morning course and one afternoon course (instead of the original two and two), and that one nonteaching day a week allows students to take care of matters in their personal life, without missing school. This extra day also allows them time to catch up on school work. We encourage independent credits (congruent with the provincial curriculum) in areas that improve both self-esteem and marketable skills, such as volunteering, cultural exploration, and participation in oral and written language proficiency tests offered by the school district.

To us, this is trauma information carefully applied to teaching in order to strategically match the students' learning needs with mandated requirements for successful completion of the mature student high school diploma.

TRAUMA, PHYSIOLOGY, AND LEARNING

Our students live with trauma and its impacts. Traumatic experiences among Indigenous adults have been demonstrated to have negative effects on memory, cognition, and learning and are detailed here for greater understanding for our readers.[33] This can manifest as decreased memory, verbal fluency, and verbal learning.[34] Sustained attention, executive functioning, and information processing speed can also suffer.[35] Chronic, traumatic experiences across the lifespan can result in changes in brain structure and brain development.[36] The age at which children are first traumatized, the duration, the severity, and the extent to which a child's caregiver was involved in inducing the trauma play a role in determining severity of neurobiological and psychological outcomes.[37]

The list of trauma-related indicators is long. Smoking, alcoholism, substance use, risky sexual behavior, poor diet, and decreased physical activity are common in Indigenous adults who have lived through adverse childhood experiences, and therefore, have experienced trauma.[38] Heart disease, diabetes, liver disease, autoimmune diseases, asthma, fibromyalgia, chronic fatigue, neck pain, back pain, digestive problems, migraines, irritable bowels, mental distress, and increased heart rate and blood pressure are also found to be correlated with having experienced increased numerous adverse childhood experiences.[39] Unhealthy coping strategies and an increased likelihood to be living with poorer health may likely contribute to increased absences from school and, possibly, a learner that is less able to expend the energy required to be an active and fully engaged learner, not to mention poor nutrition, poor sleep habits, and alcohol and drugs that impact the potential for student achievement.

Generally, people living with trauma are hypervigilant, with a heighted sense of arousal, quick to startle, quick to assume the worse, and sometimes ready to do battle to defend themselves.[40] Direct eye contact is avoided.[41] Quick to seek blame in others and a difficulty in seeing their part in the problem, along with difficulty in trusting and practicing vulnerability are other challenges inherent in this group of learners. Small incidents can quickly escalate due to dysregulated stress responses and impaired relational skills.[42] Threat of an unpredictable confrontation looms daily as a distinct possibility within the school community. Many educators are unprepared to deal with the trauma triggers, explosive outbursts, and self-destructiveness. Distrust of educators and of other students is common among traumatized Indigenous learners.⁴³ This knowledge has been extremely useful for us as we work with our learners each day.

INSIGHTS FOR EDUCATORS FROM THE TRAUMA LITERATURE

Because research and literature about the effects of trauma among Indigenous learners is in the emergent phase, we have extrapolated from the general literature. In the following paragraphs, we apply the impact of trauma to the learning context. The majority of this trauma-related literature either focuses on pedagogy, as opposed to andragogy, or working with adults in the health services, as opposed to classrooms. We have included research specific to Indigenous and adult learners whenever possible. Indigenous learners will likely experience the negative effects of trauma that are common to all learners; however, the history of Indigenous peoples in Canada adds another layer of complexity for Indigenous learners.⁴⁴ For example, classroom practices that Indigenous people associate with the authoritarian ways of residential schools may trigger or reactivate trauma-related memories and further exacerbate problematic behavior in educational settings.⁴⁵ As part of the reconciliation journey, acknowledging and confirming trauma in our learners is critical to their learning process.

When working with Indigenous adult learners through a trauma-informed lens it is imperative that one not only focuses on the aspects of how they learn but also focuses on the trauma-informed practices in place in their school. Much of the literature that speaks to creating trauma-informed care for health service providers can also be applied to adult education environments. The recommendations below are informed from both school settings and health services, but we apply them more directly to our classrooms to extend the hopeful outcomes of real reconciliation.

Some authors recommend a historically holistic approach to students. This means that just as one should assume that every adult Indigenous learner could be feeling the effects of historical trauma and concurrently experiencing ongoing trauma, one should also assume that the Indigenous adult student or people in their circle, have had their lives touched by residential school experiences.⁴⁶ Educators should anticipate that any Indigenous adult returning to ALCs, literacy programs, or upgrading programs did not have positive and successful educational experiences in their formative years and these must be acknowledged.⁴⁷ Their identities may have been deeply shaped by educators who taught them that "they are good for nothing, know nothing, and are incapable of learning anything,"⁴⁸ and by their own difficult scholastic journey.⁴⁹ Indigenous adult learners are entering the classrooms with a lot of life experience, familial and cultural influences, and a lot of baggage. Both the educator and the student may be unaware of this baggage and the extent to which it influences: the perceptions of the learning environment, the students' relationships within the school, feelings of shame, the ability of the student to learn, and modifications that could be made to increase success and positivity in the classroom, and turn a classroom from a potentially triggering experience into an opportunity for healing and growth.

Teachers are not therapists and being a trauma-informed program does not imply that students are asked to share and address their traumatic pasts.[50] Instead, we are watching, wondering, assessing, and sometimes assuming trauma, through the actions, behaviors, and attitudes in our classroom. These five core elements must animate the thinking and teaching of a trauma-informed educator:[51]

(1) Some students may be traumatized.
(2) Some content or assignments may be triggering.
(3) Some interactions and behaviors in the school community may be re-traumatizing.
(4) Certain classroom practices may be unhelpful.
(5) Self-care for everyone is important.

Understanding meanings clearly is also critical to our work. Being trauma-informed, according to Harris and Fallot[52] means:

(1) All staff are informed about the effects of trauma and victimization so that they can respond in ways that are sensitive, helpful, and avoid re-traumatization,
(2) Policies and procedures are carefully examined to ensure that they are welcoming and appropriate for the people they serve,
(3) An acknowledged understanding of how day-to-day operations may resemble terrifying experiences and designing services that accommodate these vulnerabilities,
(4) Programs are structured to allow for participant choice and feelings of self-directedness.

In this way, students and educators alike are equipped to recognize, accommodate, and navigate the consequences of trauma while engaging in the learning journey of school.

Trauma-informed schools need to use strength-based and relational approaches. These help to repair regulatory abilities, connect with their students, and allow them the safety in which to reshape their learner identity and reveal and enhance their strengths.[53] Trauma-informed educators lead by asking, "What happened to you?" as opposed to "What's wrong with you?"[54] A lot of what characterizes a person who has been affected by trauma are behaviors that could be seen by teachers in more typical classrooms as disruptive, or as lack of effort on the student's part. The better informed a teacher can be of the prevalence of trauma, possible triggers of trauma, the characteristics of a person affected by trauma, and the manifestations of trauma in a classroom, the more a teacher can support and plan for these students in his or her classroom, the better the learning experience.

Teacher and classroom practices that can support adult Indigenous learners impacted by trauma include flexibility, safety, understanding, attachment, belonging, sense of community, feeling heard and valued. This allows for student ownership, the opportunity for the student to demonstrate and reinforce their skills and abilities, support handling emotions, respect, knowledge and collaboration with outside resources, the understanding that trust must be earned, storytelling, noninterference, recognizing the importance of family and culture, humor, and empowerment.[55] The challenge for teachers working with traumatized students is that these supportive practices can be difficult to understand for those not involved in the work daily. We are grateful when we as teachers receive support and care while doing this type of work.

And so, knowledge of one's self, awareness of the effects of trauma, appraisal of the space and the curriculum content for triggers, and honest connections with students are crucial in mitigating the effects of retraumatization in adult Indigenous learners.

Some of the characteristics that trauma-affected Indigenous adult students may demonstrate can be misunderstood as learning disabilities when in fact they are based on trauma, not learning capacity.[56] For some students, this evidences as difficulty beginning new activities, having an aversion to taking risks, and difficulty maintaining self-esteem,[57] which may stem from a fear of being humiliated, punished, or rejected for making mistakes.[58] Traumatized students often resemble unmotivated students. Learners living with the effects of trauma come into the classroom significantly disadvantaged and, because of their symptoms, they may be labeled by educators as oppositional, uninterested, distracted, distant, confrontational, or unintelligent. Flexibility is a daily requirement as learners may struggle with certain tasks and they may also be frequently absent from school due to health problems, anxiety, or unstable living situations.[59] A teacher that understands trauma can better weather, and plan for, the storms that plague these learners, although the specific literature and research about trauma and learning is limited.

There are many critical ways to use the trauma-informed lens productively in the classroom as part of Canada's reconciliation journey. Understanding that frustration and panic are readily triggered among Indigenous learners who have experienced trauma when they are asked to learn something new can help teachers to be sensitive to the needs of their students when introducing new concepts.[60] Procrastination and lack of communication, which may stem from anxiety, difficult past school relationships, or an engrained sense of lack of entitlement may also characterize this type of student.[61] Paying attention, concentrating, and listening are also often challenging and could be a result of the dissociation or depersonalization experienced as a result of trauma.[62] Creating and maintaining a safe and trauma-informed environment is fundamental in helping students to being able to learn. Remembering the concepts of trauma-informed communities, focusing on strengths, and reminding oneself it is about what happened to the pupil (as opposed to what is wrong with them) can help a teacher to develop the patience, understanding, and connection required to foster an environment of healing and growth for these learners.[63]

We have learned that teachers should also be prepared and remain flexible for occasions when Indigenous adult learners disappear or self-sabotage—in particular when the student is close to reaching a goal. A deeply held belief that they are unable to be successful may plague Indigenous learners, which may prevent them from completing their work or the required courses to reach their goals.[64] We see this often at our school, where students also lack role models who have finished school, or lack families that are supportive of further education. This often results in a decreased desire, or decreased imagination to set goals and believe that persistent hard work could lead to successful attainment of their diploma. They tell us they need support and resources to access when the going gets tough, or that they need people around them who are also sharing similar experiences so that they can talk with someone who knows and is also going through it. Trying to complete school as an individual can be quite isolating and lonely if the student is the only one in the family or community in school. We recently learned about a very bright young person (all details here are anonymized) who was doing well and going far in postsecondary training. But when that person went home during break someone had smashed her windows and slashed her tires, which resulted in her missing her final exam. Fortunately, the exam proctor advocated hard for an extension and it was granted, but this is typical of many of the other challenges our students encounter.

An educator who does not consider the effects of trauma on the student's learning may question the motives and desires of such a student. An educator may also begin to withdraw from the learner with the rationale that his or her time could be better spent on another student who appears more committed to learning. The educator's response may reinforce students' feelings of incompetence and lack of self-worth, and further justify their reluctance to trust, to persist, and to try new challenges and to take risks.[65] Connecting with students, positively acknowledging them, and patiently sitting with them as they work can help to reinforce trust and meaning for the student and in the school community. In this way, we have found our consistent volunteers to be a great help. It is also important to be attuned to small successes, realizing that much of the learning that is taking place may be occurring inside the learner (like learning to trust or to regulate emotions) and is not immediately visible.[66] We strive to acknowledge strengths and accomplishments in students and their work to instill hope and meaning for their future.

Trauma survivors may also display difficulties in recognizing their feelings, taking care of themselves, feeling pleasure, or having a sense of meaning in their lives, and this is often evident in the classroom.[67] Again, these may be regarded as antisocial behaviors, rather than manifested responses to trauma. As well, because of the energy required to keep their emotions in check, deal with anxiety, and cope with disturbed sleep patterns, traumatized Indigenous learners—as with any traumatized learners—may come to school too exhausted to participate effectively.[68] These neurological changes often produce people who appear less motivated, less engaged, less enthusiastic, and less able to create healthy connections with the teacher and the other learners. In turn, teachers may feel discouraged with their inability to engage the pupil and question their dedication and effort. Understanding the lives of students outside the classroom and the students' internal turmoil has helped us as teachers, and can inform other educators in similar environments to continue to connect with learners in culturally informed and sensitive ways.

Although intimidating, and possibly triggering, school has the potential of becoming one of the few places of safety, consistency, and belonging in an Indigenous adult learner's life. Helping to establish safety and trust, a student needs to feel heard, to feel understood, to feel as though they matter, and to feel as though their feelings and responses are normal effects based on their past experiences. Choice, respect, and the opportunity to prove (seemingly to the instructor, but more likely to themselves) that they are smart should be consistent features in a trauma-informed classroom.

STRATEGIES THAT WORKED

Within our school we strive to not only educate our students' minds with the mandated subjects, but also to look at all aspects of the person and the world in which they live. Culturally, we connect with elders; traditional acts such as smudging or spirit plates at celebrations are explained and open to everyone if they choose. As funding permits, we participate with our students at a sweat lodge. We celebrate the calendar holidays (Thanksgiving, Christmas, spring feast) by sitting down and eating together with our school community. We are gentle during these times, knowing that they may not be happy times of family togetherness, feasting, and loving celebration for everyone involved.

We also do what we can to be bridges between their familiar neighborhood and the people and resources outside of their neighborhood. We recognize that a lot of mistreatment and racism may have taught our students to be apprehensive and mistrustful in the world where I and my colleagues move freely about. Not only do we go on fieldtrips to culturally significant museums, we also visit many of the mental health, employment, and educational resources in the city. Sometimes for our students, one of the hardest challenges to accessing help can be walking through the door of an organization. We realize this and try to help students walk through as many doors as possible while being welcomed and accepted, before they graduate from Maskawatisiwin.

A significant and extremely successful and meaningful project that occurred at our school was a project that connected female students with older, mostly retired women, from outside of the school's neighborhood. I created and initiated this project because I was hearing so many of my students' stories and it seemed as though they were crying out for someone to see them and hear them and tell them they were okay. So, I created a course where the students and I would move through the medicine wheel and the stages of life.

In each stage they would tell stories, first to each other and then, for one day at the end of each doorway/life stage, we would invite the outside women to join us. We would begin and end together in a circle, but the bulk of the time was spent one-on-one with a pair comprising a student and an invited woman. They met as equals, both sharing stories, asking questions, and then going away and writing their interpretation of the other person's story that was told to them.

My goals of this initiative were to connect two seemingly different and separated groups of women and have them recognize their similarities. For the students to share their story (or the parts they chose to share) with a caring, nonjudgmental person and for the students to have their story reflected back to them as a story of strength and resilience and perseverance was powerful. For the women to meet as equals, both with stories worth telling seemed transformational. The invited women caught a glimpse into the lives of the students, maybe thought "But for the grace God, go I," and took that understanding back to their lives and passed it on to some of the people they connect with. After the first nervous and apprehensive meeting everyone was excited for the next three encounters. Important relationships were formed and this project remains one of those things I am very grateful I did. Many years later, some of these pairs continue to regularly keep in touch and support each other.

CONCLUSION

Through this chapter we have strived to pull trauma literature into the realities of educating Indigenous adults. This is an important part of reconciliation. We have concluded that the trauma-informed lens is the way forward for teachers, especially those working with Indigenous adult learners. Our students are born into a world that seems to be rarely recognized as traumatic—especially by the traditional institutions of education. Most importantly, literature that includes the voices and school experiences of the traumatized Indigenous learner is sparse, and in this there is room for important research. We do know that many Indigenous persons suffer intergenerational traumas, which often manifest in daily life as abuse, neglect, addictions, racism, physical and mental health problems, and the social and economic struggles inherent with membership to a group of oppressed and marginalized people. We also know that for students like those at Maskawatisiwin, trauma is also a largely unacknowledged part of everyday life for them and for those around them.

For me, learning that there is a trauma-informed lens drastically changed my world. To use an old metaphor, it was like I did not know that I needed glasses until a doctor held up lenses to my eyes. When I began to look at our school, our students, and our role as teachers, through the trauma-informed lens, I was surprised at how sharp and clear and bright everything looked. I began to understand in ways I had not before. I also do not think the students know that their eyes are trauma-impacted eyes; they just think that that is how the world is or that these things that they are doing are just because they are not good students or good people. But again, the trauma-informed lens for us as educators has prepared us to acknowledge and address those deeply held beliefs, so that we may launch the potential in our students. It has also made us aware that we, too, are living with trauma in many forms. To continue to be strong educators for our students, we must be aware that we, too, require self-care.

Adult educators and administrators have a role to play in creating safe, trauma-informed schools where Indigenous adult learners can learn to learn, learn to heal, and have the positive educational experiences that likely eluded them their entire lives. Although trauma-informed communities have their focus on the health fields, educators are beginning to recognize the value of creating trauma-informed learning communities. Many of the recommendations for trauma-informed care or trauma-informed practices in other fields can be modified and applied to education, and especially to ALCs, for the benefits of students and teachers alike. There is little research that explains the impacts of vicarious trauma on students and on their teachers. We trust this chapter will plant seeds of inquiry so that others will undertake this important research. Because we are teachers, there are some practices we undertake because of what we have learned about trauma, but we are not counselors. We are careful to know our boundaries, to strive to understand and acknowledge the effects of vicarious trauma, to be aware of our need for extra administrative support, and to practice self-care. These are important parts of the trauma-informed lens. This will, in turn, better equip all of us who teach and learn alongside one another in this difficult yet rewarding work.

NOTES

1. All names and identifying features except Canada have been replaced with pseudonyms.

2. Indigenous is a globally recognized reference to people who can trace their ancestry to the original inhabitants of a land mass. In Canada, "Aboriginal" is the legal term for the Indigenous people, but the people groups are recognized as First Nations, Métis, Inuit. First Nations people (identified as Indian people in legislation) have a unique and constitutionally protected relationship with the Canadian government.

3. Maxine Harris and Roger Fallot, "Envisioning a Trauma informed Service System: A Vital Paradigm Shift." *New Directions for Mental Health Services*, no. 89 (2001): 11, https://doi.org/10.1002/yd.23320018903

4. Thomas Wartenweiler, "Trauma-informed Adult Education: An Interpretative Phenomenological Analysis." *The Online Journal of New Horizons in Education* 7, no. 2 (2017): 97, https://www.tojned.net/journals/tojned/articles/v07i02/v07i02-11.pdf

5. Carolyn Knight, "Working with Survivors of Childhood Trauma: Implications for Clinical Supervision." *The Clinical Supervisor* 23, no. 2 (2004): 83, https://doi.org/10.1300/J001v23n02_06

6. Harris and Fallot, "Envisioning," 11.

7. Knight, "Working with Survivors," 83.

8. Benjamin Levin, *System-wide Improvement in Education* (Paris, France: UNESCO International Institute for Educational Planning and the International Academy of Education, 2013).

9. Laura E. Reimer, "Dropping out of School: Exploring the Narratives of Aboriginal People in one Manitoba Community through Lederach's Conflict Transformation Framework," unpublished doctoral dissertation, University of Manitoba, 2013, https://mspace.lib.umanitoba.ca/xmlui/handle/1993/22052, see 154–170.

10. Harris and Fallot, "Envisioning," 4.

11. Wartenweiler, "Trauma-informed Education," 97.

12. Bessel van der Kolk, *The Body Keeps the Score: Brain, Mind, and Body in the Healing of Trauma* (New York: Viking, 2014), 349.

13. Laura E. Reimer, "Canadian Democracy and Aboriginal Relations." *The Global Journal of Peace Research and Praxis* 1, no. 1 (2014): 32-45.

14. Amy Bombay, Kim Matheson, and Hymie Anisman, "Intergenerational Trauma: Convergence of Multiple Processes among First Nations peoples in Canada." *Journal of Aboriginal Health* 5, no. 3 (2009): 7, http://search.proquest.com/doc

view/1138545041/; Lori Haskell and Melanie Randall, "Disrupted Attachments: A Social Context Complex Trauma Framework and the Lives of Aboriginal Peoples in Canada," *Journal of Aboriginal Health* 5, no. 3 (2009): 48–99, http://search.proquest.com/docview/1138543076/; Teresa Marsh, David Marsh, Julie Ozawagosh, and Frank Ozawagosh, "The Sweat Lodge Ceremony: A Healing Intervention for Intergenerational Trauma and Substance Use," *International Indigenous Policy Journal* 9, no. 2 (2018), https://doi.org/10.18584/iipj.2018.9.2.2

15. Haskell and Randall, "Disrupted Attachments," 48; Piotr Wilk, Alana Maltby, and Martin Cooke, "Residential Schools and the Effects on Indigenous Health and Well-being in Canada-a Scoping Review." *Public Health Reviews* 38, no. 1 (2017): 8, https://doi.org/10.1186/s40985-017-0055-6

16. Blythe Shepard, Linda O'Neill, and Francis Guenette, "Counselling with First Nations Women: Considerations of Oppression and Renewal." *International Journal for the Advancement of Counselling* 28, no. 3 (2006): 227–240. doi:10.1007/s10447-005-9008-8; Andrew Armitage, *Comparing the Policy of Aboriginal Assimilation: Australia, Canada, and New Zealand* (Vancouver, BC: University of British Columbia Press, 1998).

17. For a comprehensive understanding of the residential school policy and its impact, see *Final Report: Truth and Reconciliation Commission of Canada*, 2015, www.trc.ca.

18. See Maria Brave Heart, "The Historical Trauma Response among Natives and its Relationship with Substance Abuse: A Lakota Illustration." *Journal of Psychoactive Drugs* 35, no. 1 (2003): 7–13; see also Kirmayer, Laurence J., Gregory M. Brass, and Caroline L. Tait, "The Mental Health of Aboriginal Peoples: Trans-formations of Identity and Community." *Canadian Journal of Psychiatry* 45, no. 7 (2000): 607–616.

19. Amy Bombay, Kim Matheson, and Hymie Anisman, "Intergenerational Trauma: Convergence of Multiple Processes among First Nations Peoples in Canada." *Journal of Aboriginal Health* 5, no. 3 (2009): 7, http://search.proquest.com/docview/1138545041/

20. Addictions Foundation of Manitoba, 2008, http://trauma-informed.ca/wp-content/uploads/2013/06/Trauma-informed-toolkit-web-Jun6.pdf, 47.

21. Ashley Quinn, "Reflections on Intergenerational Trauma: Healing as a Critical Intervention." *First Peoples Child & Family Review* 3, no. 4 (2007): 72–82.

22. Les Whitbeck, Gary Adams, Dan Hoyt, and Xiaojin Chen, "Conceptualizing and Measuring Historical Trauma among American Indian People." *American Journal of Community Psychology* 33, no. 3–4 (2004): 119–130, https://doi.org/10.1023/B:AJCP.0000027000.77357.31

23. Lisa Blitz, Elizabeth Anderson, and Monique Saastamoinen, "Assessing Perceptions of Culture and Trauma in an Elementary School: Informing a Model for Culturally Responsive Trauma-Informed Schools." *The Urban Review* 48, no. 4 (2016): 520–542. https://doi.org/10.1007/s11256-016-0366-9; Vincent Felitti, Robert Anda, Dale Nordenberg, David Williamson, Allison Spitz, Valerie Edwards, Mary Koss, and James Marks, "Relationship of Childhood Abuse and Household Dysfunction to Many of the Leading Causes of Death in Adults: The Adverse Childhood Experiences

(ACE) Study." *American Journal of Preventive Medicine* 14, no. 4, (1998): 245–258, https://doi.org/10.1016/S0749-3797(98)00017-8.

24. Karyn Freedman, *One Hour in Paris* (Calgary, AB: Freehand Books, 2014); Bessel van der Kolk, "The Neurobiology of Childhood Trauma and Abuse." *Child and Adolescent Psychiatric Clinics of North America* 12, no. 2 (2003): 293–317, https://doi.org/10.1016/S1056-4993(03)00003-8

25. Tom Brunzell, Helen Stokes, and Lea Waters, "Shifting Teacher Practice in Trauma-Affected Classrooms: Practice Pedagogy Strategies within a Trauma-Informed Positive Education Model." *School Mental Health* (2019): 220, https://doi.org/10.1007/s12310-018-09308-8; Bessel van der Kolk, *The Body Keeps the Score: Brain, Mind, and Body in the Healing of Trauma* (New York: Viking, 2014), 80.

26. For a detailed narrative of the development process and the Adult Learning Centre concept, see Jim Silver, *In their Own Voices: Building Urban Aboriginal Communities* (Halifax, NS: Fernwood, 2006).

27. City of Winnipeg, Census and National Household Survey Data, 2011.

28. City of Winnipeg.

29. L. Battleford (pseudonym), personal correspondence, 2012.

30. Canadian Centre for Policy Alternatives, *Step by Step: Stories of Change in Winnipeg's Inner City*. State of the Inner City Report: 2007, 4.

31. Levin Levin, *System-wide Improvement in Education*.

32. James S. Coleman, "Social Capital in the Creation of Human Capital." *American Journal of Sociology* 94 (1988): S95–S120.

33. Aimee Karstens, Olusola Ajilore, Leah Rubin, Shoalin Yang, Aifeng Zhang, Alex Leow, Anand Kumar, and Melissa Lamar, "Investigating the Separate and Interactive Associations of Trauma and Depression on Brain Structure: Implications for Cognition and Aging." *International Journal of Geriatric Psychiatry* 32, no. 11 (2017): 1190–1199, https://doi.org/10.1002/gps.4755; Aimee Karstens, Leah Rubin, Stuart Shankman, Olusola Ajilore, David Libon, Anand Kumar, and Melissa Lamar, "Investigating the Separate and Interactive Associations of Trauma and Depression on Neurocognition in Urban Dwelling Adults." *Journal of Psychiatric Research* 89 (2017): 6–13. https://doi.org/10.1016/j.jpsychires.2017.01.008

34. Aimee Karstens et al., "Investigating Implications," 2017.

35. Aimee Karstens et al., "Investigating Implications," 2017; Aimee Karstens et al., "Investigating Neurocognition", 2017.

36. Aimee Karstens et al., "Investigating Implications," 2017; Aimee Karstens et al., "Investigating Neurocognition", 2017; Bessel van der Kolk, *The Body Keeps the Score*, 2014.

37. Bessel van der Kolk, "The Neurobiology of Childhood Trauma and Abuse," *Child and Adolescent Psychiatric Clinics of North America* 12, no. 2 (2003): 293–317, https://doi.org/10.1016/S1056-4993(03)00003-8

38. Vincent Felitti, Robert Anda, Dale Nordenberg, David Williamson, Allison Spitz, Valerie Edwards, Mary Koss, and James Marks, "Relationship of Childhood Abuse and Household Dysfunction to Many of the Leading Causes of Death in Adults: The Adverse Childhood Experiences (ACE) Study." *American Journal of Preventive Medicine* 14, no. 4 (1998): 245–258, https://doi.org/10.1016/S0749-3797(

98)00017-8; Leah Gilbert, Matthew Breiding, Melissa Merrick, William Thompson, Derek Ford, Satvinder Dhingra, and Sharyn Parks, "Childhood Adversity and Adult Chronic Disease: An Update from Ten States and the District of Columbia, 2010: An Update from Ten States and the District of Columbia, 2010." *American Journal of Preventive Medicine* 48, no. 3 (2015): 345–349, https://doi.org/10.1016/j.amepre.2014.09.006

39. Felitti et al., "Relationship of Childhood Abuse"; van der Kolk, *The Body Keeps Score*.

40. Brunzell, Stokes, and Waters, "Shifting Teacher Practice"; van der Kolk, *The Body Keeps Score*.

41. van der Kolk, *The Body Keeps Score*.

42. Brunzell et al., "Shifting Teacher Practice."

43. Candice L. Seti, "Causes and Treatment of Burnout in Residential Child Care Workers: A Review of the Research," *Residential Treatment for Children & Youth* 24, no. 3 (2008): 197–229. doi:10.1080/08865710802111972

44. Amy Bombay et al., "Intergenerational Trauma," 2009.

45. Peter Menzies, "Developing an Aboriginal Healing Model for Intergenerational Trauma." *International Journal of Health Promotion and Education* 46, no. 2 (2008): 41–48. https://doi.org/10.1080/14635240.2008.10708128.

46. Travis Hales, Nancy Kusmaul, and Thomas Nochajski, "Exploring the Dimensionality of Trauma-Informed Care: Implications for Theory and Practice." *Human Service Organizations: Management, Leadership & Governance* 41, no. 3, (2017): 317–325, https://doi.org/10.1080/23303131.2016.1268988; Elaine Mordoch and Rainy Gaywish, "Is There a Need for Healing in the Classroom? Exploring Trauma-informed Education for Aboriginal Mature Students." *In Education* 17, no. 3 (2011): https://ineducation.ca/ineducation/article/view/75.

47. Wartenweiler, "Trauma-informed Education."

48. Ibid., 97.

49. Reimer, "Canadian Democracy and Aboriginal Relations," 2013.

50. Brunzell et al., "Shifting Teacher Practice"; Susan McDonald, "A Touch of … Class!" *The Canadian Modern Language Review* 56, no. 4, (2000): https://www.utpjournals.press/doi/abs/10.3138/cmlr.56.4.690

51. Developed by Janice Carello and Lisa Butler, "Practicing What We Teach: Trauma-Informed Educational Practice." *Journal of Teaching in Social Work* 35, no. 3 (2015): 262–278. https://doi.org/10.1080/08841233.2015.1030059

52. Harris and Fallot, "Envisioning," 10–20.

53. Lisa Blitz, Elizabeth Anderson, and Monique Saastamoinen, "Assessing Perceptions of Culture and Trauma in an Elementary School: Informing a Model for Culturally Responsive Trauma-Informed Schools." *The Urban Review* 48, no. 4 (2016): 520–542, https://doi.org/10.1007/s11256-016-0366-9; Brunzell et al., "Shifting Teacher Practice."

54. Wartenweiler, "Trauma-informed Education," 103.

55. Knight, "Working with Survivors."

56. Macdonald, "A Touch of …Class!."

57. Wartenweiler, "Trauma-informed Education."

58. McDonald, "A Touch of … Class!."
59. Brunzell et al., "Shifting Teacher Practice"; Haskell and Randall, "Disrupted Attachments"; van der Kolk, *The Body Keeps Score*.
60. Brunzell et al., "Shifting Teacher Practice."
61. Gladwell, *Outliers: The Story of Success*.
62. Sandra Bloom, "Bridging the Black Hole of Trauma: The Evolutionary Significance of the Arts Part 2: The Arts and Evolution – What Is Art For"? *Psychotherapy and Politics International* 9, no. 1 (2011): 67–82. https://doi.org/10.1002/ppi.229; McDonald, "A Touch of … Class!"; van der Kolk, *The Body Keeps Score*.
63. Wartenweiler, "Trauma-informed Education," 2017.
64. Brunzell et al., "Shifting Teacher Practice"; Elaine Mordoch and Rainy Gaywish, "Is There a Need for Healing in the Classroom? Exploring Trauma-informed Education for Aboriginal Mature Students." *In Education* 17, no. 3 (2011), https://ineducation.ca/ineducation/article/view/75
65. Mordock and Gaywish, "Is There a Need for Healing in the Classroom?"; Wartenweiler, "Trauma-informed Education".
66. McDonald, "A Touch of … Class!".
67. van der Kolk, *The Body Keeps Score*.
68. Mordock and Gaywish, "Is There a Need for Healing in the Classroom?" 2011.

BIBLIOGRAPHY

Addictions Foundation of Manitoba (AFM), 2008, http://trauma-informed.ca/wp-content/uploads/2013/06/Trauma-informed-toolkit-web-Jun6.pdf.

Armitage, Andrew. *Comparing the Policy of Aboriginal Assimilation: Australia, Canada, and New Zealand* (Vancouver, BC: University of British Columbia Press, 1998).

Barnett, Erin, Cassie Yackley, and Elizabeth Licht. "Developing, Implementing, and Evaluating a Trauma-informed Care Program within a Youth Residential Treatment Center and Special Needs School." *Residential Treatment for Children & Youth* 35, no. 2 (2018): 95–113. doi:10.1080/0886571X.2018.1455559

Blackstock, Cindy. "First Nations Child and Family Services: Restoring Peace and Harmony in First Nations Communities." In *Child Welfare: Connecting Research, Policy, and Practice,* ed, Kathleen Kufeldt and Brad McKenzie, 331–342 (Waterloo, ON: Wilfrid Laurier University Press, 2003).

Blitz, Lisa, Elizabeth Anderson, and Monique Saastamoinen. "Assessing Perceptions of Culture and Trauma in an Elementary School: Informing a Model for Culturally Responsive Trauma-Informed Schools." *The Urban Review* 48, no. 4 (2016): 520–542, https://doi.org/10.1007/s11256-016-0366-9

Bloom, Sandra. "Bridging the Black Hole of Trauma: The Evolutionary Significance of the Arts Part 2: The Arts and Evolution – What Is Art For"? *Psychotherapy and Politics International* 9, no. 1 (2011): 67–82, https://doi.org/10.1002/ppi.229

Bombay, Amy, Kim Matheson, and Hymie Anisman. "Intergenerational Trauma: Convergence of Multiple Processes among First Nations Peoples in Canada."

Journal of Aboriginal Health 5, no. 3 (2009): 6–47, http://search.proquest.com/docview/1138545041/

Brave Heart, Maria. "The Historical Trauma Response among Natives and its Relationship with Substance Abuse: A Lakota Illustration." *Journal of Psychoactive Drugs* 35, no. 1 (2003): 7–13.

Brave Heart, Maria, and Lemyra DeBruyn. "The American Indian Holocaust: Healing Historical Unresolved Grief." *American Indian & Alaska Native Mental Health Research* 8, no. 2 (1998): 60–82.

Brunzell, Tom, Helen Stokes, and Lea Waters. "Shifting Teacher Practice in Trauma-Affected Classrooms: Practice Pedagogy Strategies within a Trauma-Informed Positive Education Model." *School Mental Health* (2019), https://doi.org/10.1007/s12310-018-09308-8

Canadian Centre for Policy Alternatives. *Step by Step: Stories of Change in Winnipeg's Inner City.* State of the Inner City Report: 2007. Canadian Centre for Policy Alternatives – Manitoba.

Carello, Janice, and Lisa Butler. "Practicing What We Teach: Trauma-Informed Educational Practice." *Journal of Teaching in Social Work* 35, no. 3 (2015): 262–278, https://doi.org/10.1080/08841233.2015.1030059

Coleman, James S., "Social Capital in the Creation of Human Capital." *American Journal of Sociology* 94 (1988): S95–S120.

Denham, Aaron. "Rethinking Historical Trauma: Narratives of Resilience." *Transcultural Psychiatry* 45, no. 3 (2008): 391–414.

Duran, Eduardo, Bonnie Duran, Marie Brave Heart and Susan Y. Horse-David. "Healing the American Indian Soul Wound." In *International Handbook of Multigenerational Legacies of Trauma,* ed. Yael Danieli, 341–354 (New York: Plenum Press, 1998).

Felitti, Vincent, Robert Anda, Dale Nordenberg, David Williamson, Allison Spitz, Valerie Edwards, Mary Koss, James Marks. "Relationship of Childhood Abuse and Household Dysfunction to Many of the Leading Causes of Death in Adults: The Adverse Childhood Experiences (ACE) Study." *American Journal of Preventive Medicine* 14, no. 4 (1998): 245–258, https://doi.org/10.1016/S0749-3797(98)00017-8

Freedman, Karyn. *One Hour in Paris* (Calgary, AB: Freehand Books, 2014).

Gagné, Mari-Anik. "The Role of Dependency and Colonialism in Generating Trauma in First Nations Citizens: The James Bay Cree." In *International Handbook of Multigenerational Legacies of Trauma,* ed. Yael Danieli, 355–372 (New York, NY: Plenum Press, 1998).

Gilbert, Leah, Matthew Breiding, Melissa Merrick, William Thompson, Derek Ford, Satvinder Dhingra, and Sharyn Parks. "Childhood Adversity and Adult Chronic Disease: An Update from Ten States and the District of Columbia, 2010: An Update from Ten States and the District of Columbia, 2010." *American Journal of Preventive Medicine* 48, no. 3 (2015): 345–349, https://doi.org/10.1016/j.amepre.2014.09.006

Gladwell, Malcolm. *Outliers: The Story of Success* (New York, NY: Back Bay Books, 2011).

Gray, Robin. "Visualizing Pedagogy and Power with Urban Native Youth: Exposing the Legacy of the Indian Residential School System." *Canadian Journal of Native Education* 34, no. 1 (2011): 9–27.

Hales, Travis, Nancy Kusmaul, and Thomas Nochajski. "Exploring the Dimensionality of Trauma-Informed Care: Implications for Theory and Practice." *Human Service Organizations: Management, Leadership & Governance* 41, no. 3 (2017): 317–325, https://doi.org/10.1080/23303131.2016.1268988

Harris, Maxine and Roger Fallot. "Envisioning a Trauma Informed Service System: A Vital Paradigm Shift." *New Directions for Mental Health Services* 2001, no. 89 (2001): 3–22, https://doi.org/10.1002/yd.23320018903

Haskell, Lori, and Melanie Randall. "Disrupted Attachments: A Social Context Complex Trauma Framework and the Lives of Aboriginal Peoples in Canada." *Journal of Aboriginal Health* 5, no. 3 (2009): 48–99, http://search.proquest.com/docview/1138543076/

Karmali, Shazeer, Kevin Laupland, A. Robert Harrop, Christs Findlay, Andrew Kirkpatrick, Brent Winston, John Kortbeek, Lindsay Crowshow and Morad Hameed. "Epidemiology of Severe Trauma among Status Aboriginal Canadians: A Population-based Study." *Canadian Medical Association Journal* 172, no. 8 (2005): 1007–1011.

Karstens, Aimee, Olusola Ajilore, Leah Rubin, Shoalin Yang, Aifeng Zhang, Alex Leow, Anand Kumar, and Melissa Lamar. "Investigating the Separate and Interactive Associations of Trauma and Depression on Brain Structure: Implications for Cognition and Aging." *International Journal of Geriatric Psychiatry* 32, no. 11 (2017): 1190–1199, https://doi.org/10.1002/gps.4755

Karstens, Aimee, Leah Rubin, Stuart Shankman, Olusola Ajilore, David Libon, Anand Kumar, and Melissa Lamar. "Investigating the Separate and Interactive Associations of Trauma and Depression on Neurocognition in Urban Dwelling Adults." *Journal of Psychiatric Research* 89 (2017): 6–13, https://doi.org/10.1016/j.jpsychires.2017.01.008

Kirmayer, Laurence J., Gregory M. Brass, and Caroline L. Tait. "The Mental Health of Aboriginal Peoples: Trans-formations of Identity and Community." *Canadian Journal of Psychiatry* 45, no. 7 (2000): 607–616.

Kirmayer, Lawrence J., Cori Simpson, and Margaret Cargo. "Healing Traditions: Culture, Community and Mental Health Promotion with Canadian Aboriginal Peoples. *Australian Psychiatry* 11, Suppl. (2003): S15–S23.

Knight, Carolyn. "Working with Survivors of Childhood Trauma: Implications for Clinical Supervision." *The Clinical Supervisor* 23, no. 2 (2004): 81–105, https://doi.org/10.1300/J001v23n02_06

Levin, Benjamin. *System-wide Improvement in Education* (Paris, France: UNESCO International Institute for Educational Planning and the International Academy of Education, 2013).

Marsh, Teresa, Sheila Cote-Meek, Nancy Young, Lisa Najavits, and Pamela Toulouse. "Indigenous Healing and Seeking Safety: A Blended Implementation Project for Intergenerational Trauma and Substance Use Disorders." *International Indigenous Policy Journal* 7, no. 2 (2016), https://doi.org/10.18584/iipj.2016.7.2.3

Marsh, Teresa, David Marsh, Julie Ozawagosh, and Frank Ozawagosh. "The Sweat Lodge Ceremony: A Healing Intervention for Intergenerational Trauma and Substance Use." *International Indigenous Policy Journal* 9, no. 2 (2018), https://doi.org/10.18584/iipj.2018.9.2.2

Mccormack, Lynne and Natalie Katalinic. "Learning to Heal from Those Who Know! The "Lived" Experience of a Peer Support Program for Adult Survivors of Childhood Trauma." *Journal of Aggression, Maltreatment & Trauma* 25, no. 10 (2016): 1021–1042, https://doi.org/10.1080/10926771.2016.1223247

McDonald, Susan. "A Touch of … Class!." *The Canadian Modern Language Review* 56, no. 4 (2000), https://www.utpjournals.press/doi/abs/10.3138/cmlr.56.4.690

Menzies, Peter. "Developing an Aboriginal Healing Model for Intergenerational Trauma." *International Journal of Health Promotion and Education* 46, no. 2 (2008): 41–48, https://doi.org/10.1080/14635240.2008.10708128

Merrick, Melissa, Katie Ports, Derek Ford, Tracie Afifi, Elizabeth Gershoff, and Andrew Grogan-Kaylor. "Unpacking the Impact of Adverse Childhood Experiences on Adult Mental Health." *Child Abuse & Neglect* 69 (2017): 10–19, https://doi.org/10.1016/j.chiabu.2017.03.016

Mordoch, Elaine and Rainy Gaywish. "Is There a Need for Healing in the Classroom? Exploring Trauma-informed Education for Aboriginal Mature Students." *In Education* 17, no. 3 (2011), https://ineducation.ca/ineducation/article/view/75.

Morrissette, Patrick. J. and Michelle Naden. "An Interactional View of Traumatic Stress Among First Nations Counselors." *Journal of Family Psychotherapy* 9, no. 3 (1998): 43–60.

No Author. *The Trauma-informed Toolkit: A Resource for Service Organizations and Providers to Deliver Services that Are Trauma-informed* (Winnipeg, MB: Klinic Community Health Centre, 2008).

Quinn, Ashley. "Reflections on Intergenerational Trauma: Healing as a Critical Intervention." *First Peoples Child & Family Review* 3, no. 4 (2007): 72–82.

Royal Commission on Aboriginal Peoples. *People to People, Nation to Nation: Highlights from the Report of the Royal Commission on Aboriginal Peoples* (Cat. No. Z1-1991/1-6E). Ottawa, ON: Ministry of Supplies and Services Canada, 1996.

Sailas, Eila, and Mark Fenton. "Seclusion and Restraint for People with Serious Mental Illnesses." *Cochrane Database Systematic Reviews* 1 (2000). Art. No.: CD001163. doi:10.1002/14651858.CD001163

Seti, Candice. L. "Causes and Treatment of Burnout in Residential Child Care Workers: A Review of the Research." *Residential Treatment for Children & Youth* 24, no. 3 (2008): 197–229. doi:10.1080/08865710802111972

Shepard, Blythe, Linda O'Neill, and Francis Guenette. "Counselling with First Nations Women: Considerations of Oppression and Renewal." *International Journal for the Advancement of Counselling* 28, no. 3 (2006): 227–240. doi:10.1007/s10447-005-9008-8

Silver, Jim. *In their Own Voices: Building Urban Aboriginal Communities*. Halifax, NS: Fernwood Publishing, 2006.

van der Kolk, Bessel. *The Body Keeps the Score: Brain, Mind, and Body in the Healing of Trauma* (New York: Viking, 2014).

van der Kolk, Bessel. "The Neurobiology of Childhood Trauma and Abuse." *Child and Adolescent Psychiatric Clinics of North America* 12, no. 2 (2003): 293–317, https://doi.org/10.1016/S1056-4993(03)00003-8

Van Niel, Cornelius, Lee Pachter, Roy Wade, Vincent Felitti, and Martin Stein. "Adverse Events in Children: Predictors of Adult Physical and Mental Conditions." *Journal of Developmental & Behavioral Pediatrics* 35, no. 8 (2014): 549–551, https://doi.org/10.1097/DBP.0000000000000102

Wartenweiler, Thomas. "Trauma-informed Adult Education: An Interpretative Phenomenological Analysis." *The Online Journal of New Horizons in Education* 7, no. 2 (2017): 96–106, https://www.tojned.net/journals/tojned/articles/v07i02/v07i02-11.pdf

West, Shantel, Angelique Day, Cheryl Somers, and Beverly Baroni. "Student Perspectives on How Trauma Experiences Manifest in the Classroom: Engaging Court-involved Youth in the Development of a Trauma-informed Teaching Curriculum." *Children and Youth Services Review* 38, no. C (2014): 58–65, https://doi.org/10.1016/j.childyouth.2014.01.013

Whitbeck, Les, Gary Adams, Dan Hoyt, and Xiaojin Chen. "Conceptualizing and Measuring Historical Trauma among American Indian People." *American Journal of Community Psychology* 33, no. 3–4 (2004): 119–130, https://doi.org/10.1023/B:AJCP.0000027000.77357.31

Wilk, Piotr, Alana Maltby, and Martin Cooke. "Residential Schools and the Effects on Indigenous Health and Well-being in Canada- A Scoping Review." *Public Health Reviews* 38, no. 1 (2017): 8–8, https://doi.org/10.1186/s40985-017-0055-6.

Chapter 6

Reconciliation through Education
The University of Winnipeg
Annette Trimbee

The University of Winnipeg (UWinnipeg), located on Treaty 1 territory in the heart of the Métis homeland, is situated in one of the most diverse communities in Canada. Winnipeg is home to the largest Indigenous population of any census metropolitan area in the nation[1] and is at the epicenter of an Indigenous resurgence that is taking place throughout Canada. According to economists Sabrina Bond and Stephen Spence, Manitoba's population will grow approximately 1.1%, per year, with the growth of the Indigenous population contributing between 0.2% and 0.4% of total population growth from 2016 to 2036.[2] Bond and Spence note that the Indigenous population of Manitoba is younger than the rest of the province.[3] Overall, Manitoba's population is relatively younger than the rest of Canada, so policies that "promote labor force participation could result in stronger economic growth for Manitoba relative to other provinces in the long term."[4] This provides important context in understanding the tremendous impact that Indigenous people will have on the future of Manitoba. It is critical that we develop meaningful connections and relationships with Indigenous people and communities by including Indigenous perspectives and experiences in our organizations, recognizing and employing Indigenous talent and knowledge, and supporting future Indigenous leaders and learners.

After living away from Manitoba for many years, I was drawn home to Winnipeg to take on the role of president and vice-chancellor of UWinnipeg in 2014 for two reasons. First, when I was growing up, my family had no expectation that I would attend university, so I am grateful to UWinnipeg for tapping me on the shoulder, offering me a significant scholarship, providing a quality education, and giving me my start. Secondly, as a Métis person who left Winnipeg with two university degrees, I had little to no knowledge of treaties, residential schools, or my own Métis history. I found my heritage later in life, which helped to shape my identity. I was inspired to be engaged with and positively influence the Indigenous inclusion and reconciliation efforts I observed unfolding at UWinnipeg.

My predecessor at UWinnipeg, Dr Lloyd Axworthy, significantly reshaped how people think about the role of postsecondary institutions in providing opportunities for Indigenous students, and in particular, how universities can and should connect with their surrounding communities. Dr Axworthy accomplished a great deal of work in creating pathways to university for traditionally underrepresented students, including refugees and war-affected youth and Indigenous people. These demographics are present in high concentrations in the neighborhoods surrounding UWinnipeg. During his tenure from 2004 to 2014, Dr Axworthy helped to shift the narrative from university as a place for the privileged to university as a place for everyone, regardless of socio-economic or cultural background. Owing to his leadership, UWinnipeg is regarded as a national leader in this area with an extensive array of programs and initiatives that support accessibility and inclusion. The vast majority of these programs are supported through private fundraising and ad hoc government grants. This part of UWinnipeg's history and the impact of these programs, many of which are still being offered today, will be discussed later in more detail.

At the time of my installation as president and vice-chancellor of UWinnipeg in 2014, the government of Canada's Truth and Reconciliation Commission's (TRC) report and its seminal *Calls to Action* were widely anticipated. UWinnipeg was fortunate to host a launch of the report in 2015. The *Calls to Action* provide a framework and a continuous source of inspiration as we move forward on our journey of reconciliation.

In 2015, the UWinnipeg Board of Regents approved five strategic directions for the University, one of which is indigenization.[5] While the launch of the strategic directions framework made indigenization an explicit institutional priority, the presence of initiatives that support the mandate of indigenization and the broader work of reconciliation have long preceded this date. UWinnipeg's wide-ranging efforts related to indigenization involve incorporating Indigenous knowledge in curricula and teaching practices, hiring Indigenous academics and employees, supporting faculty to conduct research that benefits and aligns with Indigenous communities, creating community partnerships to facilitate transitions to postsecondary education for Indigenous youth, and supporting an increased number of Indigenous students to succeed in our various academic programs. Despite this span of work, the term *indigenization* is not universally understood or utilized throughout our campus community. Indigenization is viewed by some at our institution as an extension of the work that began in earnest in 2004 by enhancing the inclusion of Indigenous peoples and extending the role of the university beyond its core mission into the surrounding community. It is seen by others as a concerted effort to adapt and change our institution—both academically and physically—to become more Indigenous. Others still, understand indigenization as relating explicitly to the *Calls to Action* of the TRC Final Report, which positions education as central to processes of reconciliation. Many of the TRC *Calls to Action* focus on the need for all Canadians to better understand our colonial history and our relationship with each other as non-Indigenous and Indigenous peoples. In this sense, education is an essential bridge. In reality, indigenization encompasses all of the above, and our understanding is continually evolving.

UNDERSTANDING *INDIGENIZATION*

The scholarship of Gaudry and Lorenz (2018)[6] conceptualizes indigenization as a three-part spectrum naming Indigenous inclusion, reconciliation indigenization, and decolonization indigenization as related models. This conceptualization of indigenization has provided UWinnipeg with a useful framework to categorize and contextualize indigenization efforts. The first of the three "visions of indigenization" Gaudry and Lorenz describe is *Indigenous inclusion*."[7] Indigenous inclusion retains the institution's structures and "support[s] the adaption of Indigenous people to the current (often alienating) culture of the Canadian academy."[8] In this model, Gaudry and Lorenz note that the "burden of change" is placed on Indigenous people while "naturalizing the status quo of academic culture."[9] They conclude that inclusion is a part of "building toward systemic indigenization," but should not be an institution's ultimate objective.[10]

According to Gaudry and Lorenz, the second model is *reconciliation indigenization* and seeks to establish "common ground between Indigenous and Canadian ideals."[11] This model supports Indigenous inclusion and is also "an attempt to alter the university's structure, including educating Canadian faculty, staff, and students to change how they think about, and act toward, Indigenous people."[12] *Reconciliation indigenization* can include the creation of an Indigenous course requirement (ICR); however, this has not been widely adopted by universities.[13] Gaudry and Lorenz write that "power sharing, a transformation of decision-making processes, and a reintegration of Indigenous peoples, faculty, staff, and students into policymaking that affects them, and their Canadian peers" is necessary to move beyond "rhetorical shifts to aspirational reconciliation."[14]

The third model described by Gaudry and Lorenz is *decolonial indigenization* and requires "the wholesale overhaul of the academy to fundamentally reorient knowledge production based on balancing power relations between Indigenous peoples and Canadians, transforming the academy into something dynamic and new."[15] There are two components to *decolonial indigenization*, the first of which is the creation of treaty-based relationships, perhaps in a "dual university structure" with "the return of control to Indigenous people, communities, and programs to better govern themselves in ways that the traditional university structure respects and supports, as an autonomous partner connected by a common institutional commitment."[16] The second is Indigenous resurgence. Gaudry and Lorenz note that if "indigenization does not strengthen Indigenous communities and support the resurgence of Indigenous intellectual traditions, then it is not indigenization." They write that this is achieved by supporting Indigenous methods of knowledge production, evaluation, and transmission.

Indigenization in Canadian Postsecondary Institutions

In 2015, Universities Canada adopted a set of principles outlining a commitment to indigenizing higher education and fostering reconciliation efforts in postsecondary institutions.[17] Considered in the context of Gaudry and Lorenz's framework, these principles fall mainly into the *reconciliation indigenization* category. The principles call for increased Indigenous representation within governance structures, staff, and student bodies and enhanced consultation and collaboration with Indigenous communities to ensure Indigenous students' needs are met. A central distinction between *reconciliation indigenization* and *decolonization indigenization* relates to where power is situated in decision-making processes. The principles do not necessitate the distribution of power to Indigenous communities.

Similarly, the Manitoba Indigenous Education Blueprint (2015), signed by the president of each postsecondary institution in Manitoba, is primarily a form of *reconciliation indigenization*. Of note, the commitments articulated in the Blueprint speak to the need for: engaging with Indigenous peoples in respectful reciprocal relationships, bringing Indigenous knowledge, languages, intellectual traditions, models, and approaches into curriculum and pedagogy, increasing access to services, building cultural safety, increasing the participation rates of Indigenous students in postsecondary, and reflecting the diversity of Indigenous peoples in governance and staffing policies and practices.

The Universities Canada principles, as well as the commitments outlined in the Manitoba Indigenous Education Blueprint are aspirational and speak primarily to the importance of inclusion, which is where most efforts are situated. The application of Gaudry and Lorenz's framework highlights the need for deeper levels of indigenization within Canadian higher education. They have provided us with a way to understand where we have been and where we should go. We now have something to relate to as we evolve.

With respect to indigenization in Canadian universities, Samson has noted a few examples of *decolonial indigenization* on Canadian campuses, where centers or faculties have autonomous decision-making power.[18] These include "the National Centre for Truth and Reconciliation at the University of Manitoba, the Indian Residential School History and Dialogue Centre at the University of British Columbia, the Yellowhead Institute at Ryerson University, and the Faculty of Native Studies at the University of Alberta."[19]

What Others Have Said

Perspectives regarding indigenization in Canadian postsecondary institutions are varied and diverse. Deborah Saucier has stated that Canadian higher education "continues to fail Indigenous peoples."[20] Saucier notes that Indigenous people are much less likely than non-Indigenous Canadians to have obtained a university degree, but the removal of barriers is possible.[21] As president of MacEwan University in Edmonton, Saucier oversaw a number of initiatives related to indigenization, such as the *pimâcihisowin* Foundation Program for upgrading high school qualifications, plaques installed at each entrance that acknowledge their location in Treaty 6 territory, engaging in ceremonies, and developing land-based learning opportunities in partnership with Indigenous institutions.[22]

According to Sheila Cote-Meek, Vice-President, Equity, People, and Culture at York University, postsecondary institutions responded positively to the TRC's call to take a leadership role. She notes that, while this is a hopeful sign of change, it is necessary to "determine how to undertake this leadership role in a way that ensures educators recognize the long-standing colonial practices that have profoundly affected many Indigenous people. Responding meaningfully to the Calls to Action requires understanding more fully that these practices remain embedded in our educational systems."[23] Cote-Meek lists four actions postsecondary institutions should take to make progress toward reconciliation: "addressing the systemic under-representation of Indigenous peoples in the academy; providing sufficient resources to any program or change that is put in place; changing the structure by way of decision-making; and changing the culture of the institution."[24] Using Gaudry and Lorenz's framework, these actions address inclusion and reconciliation, and move into decolonization.

Ron Deganadus McLester, Vice-President, Truth, Reconciliation, and Indigenization at Algonquin College, described reconciliation in postsecondary institutions in an Academica Forum interview with Rod Skinkle. Using the Two-Row Wampum belt as a foundation for this framework, McLester notes that for Indigenous peoples, the colonists agreed to travel in parallel in a relationship "based on three tenets: peace, friendship, and respect."[25] For most institutions, he says, indigenization means "new campus spaces and a greater emphasis on hiring Indigenous faculty," but now institutions are realizing that they can "change basic institutional processes to have them better integrate and benefit from Indigenous ways of knowing."[26] To do this, Algonquin has developed practices that incorporate Indigenous perspectives. For instance, departments are correlated with the ceremonial calendar and they are celebrated in turn with "lecture series, professional development, or whatever other initiatives we choose" for seven weeks.[27]

Canadian journalist Sarah Treleaven writes that universities responded to the TRC's ninety-four Calls to Action by focusing on "recruiting and retaining more Indigenous students, hiring Indigenous faculty, and creating Indigenous spaces."[28] Treleaven notes that University of Saskatchewan decided that "each degree program should have significant Indigenous content" with some differences throughout the university's colleges and schools.[29]

UWINNIPEG'S JOURNEY: AN OVERVIEW OF OUR PROGRAMS AND PROGRESS, RESULTS, AND ANALYSIS

Leadership and Governance

UWinnipeg's approach to indigenization and reconciliation involves working within and beyond the borders of our campus and seeking new partnerships, while strengthening existing ones, with surrounding community, organizations, and schools. We make efforts to engage and take our cues on indigenization from Indigenous students, faculty, elders and traditional knowledge keepers, staff, and community members. For example, over the past decade, UWinnipeg has received counsel from an Indigenous Advisory Circle that provides ongoing advice and guidance to the president and vice-chancellor. In addition, an associate vice-president of Indigenous Engagement reports directly to the president and vice-chancellor and an Indigenous Academic Lead role reports directly to the provost and vice-president, Academic. The inclusion of Indigenous perspectives at the highest levels of decision-making has had a significant impact on UWinnipeg's approach to reconciliation and indigenization.

University-Bound Programs and Initiatives

Building on the work that was started more than a decade ago, UWinnipeg has focused on strengthening the transition to postsecondary from the elementary and secondary education system. For example, Indspire Canada, the Winnipeg School Division (WSD), and UWinnipeg's Faculty of Education have collaborated to deliver the *Build From Within—Ozhitoon Onji Peenjiiee* program providing a pathway for Indigenous high school students into our Bachelor of Education program. Students complete grade 12 with both a high school diploma and an educational assistant diploma from UWinnipeg. Following high school, students are assigned to a school in the WSD to work part-time as an educational assistant while completing their Integrated Bachelor of Arts and Bachelor of Education degrees at UWinnipeg. Tuition is provided, as well as a monthly bus pass, access to cultural activities and mentors, and summer job opportunities.[30]

Support for Indigenous culture and languages is an essential part of reconciliation.[31] UWinnipeg's Wii Chiiwaakanak Learning Centre is a community partnership initiative that provides educational and capacity building opportunities to Winnipeg's Indigenous and inner-city communities. The Centre provides innovative programming to over 20,000 community members per year, including after-school youth programs focusing on culturally appropriate activities and Indigenous language programs in Cree and Ojibwe. Through these programs, Wii Chiiwaakanak supports inner-city children and their families in developing a university-bound identity.

The Indigenous Science, Technology, Engineering, Arts and Math (STEAM) Summer Camp provides opportunities for children and youth to combine Indigenous knowledge with subjects such as chemistry, physics, computer science, and biology. The Faculty of Education has offered a science outreach program, Design It Science, where students from local schools were introduced to engineering concepts through the process of designing and building a structure that illustrated an important place in their own lives.

UWinnipeg's Wii Chiiwaakanak Learning Centre and Innovative Learning Centre programs were recently evaluated by Axworthy, DeRiviere, and Rattray. They found five themes that denoted success in these community-driven programs:

> (1) support and connection with the community through free culturally-based educational opportunities; (2) strengthened community partnerships; (3) building social capital among youth through peer mentoring and role modeling opportunities; (4) encouraging connections of youth to education, employment, leadership opportunities, and civic responsibility; (5) fostering a sense of belonging to the university community in children, youth, and their families.[32]

Culturally relevant programs, such as the Pow Wow Club and Let's Speak Ojibway, were enjoyed by participants because they "provided meaningful learning opportunities, built stronger family units, and enhanced the community's capacity to see itself as learners."[33] Programs used "hands-on or experiential learning opportunities" and "celebrate[d] First Nations, Métis, and Inuit accomplishments and contributions."[34] Participants viewed these programs "as a family celebration of learning about culture and as an intergenerational transfer of knowledge."[35] Participants found that the Wii Chiiwaakanak Learning Centre strengthened community partnerships because "it is a link that connects Indigenous people and families to one another by giving them an opportunity to participate in activities together, such as crafting, beading, and other cultural activities."[36]

Programs such as UWinnipeg's Model School help build social capital among youth through mentorship and the development of leadership skills.[37] The Model School is located within the UWinnipeg Collegiate, with fifty students from grades 9 through 12 enrolled each year. Model School students are identified by public school educators and non-profit organizations as having academic potential, but experiencing various barriers that could prevent them from reaching their potential in the absence of appropriate guidance and support. Model School students are provided tuition and access to the intimate learning environment at the Collegiate, supported academically by individualized education plans, and engaged in leadership initiatives and employment-readiness programs. All Model School students are enrolled in the University's Opportunity Fund Tuition Credit Account Program, where they can earn up to $4,000 in tuition credits that can be used upon completion of grade 12 to attend UWinnipeg undergraduate programming.

An evaluation of the Model School found that 84.6% of students reported that their decision to continue education after high school was influenced by their experiences at the Model School.[38] Participants in the Model School, as well as participation in programs like the Sacred Seven Healthy Relationships, Adventure Kids Summer Camp, and Math Camp gained skills and identified education needed for future employment.[39] Access to the university campus reduced students' nervousness about being on campus, as all of the evaluated programs "showed evidence of improvements in the participants' sense of belonging in a postsecondary environment."[40]

Promoting Access to Education for Indigenous Students

UWinnipeg has a long-standing commitment to ensuring that all students have equal access to higher learning. To this end, we established the Opportunity Fund over ten years ago to support Indigenous students, young people from war-affected areas and refugee populations, and youth from inner-city neighborhoods through fast-track bursaries and tuition credits, as well as tuition waivers for youth who have grown up in the child welfare system.

Since 2007, over US$3 million in assistance has been awarded to over 3,000 students.

Promoting Indigenous Student Success in Undergraduate Programs

Indigenous students at UWinnipeg have access to the Aboriginal Student Services Centre (ASSC), a culturally safe, educational, and supportive environment. The ASSC assists students through academic advising, the university preparatory program, tutoring, cultural and social activities, and access to elders in residence. The ASSC also liaises with UWinnipeg faculties and staff, education authorities, and sponsorship agencies. High school visits to UWinnipeg and community presentations are also facilitated by the ASSC.

The Merchants Hotel on Selkirk Avenue in Winnipeg's North End neighborhood (which has one of the highest concentrations of urban Indigenous people in Canada) has been transformed into a community-based educational and cultural hub, which houses UWinnipeg's Department of Urban and Inner-City Studies (UIC). A key aspect of its operations is community-outreach programming, which seeks to identify and encourage Indigenous youth to pursue higher education.

In 2018/19, 444 students enrolled in 23 UIC courses. Approximately 40% of UIC students are Indigenous and multi-barriered. A high percentage of these students have had a negative experience with education. To make university more accessible, more comfortable, and to improve retention rates, UIC provides tools for success. UIC offers five courses that satisfy UWinnipeg's ICR, an Indigenous Elder is on site one day per week, and an Academic Advisor with specific expertise working the aforementioned population of adult learners is available.

UIC offers a Beginning University Successfully (BUS) program, designed for multi-barriered adult learners. Of these students, 85% identify as Indigenous and at least 60% of them are expected to continue their education at UWinnipeg. In contrast, approximately 60% of the students taking UIC courses are more typical university students. The participation and interaction of students from different experiences is an important part of the program and an important part of reconciliation. Dr Shauna MacKinnon, associate professor and chair of UIC, writes that "students talk about the importance of learning with students from different backgrounds and experiences in the unique learning environment that UIC provides, and they tend to emphasize how much they learn from each other."[41] MacKinnon writes that UIC students have found the program meaningful and transformative.[42] She notes that, on the last day of classes, an Indigenous student told her classmates that "we [Indigenous students] have shared with you openly about our painful experiences as a result of residential schools, the sixties scoop, and the continued systemic racism that we encounter every day in our city. It is now your responsibility to do something about it."[43]

As part of UWinnipeg's commitment to provide hands-on, cooperative, experiential and work-integrated learning opportunities for undergraduate and graduate students, UWinnipeg offers a variety of courses are offered that focus on Indigenous culture and ways of knowing. Land-based learning opportunities are available to UWinnipeg students through our Spring and Summer Institutes. Past institutes have included Indigenous ethnobotany and Indigenous food systems. UWinnipeg also offers a summer course, Shoal Lake to Winnipeg: Practicing Land-Based Reconciliations, which brings together UWinnipeg students and youth from Shoal Lake 40. In previous offerings, participants had the opportunity to build relationships and discuss colonization and reconciliation while learning about the land. It is important to note that the City of Winnipeg draws its drinking water from Shoal Lake and has done so for over 100 years. The First Nations residents of Shoal Lake 40 have been under a boil water advisory for over twenty years.

The ICR

In 2015, the UWinnipeg became one of the first postsecondary institutions in Canada to approve an ICR, making Indigenous learning a component of the undergraduate degree requirements for all new undergraduate students. To fulfill this requirement, students may choose from a wide range of three credit-hour courses in which the greater part of the content is local Indigenous material, derived from or based on an analysis of the cultures, languages, history, ways of knowing, or contemporary reality of the Indigenous peoples of North America. The decision exemplifies UWinnipeg's leadership in responding to the recommendations made in the Final Report of the Truth and Reconciliation Commission.

UWinnipeg has increased the number of approved ICR courses since its inception. As of May 2019, there are fifty-seven unique courses that fulfill the ICR. Two years after implementation, 940 UWinnipeg students have completed an ICR approved course. Williamson conducted an evaluation of UWinnipeg's ICR that asked faculty to respond to the following: "differences between teaching an ICR course and a non-ICR course; what was going well in the ICR course; the challenges of teaching an ICR course; supports and resources that would be helpful; and how they assess student learning."[44] Williamson notes that faculty reported some differences in teaching ICRs, such as inviting more guest speakers as experts, or incorporating Indigenous pedagogies in class.[45] As the number of non-Indigenous students in these courses has risen, there is a growing challenge to "manage and anticipate responses to content that is often deeply political and sometimes triggering."[46] Strategies and approaches that have worked well include guest speakers, circles, a less formal classroom, small class sizes, small group work and discussion, and using UWinnipeg resources such as the ASSC and elders in residence.[47]

ICR challenges included "racism—performed as fear, stereotyping, or sheer ignorance," caring for students in large classes, and feeling "not necessarily trained to handle emotional responses."[48] Faculty noted that administrative support in the form of financial support for guest speakers, an online hub for ICR faculty, dedicated library staff, and professional development are helpful in delivering the ICR.[49] Student learning is assessed through formal assignments, in-class interactions, and relationship building.[50] Williamson concludes that the ICR is a "vital step toward reconciliation" and that it is possible for the program to succeed by engaging in "respectful, responsive relationship building."[51]

According to Lepp-Friesen's survey of student and faculty experiences after the first year of the ICR, 72% of student participants had a positive experience.[52] These students "appreciated the open conversations and the acquisition of new vocabulary to be able to participate in the dialogue in a respectful way."[53] Of the students, 28% reported a negative experience for some of the following reasons: a class "did not meet their expectations," they "felt forced to take a class they did not want," and "reconciliation was a waste of time."[54] Lepp-Friesen collected recommendations from respondents for improving the ICR, including "providing students with more information and intent about the ICR, more support services, pedagogical training, and debrief mechanisms for all involved."[55]

Supporting the Transition from Undergraduate to Graduate Studies

Over the past three years, UWinnipeg has offered the Indigenous Summer Scholars Program (ISSP), which allows senior undergraduate students and recent graduates of undergraduate programs who identify as Indigenous to explore the possibilities of graduate studies. The ISSP has three goals: to strengthen the pathways for Indigenous students to move into graduate school and leadership roles within the academy and beyond; to recognize the importance and centrality of Indigenous peoples, ways of knowing, and experiences at UWinnipeg; and to create a network of Indigenous scholars and allies on campus.

The ISSP begins with an orientation week where students participate in a series of workshops and events designed to give them an introduction to the centrality of research in graduate studies, to Indigenous knowledge in the academy, and to skills needed to succeed in graduate studies (e.g., research presentations, research proposal writing). For the following eleven weeks, students participate as members of research teams, undertaking research on a project under the supervision of a UWinnipeg faculty or staff researcher. Students receive an award of $5,000 for their participation over the twelve weeks. UWinnipeg's Pathways to Graduate Studies (P2GS) program is an opportunity for UWinnipeg Indigenous students majoring in science to engage in science learning and research. The intent of this program is to support Indigenous students in STEM fields, introduce students to research opportunities, and encourage students to continue with their undergraduate programs and eventually into graduate programs.

Indigenous-focused Graduate Programs

Ten years ago, UWinnipeg launched a unique graduate-level program: the Master's in Development Practice in Indigenous Development (MDP) with the support of the MacArthur Foundation. The Foundation invested in over 30 MDP programs on six continents to train a new generation of development practitioners with the technical and practical skills necessary to diagnose and address the interlinked global problems of sustainable development and poverty. Through classes, case studies, group projects, and a field placement, students build the skills needed to be a development practitioner. At UWinnipeg, the MDP uniquely focuses on Indigenous development—the only MDP program to focus on how Indigenous knowledge and experience can help shape a sustainable path for development, rooted in culture and identity.

In 2008, UWinnipeg also created a Master of Arts in Indigenous Governance (MAIG) program. Students in this program examine Indigenous governance through Indigenous wisdom and multidisciplinary coursework in fields such politics, anthropology, human ecology, sociology, law, history, religion and culture, and conflict resolution studies. The program recognizes and honors the central role of language as carrier of culture, conveyor of tradition and knowledge, and signifier of individual and community identity by supporting the teaching of the Indigenous languages Ojibwe and Cree. An international focus will prepare students to take leadership positions in the private and public sectors, to create and influence policy, to creatively approach development and governance from an Indigenous perspective, and to promote the visibility and recognition of sovereign Indigenous peoples and communities in Canada and abroad. As both the MDP and MAIG have existed for the past ten years, UWinnipeg faculty and administration members will be reviewing the programs, in partnership with Indigenous elders, traditional knowledge keepers and program alumni to ensure they are still meeting their objectives.

Supporting Transitions to Work

One of UWinnipeg's experiential learning opportunities for students is the Youth United inner-city work study program. A partnership with the City of Winnipeg and numerous community-based organizations, the program focuses on reconciliation and the concept of breaking barriers and building bridges. The students come from a diversity of backgrounds, both suburban and inner-city, with the intent of fostering new relationships and the exchange of ideas and perspectives. Students spend one day a week in the classroom, and four days a week working in community-based organizations. The curriculum exposes them to a variety of community settings and cultural experiences.

UWinnipeg also recently signed a memorandum of understanding with the federal government to promote the recruitment of recent graduates, particularly Indigenous graduates, into the federal public service.

Community Engagement: Indigenous Insights, Executive Leadership Course in Indigenous and Human Rights, Walls to Bridges

UWinnipeg offers a range of programs designed to engage with outside audiences. Indigenous Insights is a flexible learning program designed to advance reconciliation across Canada by starting with employee training. The program highlights Indigenous peoples' history, rights, and relationship with Canada, and provides a foundation for organizations seeking to understand and respond to the TRC *Calls to Action*. The program, designed for mid-career professionals who may not have encountered Canada's history of residential schools and colonialism, was created by Indigenous people, including academics, professionals, and community members.

UWinnipeg and the Canadian Museum for Human Rights (CMHR) have developed a joint program called "Indigenous and Human Rights: An Executive Leadership Program" intended to help business executives and organizational leaders shape workplace cultures that respect Indigenous and human rights. This is an intensive course delivered by UWinnipeg faculty and draws upon the expertise, programs, and relationships of both institutions. The robust program includes presentations and discussions with Indigenous leaders, activists, educators and human rights scholars, exploration of relevant, interactive museum exhibits for in-gallery learning, and first-hand perspectives from Indigenous peoples, including survivors of Indian residential schools. In 2014, UWinnipeg began offering the Walls to Bridges program, which brings together incarcerated and campus-enrolled students to study at correctional facilities. While earning degree credit as equals, students share their perspectives as they analyze social issues together.

CONCLUSION AND PERSONAL REFLECTION

To understand Indigenous postsecondary students' experiences as institutions move toward reconciliation, Indspire sent a survey to 2,000 students in the summer of 2018.[56] The Indspire report offers insight into the progress that has been made and the many challenges that lie ahead. Students reported insufficient funding for school and living expenses and a lack of funding coordination between schools and home communities. Students noted that funding was inconsistent across institutions and some noted that "funding that looks at the needs of Indigenous students in a holistic way" is needed.[57] Students reported feeling isolated and felt that "Indigenous student services can anchor the students' connection to their culture identity."[58] Students reported that instructors need to be educated on Indigenous history and should be respectful of Indigenous cultures.[59] They want Indigenous representation in all disciplines and do not want the burden of being asked to "speak to all things Indigenous."[60] Some students felt that they would, however, work with schools to determine what content should be incorporated in curricula.[61] Of the students, 45% reported racism, isolation, and marginalization on campus.[62] Many said that, while attending a non-Indigenous school, they were most comfortable in Indigenous spaces and programs and felt welcomed when school initiatives included their cultural practices.[63] The results of the Indspire survey show that there is still much more to do with respect to indigenization. Of particular importance, the survey found that students feel least safe in classrooms. Confronting this reality must be front and center.

At UWinnipeg, we remain committed to advancing reconciliation. As we reflect back on Gaudry and Lorenz's framework, we strive to implement initiatives that fall under their definition of *decolonial indigenization*. For example, in 2018, UWinnipeg and the Manitoba Métis Federation (MMF) signed a ten-year agreement to partner in addressing policy research questions designed and developed by the MMF. As part of this agreement, UWinnipeg will host postdoctoral researchers who work closely with UWinnipeg faculty and MMF representatives to conduct research and provide answers to the MMF's questions. In 2019, UWinnipeg and the MMF published a research report on the school readiness of Métis children in Manitoba. UWinnipeg is actively pursuing a number of other partnerships, particularly in the area of Indigenous language and traditional knowledge education that fit with decolonization.

I came to UWinnipeg in 2014 with good intentions. My identity as a Métis woman is based on my family history and my own personal journey to understand and connect with my heritage. I am learning more all the time. There are strong linkages between my journey, UWinnipeg's journey, and Canada's journey toward reconciliation. I understand that I was an atypical hire to be the president of an academic institution. While I hold a PhD and have completed postdoctoral studies, my career has largely been in the public service. As a Métis woman, following a powerful white male with long-standing relationships with powerful male leaders, I had to find and build my own networks and relationships. I deliberately pivoted toward grassroots, female Indigenous leaders, and faculty, while rebuilding and forming relationships with the next generation of leadership.

At the same time, I was fortunate to start building from a strong foundation at UWinnipeg, established by Dr Axworthy, faculty, and staff and informed by our location in the heart of Winnipeg, with one of the highest urban Indigenous populations, on Treaty 1 territory, in the homeland of the Métis nation. The work of UWinnipeg to 2014 moved us from access to inclusion. In this regard, UWinnipeg is perhaps ahead of some other Canadian institutions, while I also recognize that pathways to reconciliation are informed by people and location, and are relative to local conditions and ideas.

The Truth and Reconciliation Commission's *Calls to Action* provide us with a road map and challenge universities to assume a leadership role and do more to include Indigenous students and work with Indigenous people and communities to build understanding. By and large, universities have embraced this challenge, have made public commitments, and have followed through with action. The commitments, though, are ahead of results as system and culture change takes time and effort. We are also evolving our understanding of reconciliation and indigenization. This is a period of "first-evers" and it sometimes feels like universities are competing with each other, as much as we are also working together.

Indigenization is about cultural change, internally at UWinnipeg and externally in the community and across Canada. For me, it is also personal. A great deal of work had already been done when I arrived in 2014, which meant that the next steps were transformative, such as the ICR, and the deeper work associated with reconciliation and decolonization. I am aware of the need to make progress and continue our journey, while also working in a way to ensure the confidence of the UWinnipeg community.

UWinnipeg's resources continue to be stretched and we are faced with a range of things that need to be done, all of which require funding, time, and attention. We do not have the ability to make cluster hires or build standalone Indigenous centers. Larger universities in Canada have proportionately larger influence when it comes to calling for resources and investments, much of which is provided by federal and provincial governments looking for the biggest possible impact. There is also an issue of alignment between provincial and federal government, where the priorities of one level of government may not be supported by another level of government, even though there are cost-sharing requirements in most infrastructure programs. We need to be strategic then about advancing our priorities and look for synergies and opportunities to partner with Indigenous people, organizations, and communities. This has forced a realization that we cannot (and should not) do it alone, or even on our own campus. Despite these challenges, we have found opportunities. In June 2019, we honored four Indigenous elders and traditional knowledge keepers with honorary doctorates, thus communicating the message that Indigenous knowledge and language, and the efforts to preserve and revitalize it, are on the same level as other knowledge and effort. UWinnipeg also announced the appointment of three new Indigenous-focused Canada Research Chairs, all of whom are women.

At UWinnipeg, we are moving forward on a journey of reconciliation and indigenization. Gaudry and Lorenz have provided a useful framework through which we can categorize and assess what we are doing. We know that what we are doing is having an impact and contributing to a more positive future. We also acknowledge that there is more to be done. We will continue our journey in partnership with Indigenous peoples, so we may all succeed together.

NOTES

1. Statistics Canada, 2016 Canadian Census, September, 2018.
2. Sabrina Bond and Stephen Spence, "Maximizing Manitoba's Potential: Manitoba Research Centre," The Conference Board of Canada, Jan. 25, 2017, iii.
3. Bond and Spence, "Maximizing Manitoba's Potential," 7.
4. Ibid., 8.
5. Indigenization is fully explained below and in the next section.
6. Adam Gaudry and Danielle Lorenz, "Indigenization as Inclusion, Reconciliation, and Decolonization: Navigating the Different Visions for Indigenizing the Canadian Academy." *AlterNative: An International Journal of Indigenous Peoples* 14, no. 3 (2018): 218. doi:10.1177/1177180118785382.
7. Gaudry and Lorenz, "Indigenization as Inclusion, Reconciliation, and Decolonization," 218.
8. Ibid., 218.
9. Ibid., 220.
10. Ibid., 221.
11. Ibid., 219.

12. Ibid., 222.
13. Ibid., 222.
14. Ibid., 223.
15. Ibid., 219.
16. Ibid., 224.
17. Universities Canada, "Principles on Indigenous Education," June 29, 2015.
18. Natalie Samson, "Indigenization Efforts Vary Widely on Canadian Campuses, Study Finds," University Affairs, April 16, 2019, https://www.universityaffairs.ca/news/news-article/indigenization-efforts-vary-widely-on-canadian-campuses-study-finds/.
19. Samson, "Indigenization Efforts Vary Widely on Canadian Campuses, Study Finds."
20. Deborah Saucier, "Reconciliation on University Campuses: 'Two realities, side by side,'" Maclean's, October 11, 2018, https://www.macleans.ca/education/reconciliation-on-university-campuses-two-realities-side-by-side/.
21. Saucier, "Reconciliation on University Campuses."
22. Ibid.
23. Sheila Cote-Meek, "Postsecondary Education and Reconciliation," *Policy Options*, February 16, 2017, https://policyoptions.irpp.org/magazines/february-2017/post-secondary-education-and-reconciliation/.
24. Cote-Meek, "Postsecondary Education and Reconciliation."
25. Rod Skinkle and Ron Deganadus McLester, "What It Means for an Institution to Indigenize," *Academica Forum*, June 18, 2019, https://forum.academica.ca/forum/what-it-means-for-an-institution-to-indigenize.
26. Skinkle and McLester, "What It Means for an Institution to Indigenize."
27. Ibid.
28. Sarah Treleaven, "How Canadian Universities Are Responding to the TRC's Calls to Action," Maclean's, December 8, 2018, https://www.macleans.ca/education/how-canadian-universities-are-responding-to-the-trcs-calls-to-action/.
29. Treleaven, "How Canadian Universities Are Responding to the TRC's Calls to Action."
30. Winnipeg School Division, "Build from Within – Ozhitoon Onji Peenjiiee," Winnipeg School Division, https://www.winnipegsd.ca/Education%20Services/EquityDiversity/indigenous-education/Pages/Build-From-Within.aspx.
31. Andrea Sterzuk and Russell Fayant, "Towards Reconciliation through Language Planning for Indigenous Languages in Canadian Universities," *Current Issues in Language Planning* 17(3–4).
32. Lloyd Axworthy, Linda DeRiviere, and Jennifer Rattray, "Chapter 4: Beyond Access to Inclusion: The Axworthy Years 2004–14," in *From Access to Engagement: Initiatives at the University of Winnipeg in Support of Educationally Marginalized Children and Youth, 1988–2017*. 2018, 4–12, https://www.uwinnipeg.ca/community-engagement/Research/about-research.html.
33. Ibid., 4–12–4–13.
34. Ibid., 4–14.
35. Ibid., 4–15.

36. Ibid., 4–16.
37. Ibid., 4–16.
38. Ibid., 4–18.
39. Ibid., 4–19.
40. Ibid., 4–22.
41. Shauna MacKinnon, "Urban and Inner-City Studies: Looking Back at 2018," February 5, 2019, http://www.shaunamac.com/2019/02/.
42. Shauna MacKinnon, "Truth, Reconciliation and Responsibility Beyond the Classroom," May 29, 2019, http://www.shaunamac.com/2019/05/.
43. MacKinnon, "Truth, Reconciliation and Responsibility Beyond the Classroom."
44. Tara Williamson, "Be a Part of History: Preliminary Evaluation and Assessment of the Indigenous Course Requirement (ICR) at The University of Winnipeg," The University of Winnipeg, January 7, 2018, 12.
45. Williamson, "Be a Part of History," 13.
46. Ibid., 13.
47. Ibid., 13.
48. Ibid., 14.
49. Ibid., 14.
50. Ibid., 15.
51. Ibid., 31.
52. Helen Lepp Friesen, "Chapter 8: "We Are All Relations": An Indigenous Course Requirement (ICR) as Part of a Good Way to Reconciliation," in *From Access to Engagement: Initiatives at the University of Winnipeg in Support of Educationally Marginalized Children and Youth, 1988–2017*, 2018, 8-25, https://www.uwinnipeg.ca/community-engagement/Research/about-research.html.
53. Friesen, "We Are All Relations," 8–25.
54. Ibid.
55. Ibid.
56. Indspire, "Truth and Reconciliation in Post-Secondary Settings: Student Experience," Indspire, November 15, 2018, 8, https://indspire.ca/wp-content/uploads/2018/11/JMGD_003_IND_TR_REPORT_FINAL_V3_NOV15_V3.pdf.
57. Ibid.
58. Ibid.
59. Ibid.
60. Ibid.
61. Ibid.
62. Ibid.
63. Ibid.

BIBLIOGRAPHY

Axworthy, Lloyd, Linda DeRiviere, and Jennifer Rattray. "Chapter 4: Beyond Access to Inclusion: The Axworthy Years 2004–14," in *From Access to Engagement: Initiatives at the University of Winnipeg in Support of Educationally Marginalized*

Children and Youth, 1988–2017, 2018, https://www.uwinnipeg.ca/community-engagement/Research/about-research.html.

Bond, Sabrina and Stephen Spence. "Maximizing Manitoba's Potential: Manitoba Research Centre," *The Conference Board of Canada*, January 25, 2017.

Cote-Meek, Sheila. "Postsecondary Education and Reconciliation," *Policy Options*, February 16, 2017, https://policyoptions.irpp.org/magazines/february-2017/post-secondary-education-and-reconciliation/.

Gaudry, Adam, and Danielle Lorenz. "Indigenization as Inclusion, Reconciliation, and Decolonization: Navigating the Different Visions for Indigenizing the Canadian Academy." *AlterNative: An International Journal of Indigenous Peoples* 14, no. 3 (2018): 218. doi:10.1177/1177180118785382.

Indspire. "Truth and Reconciliation in Post-Secondary Settings: Student Experience," November 15, 2018, https://indspire.ca/wp-content/uploads/2018/11/JMGD_003_IND_TR_REPORT_FINAL_V3_NOV15_V3.pdf

Lepp Friesen, Helen, "Chapter 8: "We Are All Relations": An Indigenous Course Requirement (ICR) as Part of a Good Way to Reconciliation." In *From Access to Engagement: Initiatives at the University of Winnipeg in Support of Educationally Marginalized Children and Youth*, 1988–2017. 2018, https://www.uwinnipeg.ca/community-engagement/Research/about-research.html.

McKinnon, Shauna, "Truth, Reconciliation and Responsibility Beyond the Classroom," May 29, 2019, http://www.shaunamac.com/2019/05/.

Samson, Natalie, "Indigenization Efforts Vary Widely on Canadian Campuses, Study Finds," *University Affairs*, April 16, 2019, https://www.universityaffairs.ca/news/news-article/indigenization-efforts-vary-widely-on-canadian-campuses-study-finds/.

Saucier, Deborah, "Reconciliation on University Campuses: 'Two realities, side by side,'" Maclean's, October 11, 2018, https://www.macleans.ca/education/reconciliation-on-university-campuses-two-realities-side-by-side/.

Skinkle, Rod and Ron Deganadus McLester. "What it Means for an Institution to Indigenize," *Academica Forum*, June 18, 2019, https://forum.academica.ca/forum/what-it-means-for-an-institution-to-indigenize.

Statistics Canada. *2016 Canadian Census*, https://www12.statcan.gc.ca/census-recensement/2016/dp-pd/index-eng.cfm.

Sterzuk, Andrea and Russell Fayant. "Towards Reconciliation through Language Planning for Indigenous Languages in Canadian Universities," *Current Issues in Language Planning*, 17(3–4).

Treleaven, Sarah. "How Canadian universities are responding to the TRC's Calls to Action." *Maclean's*, December 8, 2018, https://www.macleans.ca/education/how-canadian-universities-are-responding-to-the-trcs-calls-to-action/.

Williamson, Tara, "Be a Part of History: Preliminary Evaluation and Assessment of the Indigenous Course Requirement (ICR) at the University of Winnipeg," The University of Winnipeg, January 7, 2018.

Winnipeg School Division, School Division, "Build From Within—Ozhitoon Onji Peenjiiee," Winnipeg School Division, https://www.winnipegsd.ca/Education%20Services/EquityDiversity/indigenous-education/Pages/Build-From-Within.aspx.

Chapter 7

Ago'widiwinan (Principles of Treaties)

Loretta Ross

Our Elders tell us that in order for us to know where we are going, we must know where we came from. This teaching could not be more true. As part of this journey, we have therefore begun to explore the history of Indigenous people. This journey also provides all of Canada with the opportunity to reflect and gain a deeper understanding of the treaties and the treaty relationship. Numerous institutions have responded to the increased desire for knowledge and education by offering courses, workshops, conferences, and other events focused on various aspects of Indigenous history. The TRC issued these ninety-four *Calls to Action* calling public attention to critical issues affecting First Nations and urging immediate action in 2015 and, in 2019 we continue to see Canadians taking these *Calls to Action* to heart and reaching out to First Nations in various ways. In this context of renewed interest in reconciling the past wrongs, I want to focus on the treaties and the unique relationship between First Nations peoples and the Crown. Furthermore, I would like to challenge what we think we know about treaties and suggest that a First Nations perspective of those treaties can guide our approach to building a stronger relationship between First Nations peoples and non-First Nations people, as well as between First Nations peoples themselves in their own communities and nations.

   In the Canadian society we rely largely on the formal education system to do this for us. However, our formal education system must continue to adapt to include the histories of First Nations peoples told from the First Nations perspective. If we try to remember what we may have been taught, many will have little to no memory of treaty education. We do not even realize the impact that this has on our relationships and how we have come to view each other as First Nations and non-First Nations people. When I recall what I was taught about the treaties in the classroom during my grade 5 social studies class, I learned that the treaties were entered into with the Indians so that the land could be opened up for settlement and the railway.

I also learned that my First Nations people gave up all their land and agreed to be put on [government assigned land] reserve for this to occur. Even as a child, I could not understand why that happened and how my ancestors would allow that. I attended school on reserve and so I understood that reserves did exist and in fact if reserves did exist, then there must be some truth to my treaty lesson. But what that lesson also taught me, that if I accepted that version of events, then my people were terrible negotiators or were just not as smart as the negotiators for the Crown, and if we were placed on reserves and continued to live on those reserves, then the Crown must have enough strength to keep us there. Smart and strong, so the converse of that was to be, foolish and weak? Maybe not that extreme but certainly it left me with a feeling of "less than." This feeling remained during all of my formal educational training, right through law school. There was nothing in that formal training that challenged the perspective that as a First Nations person, I was less than a non-First Nations person. Neither did my formal schooling tell me that my history and contributions to the development of Canada as a First Nations person were worthy. In fact, when I was in law school in the early 1990s, my law course referred to the application of Canadian law to First Nations peoples. It did not mean law from the perspective of First Nations peoples. It did not even acknowledge that First Nations peoples had their own laws, governance systems, and ways of being. Despite the efforts of many people, in the forty plus years since I was in that grade 5 class, the formal educational processes in terms of including our perspectives of history have improved only slightly.

Reconciliation requires that each of us determine what it means for us, both in our personal and professional lives. We cannot expect that reconciliation is the sole responsibility of governments or institutions such as our churches and universities, but rather, it is also the responsibility of us as individuals. It is too easy to avoid responsibility and say that it was the government that orchestrated these events, so government must also effect the required change. Government certainly has the biggest responsibility, but we cannot avoid our role as well. After all, government also responds to it and as people in Canada we must continue to move toward a society that is reflective and respectful of all. Informed citizens are vital to the process.

The influence of voice is exemplified if we look back at the example of the Manitoba Indian Brotherhood (MIB) in 1971. The following powerful statement was released by the MIB through *Wahbung: Our Tomorrows*.

> The history and past policies regarding the Indian people cannot and must not be ignored, for their effects are with us all in the present Indian fact. To deny

the past and to refuse to recognize its implications is to distort the present and to distort the present is to take risks with the future that are blatantly irresponsible.[1]

This publication was prepared in response to a 1969 federal government White Paper entitled *Statement of the Government of Canada on Indian Policy*[2] which proposed to do away with special status for First Nations people as outlined in the *Indian Act*. The White Paper included abolishing the *Indian Act* and other pieces of legislation that related to Indians, eliminating reserves, and terminating the treaties that were entered between First Nations peoples and the Crown. The facts in 2019 are much the same as in 1971: First Nations people continue to experience higher representation in the justice system, the child welfare system, and suicide and mortality rates. The effects of past policies are still evident in the present, yet why have we not heeded the words of the MIB? It is not enough, however, to merely comprehend the past policies affecting First Nations peoples. We must also examine and understand the foundational agreements that were the basis of what has formed much of what we know today as Canada. The treaties between the First Nations peoples and the British Crown are the building blocks in the creation of Canada, and their significance is not one relegated to the past but continues for as long as the sun shines, the grass grows, and the rivers flow.

Canadians to examine these past policies and reflect on how these policies were not in consideration of and, in fact, breached the agreements made in the treaties. However, since 2015, many of us have embarked upon a journey of reconciliation that stems from the challenge set out in the *Calls to Action* as set out in the Final Report of the Truth and Reconciliation Commission of Canada (TRC).

WHAT DO WE KNOW ABOUT THE TREATIES?

So, what have we been taught about the treaties that informs our understanding of them today? The short answer is, that sadly, there has not been much, if any, formal education about the treaties, at least not to the level that we understand the significant role of the treaties both historically and in our modern world. The lack of education regarding treaties is evident in the broken relationship between First Nations and non-First Nations people throughout history, including contemporary times.

Generally speaking, the general public's understanding of the treaties usually centers around the belief that agreements were entered into between the Crown and the First Nations peoples, whereby the First Nations peoples surrendered their land to the Crown, so that the Crown could have access to the land for settlement and the railway that would and now does link Canada coast to coast. The First Nations peoples agreed or were put on land reserves in exchange and were provided an annual payment of five dollars per year. In all likelihood, this would be the extent of most treaty history lessons, and for most, this is all we think we need to know about the treaties. This understanding, reflective of a non-First Nations perspective of the treaties, has resulted in a number of misconceptions. Some of these misconceptions include: the treaties were simple land transactions; the treaties are frozen in time and therefore have no relevance in modern times; the treaties only benefit First Nations peoples; the written text of the treaties captured the entire agreement and that all land was surrendered thereby giving the Crown full access to it, including its resources. As a result, many Canadians believe the treaties are outdated agreements that occurred such a long time ago that they are no longer relevant in this day and age, so we don't pay any more attention. Even if some believe the treaties were important, many will view them as modernly irrelevant and absorbed or replaced by the current Canadian framework. Consequently, very little attention is given to First Nations peoples in Canadian society except perhaps to study the contemporary situation of First Nations people and the multitude of social struggles that they face. Indigenous studies courses explore some of the reasons for these struggles and in law schools one will learn about how Canadian law applies to First Nations peoples.[3] But what is it that we learn about the treaties and our relationship to each other, specifically?

While many education institutions have made considerable effort in including more courses on Indigenous history in recent years, the topic of treaties is found within over-arching topics related to Indigenous history. Treaty education is sometimes included under the heading of "Treaty and Aboriginal rights,"[4] which draws the conclusion that the treaties are about

providing certain rights to First Nations peoples. The treaties have been relegated to rights, a concept that until very recently for First Nations peoples, did not exist.

Most Canadians have accepted Canadian history in the way it has been taught to us by non-First Nations instructors, teachers and professors in European[5]-style education institutions. Generally, there is only one point of view, the European side, to this history which does not provide a proper foundation for understanding the full history of how Canada came to be. Given these understandings, it puzzles Canadians when they hear First Nations peoples calling upon the Canadian government to live up to the obligations set out in treaties. What is it about the treaties that we need to understand and what will it take for First Nations peoples to stop saying that the Canadian government must fulfill outstanding obligations and responsibilities?

Questions surrounding the treaties often include: Doesn't the government provide funding to First Nations peoples? How much money will it take for First Nations peoples to be happy? How much more do we have to give them?

To gain the understanding required to answers to these types of questions, we have to take a step back to a time to when those agreements were entered into and critically reflect on the events that led up to that time. We also have to step into the shoes of the First Nations peoples and gain an understanding of their worldview. Only then, will we have a sufficient level of comprehension to enable us to arrive at a place in time where we will no longer wonder what remains outstanding or why First Nations peoples appear to be in a continual struggle with the Canadian society.

So, let us take a step back and revisit the history of our lands and territories. Let us review each treaty party's perspectives and how they were retained and passed down to each respective generation, only then can we better understand the differences and appreciate the challenges we will be required to overcome in order to move forward.

UNDERSTANDING DIFFERING WORLD VIEWS

The non-First Nations approach to understanding the treaties relies heavily upon the written documents.[6] The historical written records of government, journalists, and journals of others that present at the time of treaty, such as the treaty commissioners, are common tools used by historians to interpret what was intended by the parties through the treaties. While the written record has attempted to provide an objective view of the events of the day, they are inherently reflective of the values, culture and perspectives of the people recording the information (the Crown's Treaty Commissioners, not the First Nations in attendance), and therefore cannot be assumed to be neutral reflections. The treaty commissioners for example had written instructions that they were to follow, and their written accountings had to reflect adherence to those instructions. As political appointees of the government, they had a mandate to follow and needed to reflect the fact that they had followed their mandate. Fortunately, as the values and cultures of those times have changed, we can now reflect back on events and deepen previous understandings. The perspective of First Nations, on the other hand, is recorded in the oral history of the people.

> A fundamental law that respects the sacredness of these Creator made laws is the requirement that one cannot embellish, add to, or change these laws..... Oral history preserves traditions, transfers knowledge, and records events. The elders describe the process as very rigorous and disciplined and as one which emphasizes the requirement for preserving accuracy, precision and procedural protocols. This procedural and substantive knowledge is passed from one generation to the next. The process of preserving and transferring traditional laws and procedures is a solemn obligation and serious commitment.[7]

This discipline was followed through other forms of recording events, such as in the language itself as well as songs, dances, birch bark scrolls and wampum belts. As noted, no further information was added or deleted, including embellishments or interpretation of those events. If we consider these various ways of recording events, it reminds us that when we examine the history, we must take into account all sources of information.

First Nations peoples had their own ways of being that included elaborate systems of governance, laws, social order, family structure and spirituality. The spirituality of the First Nations peoples guided the other systems by which they lived. For example, the fundamental relationship for First Nations peoples is the one that they have with the Creator. This spiritual relationship contains the values, customs and laws and worldviews that are relied upon in all their relations, enabling them to function as successful societies, in their own right, for thousands of years both before and after European contact and into today. This belief system centers around the understanding that they are in harmony with nature, with man not being dominant or above nature, but a small and equal part of it.

This included a significant relationship to the land as it is First Nations peoples' belief that they are one with the land. The words of the First Nations chief Ay-ee-ta-pe-pe-tung, during the negotiations of Treaty 1 reflect the connection to the land:

> When first you began to travel from Fort William you saw something afar off and this is the land you saw. At that time, you thought I will have that someday or other; but behold you see before you the lawful owner of it. I understand you are going to buy this land from me. Well God made me out of this very clay that is besmeared on my body. This is what you say you are going to buy from me.[8]

Common to all First Nations peoples is this understanding that while land can be utilized for survival and that different nations occupied different territories of land, one could not own the land in the sense of private ownership.

> Creator put us on this earth, to look after wherever it is where we're living. *Ji-dibendamang*, we say, to look after it, to be care-taker of that land. To communicate with those animals, those plants, those trees, so they can show us their wisdom and knowledge for the medicine of our people, for the health and well-being of our nation, our Anishinabe people.[9]

This is a very important point in terms of differences in the European and First Nations view of treaty: if you cannot own the land; you cannot sell or surrender the land. It was also understood that everyone lived together on the land and so the land was shared for different purposes including peaceful coexistence and sharing of territories.

The territories were understood as the occupation and use of the land for livelihood, rather than ownership in the Canadian legal context. One Elder has described this relationship with the land as follows:

> All of the agreements they have had between one another as peoples and as nations were always based on [land] use-on how they were going to use that land. And...when I say that the use of that land, we had agreements between one another, hunting territories that we shared, trapping lands that we shared, gathering lands that we shared, medicinal lands that we shared [sacred lands], peace territorial lands that we designated for the shelter and safety of all people. And [the boundaries of] those lands were always laid out before these peoples .... That's how they set out things between one another. They understood use; they understood the means by which land was used.[10]

A fundamental difference in perspectives of the land therefore existed at the time of treaty making and continues through to today. However, this is not reflected in the written text of the treaty and has not been presented when we study the treaties, especially in government funded schools.

A FIRST NATIONS UNDERSTANDING

First Nations peoples also had their ways of interacting with each other. Elaborate and important protocols were followed when dealing with other Nations. As described by Indigenous scholar Aimee Craft:

> Their political, military, and trade alliances among themselves and with other Indigenous nations gave them extensive experience in treaty and alliance building, modelled on Indigenous legal traditions.[11]

We see these protocols in the many treaties and agreements that were established among First Nations themselves, but they were also relied upon in the later relationships established between First Nations peoples and the European fur traders. The Hudson Bay Company (HBC) quickly realized that the assistance of the First Nations people was critical to the ability of the HBC and its employees, to survive and thrive in this new land and, in building relationships with them, learned and adopted the many protocols of the First Nations people. As Indigenous scholar Aimee Craft has stated,

> The giving of gifts, the extension of credit, and the standards of trade were often based on Indigenous legal concepts. Traditionally, Aboriginal peoples in Canada did not transfer goods by conducting their relations with other people in a static way. Relationships were continually renewed and reaffirmed through

ceremonial customs. The idea of trade terms being "frozen" through a contract, written on paper, was an alien concept.[12]

Indigenous legal concepts, ceremonies and protocols continued to be adopted and utilized in building new relationships up to and including 1763, when the King of England issued a *Royal Proclamation* that would prove critical in the development of Canada.

The British victory in the Seven Years War in Europe (1756–1763) paved the way for the British to assert its sovereignty in the new colonies. King George III, the British ruler at the time, set out through the proclamation the rules for how the British would, among other things, engage with First Nations peoples and their lands. *The Royal Proclamation* text stated in part:

> And whereas it is just and reasonable, and essential to Our Interest and the Security of Our Colonies, that the several Nations or Tribes of Indians, with whom We are connected, and who live under Our Protection, should not be molested or disturbed in the Possession of such Parts of Our Dominions and Territories as, not having been ceded to, or purchased by Us, are reserved to them, or any of them, as their Hunting Grounds.
>
> In order, therefore, to prevent such Irregularities for the future, and to the end that the Indians may be convinced of our Justice and determined Resolution to remove all reasonable Cause of Discontent, We do, with the Advice of our Privy Council strictly enjoin and require. that no private Person do presume to make any purchase from the said Indians of any Lands reserved to the said Indians, within those parts of our Colonies where, We have thought proper to allow Settlement: but that, if at any Time any of the Said Indians should be inclined to dispose of the said Lands, the same shall be Purchased only for Us, in our Name, at some public Meeting or Assembly of the said Indians, to be held for that Purpose by the Governor or Commander in Chief.[13]

The Royal Proclamation process secured the Crown as the only entity that could acquire First Nations lands. For First Nations peoples, the *Royal Proclamation* recognizes them as separate and distinct Nations with sovereignty over their people and their lands. As Elder Bone describes,

> There are three major principles fundamental to each First Nations-the spirit of our people lives in the language, the history of or peoples is embodied in the language, and the oral history carried by our people reconciles the past and the future. These principles include the belief in the Creator, land, peoples, language, history, customs, and traditions. These teachings are referred to as the 'original laws of people'. These seven concepts are important. The United Nations has defined what a Nation is and they used these similar principles.[14]

The Royal Proclamation was issued at a time when the French and English were struggling for power in the new lands. Both sides sought the alliance and support of the Original peoples to assist them in achieving victory.

The strength and significance of Indigenous[15] people was well understood and highly respected by both the French and the English at the time. Understanding this, the British wanted to ensure that the Indigenous people of North America understood what the *Royal Proclamation* meant to their relationship. The Crown representative, William Johnson, set out to meet with the First Nations people and did this through an invitation for First Nations leaders to attend at Niagara. Indigenous Scholar, Aaron Mills describes this time in our history by connecting the *Royal Proclamation of 1763* and the 1764 Treaty of Niagara:

> The ground for the Treaty of Niagara of 1764 actually started in 1760 with the fall of New France and the need for the English for British North America to now build relationships with the Algonquin peoples who had been allies of new France. And with the exception ... The vast majority of Indigenous people on Turtle Island (except the Haudenosaunee who had long been allies with the British) and the relationship between the British colonial authority and Algonquian peoples was not going well.
>
> And so by December 24th of 1763, he [Sir William Johnston] had received King George III's Royal Proclamation and orders to publicly disseminate it and he sent Algonquin and Nipissing runners throughout Turtle Island in the winter 1763-1764. Inviting our ancestors to come to this summer congress at Niagara that following summer of 1764. So it was a historical gathering of truly epic proportions. There had been nothing of this scale ever.[16]

The Royal Proclamation, as understood by the First Nations peoples, was a declaration that there would be no interference in the internal operations and way of life of the First Nations Peoples and their territories. The epic gathering in the summer of 1763 was an opportunity for the Crown to explain the intention of the British. Written records and oral history states that the Indigenous leaders that were gathered were told of the *Royal Proclamation* in their own languages. The fact that this event had even taken place reflects that, despite the assertion of British sovereignty, the British were aware of the strength and sovereignty of the First Nations peoples. They understood that agreements would be necessary. The promises of the *Royal Proclamation* at Niagara in 1764 culminated in solidifying the Treaty of Niagara through the creation of a Wampum belt, depicted in figure 7.1.[17] The Wampum belt is solemn and symbolic representation used by First Nations in the recording of important historical events, to solidify the mutual understanding of the relationship between the Nations.

Figure 7.1   **The Treaty of Niagara Wampum Belt.** *Source*: Courtesy of Nathan Tidbridge.

Wampum belts would become the basis of the relationship, and all future agreements entered into, between the First Nations and the Crown. The Treaty of Niagara is a treaty of peace, friendship and alliance which involved an understanding of non-interference and mutual respect. It was understood that the wampum belts would be brought out each year to serve as an annual reminder to the leaders and people that entered into that relationship to honour that promise by continuing to peacefully co-exist. However, by the time of the War of 1812 the annual tradition was no longer being practiced and, by the time of Canadian Confederation in 1867, this practice had long since been forgotten by the Crown.

First Nations peoples, however, never forgot this important tradition and have always reminded the Crown of their special relationship of mutual respect and peaceful coexistence. Following the Treaty of Niagara in 1764, the 2000 plus First Nations leaders returned to their respective territories and shared this understanding with the people. It is this understanding that continues to be passed on from generation to generation. At this time in our early history with the Crown, it was still in the minds of the First Nations peoples when the time of treaty making in the province of Manitoba came about.

The First Nations' perspective tells us that they entered the treaty-making process with the understanding that they would be sharing the land with the new settlers, while maintaining their sovereignty over their land and their people. At the time of entering into the first of the Numbered Treaties in

1871, the First Nations peoples were already experiencing dramatic changes to their way of life. The buffalo had all but disappeared and the fur trade was no longer providing a viable livelihood. The impacts of diseases such as smallpox and Tuberculosis, unknown to First Nations prior to European contact, were devastating to their people. As was their practice of resilience and adaptation to changing environments, the First Nations peoples understood they understood that they had to enter into a relationship with the newcomers in order to survive.

At this point in time, there was already an increase in the numbers of newcomers, placing ongoing pressure on First Nations peoples, as more non-First Nations peoples began to occupy the land. Despite these changes, the treaty-making process was done in a manner that continued to reflect First Nations protocols and treaty-making practices, including the pipe ceremony and the exchange of gifts as important components of the process. The reliance on First Nations protocols during the Numbered treaties was not new to European settlers as they played an equally important a role during the fur trade era in Western Canada.

> First Nations peoples had well established inter-continental trade and commerce networks among each other which they had been practicing for several thousand years prior to European contact. So, at the time of these early contacts, they expected that their trade, commerce, military alliances, and peace-making protocols and practices would apply to these new relations.[18]

The early trade relations between First Nations and Europeans were built around First Nations protocols.

Trade, military and peace alliances and relations were common for Europeans as well. They had their own understanding of what would be required in forging relationships. This skill is something that served them well during the fur trade era. Certainly, in the new lands, the members of the fur trade learned from the French and saw the success of adopting Indigenous protocols and they too adopted these practices. During the treaty-making process, the Crown would have recognized many of these protocols as being an important part of building relations with the First Nations peoples through the experience of the Hudson's Bay Company during the fur trade era. First Nations peoples accepted this manner as a true and honest approach to creating the new relationship and remembered that these relations were meant to be of mutual respect and non-interference, in order to ensure an ongoing peaceful coexistence. It can be argued that these practices were clearly reflected in the early treaty making including the Selkirk Treaty of 1817, where not only were protocols of gift exchange done but the written text of the treaty reflects the acceptance of the nation to nation arrangement through the inclusion of drawings of the First Nations chiefs' clans representations.[19] This clear appreciation and recognition of First Nations peoples' governance systems demonstrate that First Nations protocols were an integral part of building relations between Nations.

Unfortunately, as the treaty-making process continued with the westward expansion of the British settlers, the written history shows that First Nations protocols that previously served as a recognition of First Nations' sovereignty as well as being foundational for building relationships, began to wane in the minds of the Crown. For example, during the negotiation of the Robinson Treaties in 1850, the Crown was engaging in activity contrary to the *Royal Proclamation* by going so far as to provide mining permits in Anishinabe territory without the prior knowledge and consent of the Anishinabe. This is seen in Chief Shingwauk's words to the Governor General (representative of the British Crown in Canada) in Montreal where he questions the actions of the Crown:

> Can you lay claim to our land? If so, by what right? Have you conquered it from us? You have not, for when you first came among us your children were few and weak, and the war cry of the Ojibway struck terror to the heart of the pale face.... Have you purchased it from us, or have we surrendered it to you? If so, when? And how? And where are the treaties?[20]

Clearly, the First Nations peoples remembered and understood the treaty-making process that the British Crown had set out for itself. As treaty making continued after 1867, the Canadian government instructions to its Crown representatives was for peaceful and friendly relations as they sought to continue to establishment settlements and gain access to First Nations land. The purchase of Rupert's Land from the fur trading HBC in 1869, without the knowledge or consent of the First Nations peoples, began a trend of Crown sovereignty assumption that ignored the *Royal Proclamation*. The First Nations people, however, were quick to remind the British Crown and sent a message through a number of actions. For instance, in what is now Northwestern Ontario and land covered in Treaty 3, the chiefs prevented settler travel through their territory. This was also done by Chief Yellowquill when he prevented settlers from travelling through his territory, which is now the area around the town of Portage la Prairie, Manitoba. The treaty-making process was also influenced by events occurring in the United States. The Crown and First Nations were well aware of events such as the northward movement of the Americans and the Indian Wars that were occurring in the United States. Neither First Nations peoples nor the Crown had a desire to incur the human and financial tolls associated with such conflicts. Both had interests in maintaining peaceful relations.

TREATY MAKING

The negotiations of the Numbered Treaties began with the Crown attempting to negotiate with the First Nations located, in what is known by many as Northwest Ontario, on lands covered by Treaty 3. This was a natural follow up to the Robinson-Huron and Robinson-Superior treaties as it would have been the logical move as the Crown representatives continued to move along the westward route. However, the First Nations of Treaty 3 were not happy with what they had witnessed with previous treaty making by the Crown and they refused to engage in negotiations. The Crown then proceeded to move on in their travels and engaged in discussions with the First Nations of what would eventually be Treaty 1. Some of the First Nations that had entered Treaty 1 had already had some treaty-making experience with the Crown through the negotiation of the Selkirk Treaty of 1817. The negotiation and entering into Treaty 1 was the first in a series of the eleven Numbered Treaties, negotiated between First Nations and the Crown from 1871 to 1921. For the Crown Treaty making occurred in two phases, the first involved treaties 1–7 and were concluded between 1871 and 1877. This phase of treaty making opened the prairies for farming and settlement and also allowed for the construction of the railway, which would eventually solidify the Crown's claim to the land north of the United States. This excerpt from the texts of these treaties reflects the Crown's intentions: "the desire of Her Majesty to open up for settlement, immigration, and such other purposes as to Her Majesty may seem meet, a tract of country bounded and described as hereinafter mentioned."[21]

The second phase of treaty making, involving treaties 8–11, occurred between 1899 and 1921. As these treaty areas were not as desirable to settlement for agricultural purposes, the Crown was slow to enter into this phase of treaty negotiations. However, this changed when events such as the gold rush in 1897 alerted the British Crown to the natural resources and minerals in those territories. In the Crown's view, these latter treaties would not only provide for access to natural resources in northern Canada, but they also opened the far West for settlement and secured a connection between British Columbia and central Canada. For the First Nations peoples, the treaties represented something considerably different.

The particular circumstances surrounding the treaty-making process was different in each of the treaty areas. Some negotiations took days and others a much shorter amount of time: they included a range of ceremony and formality. There are, however, a number of commonalities throughout any treaty-making process that should be understood.

One of those commonalities was that there was some mutuality in all of the agreements. It was understood by the First Nations that there would be exchanges between the parties, as demonstrated by Chief Mawedopenais during the Treaty 3 negotiations:

> All this is our property when you have come . . . . This is what we think, that the Great Spirit has planted us on this ground where we are, as you were where you came from . . . . Our hands are poor but our heads are rich, and it is riches that we ask so that we may be able to support our families as long as the sun rises and the water runs . . . . The sound of the rustling of the gold is under my feet where I stand; we have a rich country; it is the Great Spirit who gave us this; where we stand upon is the Indians' property, and belongs to them.
>
> It is your charitableness that you spoke of yesterday—her Majesty's charitableness that was given you. It is our chiefs, our young men, our children and great grandchildren, and those that are to be born, that I represent here, and it is for them that I ask for terms. The white man has robbed us of our riches, and we don't wish to give them up again without getting something in their place.[22]

The treaty-making process was a way of reconciling the interests of both parties and a means to building lasting and meaningful alliances that would foster future well-being between the Crown and First Nations peoples. The treaties not only secured their respective futures, but it also preserved peace and goodwill among both parties.

Securing of the future well-being of their people was a common feature of First Nations peoples' relationship building and treaty making. Certainly, the mutuality of the Numbered Treaties represented yet another relationship that was expected to provide stability and security in an increasingly changing environment. In the eyes of the First Nations peoples, the obligations of the Crown set out in the treaties were to protect their way of life and provide education, economic opportunities, and material goods to First Nations people to ensure their ongoing prosperity.

One of the most important aspects of treaty making involved honouring the Creator as being a third party to the process. First Nations people looked to their spiritual traditions for guidance during this process and their relationship with the Creator is fundamental. The Creator was viewed to have guided the discussions as well as being present during the smoking of the pipe, thus witnessing the spirit and intent of the promises that each party made to uphold the treaty. Consequently, the treaties made with and under the Creator elevated the solemnness of the treaties and the treaty relationship to be unalterable, inviolable, sacred and unbreachable. Elder Bone's words assist in this understanding:

> The first three concepts, the Creator, the Land, and the People were intrinsic to our belief systems prior to our relations with the Newcomers. They were stated by our leaders of the past echoed down to the treaty negotiations and passed onto us from the Elders. The Treaty phrase is a perfect example of our understanding

of Nationhood: Minik giizis ge-bimasiged, minik ge-mashkosiigag, minik nibi ge-bimijiwang. As long as the sun shines, the grass grows, and the waters flow. This phrase is the spirit and intent—the sun is the eye of the Creator watching over us, the grass is the fertile land on which we depend, and all sacred water including the waters that flow at the time of a birth and all other life giving water. Our relationship to Gizhe-Manidoo and the continuation of Bimaadiziwi-win is the foundation of what it means to be a Nation in our worldview.[23]

Treaty 1, concluded on August 3, 1871, probably is one of the treaties with the most written record. This record also captures some of the concerns and perspectives of the First Nations peoples that were engaged in those discussions. These same records also illustrate the differences in perspectives on a number of issues including concepts of land reserves and the surrender of land. Historians, academics and lawyers all utilize these recordings to form various interpretations of what the First Nations people understood. For example, Aimee Craft writes:

> Historians such as Jean Friesen have found that, faced with a difficult situation, the Anishinabe made the best deal they could, and that they surrendered the land, but retained some jurisdiction over resources. While I agree that the chiefs were in a sense forced to negotiate, I take a different view about the resulting agreement….It is my view, based on the evidence taken as a whole, that the Anishinabe agreed to share the land with the settlers and to allow them to use the land for agriculture. The Anishinabe also understood that they could continue to use their territory for their traditional activities. Neither party would interfere with the other…. Neither traditional harvesting nor farming were mutually exclusive, the result being that the Anishinabe would continue to use the land of Treaty One, along with the settlers, in a spirit of equality and non-interference. This is what the elders refer to as "a sharing treaty."[24]

The latter perspective is a common understanding among First Nations peoples. Concepts of surrender and cede are inconsistent with the principles of stewardship and sharing.

For the First Nations peoples, their understanding of the treaties was to build relations and an essential component was to share the land. As captured in the words of author Harold Johnston he describes the kinship relations that were expected in sharing the lands:

> When your family arrived here, Kiciwamanawak (my cousin), we expected that you would join the families already here, and, in time, learn to live like us. No one thought you would try to take everything for yourselves, and that we would have to beg for leftovers. We thought we would live as before and that you would share your technology with us. We thought that maybe if you watched how we lived, you might learn how to live in balance in this territory.

> The treaties that gave your family the right to occupy this territory were also an opportunity for you to learn how to live in this territory.[25]

We can continue to examine the various perspectives of what the treaties meant from a First Nations perspective; the Spirit and Intent of those treaties must be paramount in understanding. The literal word of the written text cannot be the only means that we utilize when we strive to gain a better understanding of these relationships.

We cannot just relegate the First Nations peoples' practice of treaty making to relics of the past, for the values that guided those treaty making and relationship building practices, remain alive in contemporary First Nations peoples' culture and practices to guide our reconciliation journey. First Nations peoples have utilized treaty making in all of their relationships with all Creation, whether those relationships were with plants, animals or other Nations. Therein lies the difference in the world views of First Nations and non-First Nations people and their concept of relationships. For First Nations peoples "we are of the land."

> Without the land, air and water, all forms of life on the Ninge'aki would not exist. This is our strength. We always say Gishe-manidoo put us here for a reason. We are the voice for the animals, the plants and the water. We are the ones gifted with Anishinaabemowin. At first there was the Gizhe-manidoo, then Ninge'aki and then the Anishinaabeg (people). That is why we were last—we were given a responsibility to speak for all the animals and plants.[26]

First Nations peoples viewed themselves as but one part of the world that relied on all of its parts to maintain a natural balance. The "western"[27] view of man as the ruler of the world and dominant over the natural world and all it has to offer is substantially different. Reconciliation requires us to change the way we think about ourselves and our world. It requires that we examine the relationship through the eyes of First Nations people, and for many, this is extremely difficult to do.

An Elder once told me, that Reconciliation for him means "the truth." To understand the true history, the true relationship means understanding the First Nations perspective, history and understanding of the relationship. The First Nations perspective not only comes from their world views and values, but from the words of the early treaty commissioners. For example, Alexander Morris, through his own words records some of the promises made to the First Nations peoples in the late 1870s.

> I see the Queen's councilors taking the Indian by the hand saying we are brothers, we will lift you up, we will teach you, if you will learn, the cunning of the

whiteman. All along that road I see Indians gathering, I see gardens growing and houses building; I see them receiving money from the Queens Commissioners to purchase clothing for their children; at the same time I see them enjoying their hunting and fishing as before, I see them retaining their old mode of living with the Queen's Gift in addition.[28]

The First Nations perspective understands this to be assistance in the transition to a new way of life. The phrase: "What I offer you is on top of what you already have" was expected to be in addition to what First Nations peoples already possessed which was freedom, mobility and access to their land and a way of life that had sustained them as a People for centuries.

A DIFFERENT LENS

Now that we have a glimpse of the perspective of First Nations peoples of the treaties, what is our understanding? We should understand at the very least that the treaties are not just about historical documents signed in 1871 (Treaty 1) for example: they are not just the written text of the treaties; they were not land surrenders or real estate transactions; they are not just about hunting and fishing rights. Quite simply, the treaties are about relationships. Relationships between First Nations peoples and the Crown also means relationships between the citizens of those parties: ongoing relationships that live and breathe and change over time but never go away. Relationships that need to involve a respect for, and mutual understanding of, our different cultures and histories. We do so because knowing the true history triggers our responsibility to act. Not out of obligation but out of our basic human decency and the desire to help our fellow human beings. We cannot unknow this information. The onus is now on us to do something with it.

Reconciliation requires us to become aware of the relationship, and that we must seek to understand that relationship. Only then can we make the substantive changes required to address some major assumptions in the way that we move forward in rectifying that relationship. The way in which we look at each other as non-First Nations and First Nations peoples or Indigenous and non-Indigenous peoples, we have to do so with a better understanding of who we are as a people. We all have to take up this challenge. We have been called upon to recognize and understand our past, which include the many policies to which Wahbung refers. There have been many events that have impacted the spirit and intent of treaties. Since the treaties were entered, numerous Canadian government policies were implemented. Some include the Pass System which limited the mobility of First Nations peoples, the

Indian Act which affected the traditional form of governance and citizenship, and the Sixties Scoop which resulted in thousands of First Nations children being apprehended from their families in the 1960s. Each policy individually had damaging effects on the relationship but when you examine the totality of these policies, you realize how the original spirit and intent of the treaties has been all but removed from the memory of Canadian society and its institutions.

However in 2019, we find ourselves at another crossroads in this treaty relationship and we are faced with the opportunity and a strong desire to make the required changes. These changes must be done collaboratively and in a manner that reflects the intentions of the original relationships. Our efforts cannot be impeded by the existing Canadian legal and political constraints. We must be willing to look beyond the walls of the current frameworks and create a society that represents the coexistence envisaged at the time of treaty making.

These efforts may seem overwhelming given that we cannot change what we cannot control. So, let us look at what it is that is within our control, as institutions, governments and as individuals. We can change the manner and content in which we learn about our history and each other; we can change our structures to include Indigenous perspectives; we can make space for First Nations institutions; and we can change the way in which we look at each other. As Aaron Mills states:

> How I come to understand a meaning of treaty as lived out as ordinary people in our day to day relationships attending as thoughtfully and carefully as we can to each other needs are and sharing those gifts that we've been given to carry with them to help each other. It's something we do at our kitchen tables. It's something we do out in the community and it can work today as well as it did in 1764.[29]

As the Elders continue to say, if it is not uncomfortable or inconvenient, then it is not really change. We have to be prepared for those inconveniences to get to the place where it is comfortable for all.

Miigwech (Thank you)!

NOTES

1. Manitoba Indian Brotherhood, *Wahbung Our Tomorrows, Special 40th Anniversary Edition. Prev. ed.* (Winnipeg, Manitoba: Manitoba Indigenous Cultural Education Centre, 2011), 20.

2. Government of Canada, *Indian Policy: Statement of the Government of Canada on Indian Policy, 1969* (Ottawa: Queen's Printer, 1969).

3. Many terms have been used to describe First Nations people, and First Nations peoples have been included in terminology that includes the Metis and Inuit. For instance, "Indigenous peoples" is currently used to include First Nations, Metis, and Inuit. However, legally, the term "Aboriginal peoples" has been used to describe First Nations, Metis, and Inuit. The term Aboriginal peoples is used in the Canadian Constitution.

4. The phrase "Treaty and Aboriginal rights" is a phrase included in the Canadian Constitution.

5. The term European is one that reflects the population at the time when the treaties were entered and while the current non-First Nations population consists also of non-European settlers, most of the Canadian systems, including its education, legal and political systems were built around European ideals and values.

6. The Rule of Law, established in England as a written document in the 1215 Magna Carta (Bill of Rights), holds that everyone, including the King, is subject to the law, and so established the high regard of the Western worldview for the written word.

7. Office of the Treaty Commissioner, *Statement of Treaty Issues: Treaties as a Bridge to the Future* (October 1998), 12.

8. Jean Friesen, "Magnificent Gifts: The Treaties of Canada with the Indians of the Northwest 1869–1876," Chapter 8 in Douglas Sprague, *Post Confederation Treaties of Canada* (Canada, Prentice-Hall, 1990), 207.

9. D'Arcy Linklater, Harry Bone and the Treaty and Dakota Elders of Manitoba with contributions by the AMC Council of Elders, *Ka'esi Wahkotumahk Aski—Our Relations with the Land: Treaty Elders' Teachings Volume 2* (Winnipeg: Treaty Relations Commission of Manitoba and Assembly of Manitoba Chiefs, 2014), 39.

10. Office of the Treaty Commissioner, *Treaty Elders of Saskatchewan* (2002), 39.

11. Aimee Craft, *Breathing Life into the Stone Fort Treaty: An Anishinabe Understanding of Treaty One,* (Saskatoon, Saskatchewan: Purich Publishing Limited, 2013), 20.

12. Craft, *Breathing Life into the Stone Fort Treaty*, 28.

13. Canada, Royal Commission on Aboriginal Peoples, *Report of the Royal Commission on Aboriginal Peoples*, vol. 1, *Looking Forward Looking Back* (Ottawa: Canada Communication Group, 1996), 116.

14. Doris Pratt, Harry Bone, and the Treaty and Dakota Elders of Manitoba, with contributions by the Assembly of Manitoba Chiefs Council of Elders and Darren H. Courchene, *Untuwe Pi Kin He-Who We Are: Treaty Elders Teachings*, vol. 1 (Winnipeg: Treaty Relations Commission of Manitoba and Assembly of Manitoba Chiefs, 2011), 114.

15. *The Royal Proclamation* was signed before the founding of Canada or the United States. First Nations peoples are only in Canada according to the terms of the *Indian Act.*

16. Treaty Relations Commission of Manitoba website: Treaty Relations Commission of Manitoba, *Episode 15* (2018), accessed December 6, 2019, https://www.youtube.com/watch?v=3PPlxmA0xGU&list=UUygGVnfn4nSuSsONMDVr5-Q&index=2&t=0s.

17. Wampum belts are belts made of the wampum bead that was used for many important events such as ceremony, diplomacy as well agreements. The wampum belt was a means of recording the agreements including treaties and other covenants.
18. Craft, *Breathing Life into the Stone Fort Treaty*, 20.
19. Treaty Relations Commission of Manitoba website: *Episode 49* (2018).
20. Canada, Royal Commission on Aboriginal Peoples, 158.
21. Alexander Morris, *The Treaties of Canada with the Indians of Manitoba and the North-West Territories* (Saskatoon: Fifth House, 1991), 313–314.
22. Morris *The Treaties of Canada*, 59.
23. Pratt et al., *Untuwe Pi Kin He-Who We Are*, 114.
24. Craft, *Breathing Life into the Stone Fort Treaty*, 61.
25. Harold Johnson, *Two Families: Treaties and Government* (Saskatoon: Purich, 2007), 21.
26. Pratt et al, *Untuwe Pi Kin He-Who We Are*, 123.
27. Western is used to incorporate European, Christian world views.
28. Morris, *The Treaties of Canada*, 59.
29. Treaty Relations Commission of Manitoba website: Episode 15.

BIBLIOGRAPHY

Canada Royal Commission on Aboriginal Peoples. *Report of the Royal Commission on Aboriginal Peoples, Looking Forward Looking Back* (Ottawa: Canada Communication Group, vol. 1, 1996), 116, 158.

Cardinal, Harold and Walter Hildebrandt. *Treaty Elders of Saskatchewan* (University of Calgary Press, 2002).

Craft, Aimee. *Breathing Life into the Stone Fort Treaty: An Anishinabe Understanding of Treaty One* (Saskatoon, Saskatchewan: Purich Publishing Limited, 2013).

Friesen, Jean. "Magnificent Gifts: The Treaties of Canada with the Indians of the Northwest 1869–1876." In Douglas Sprague. *Post Confederation Treaties of Canada* (Toronto, ON: Prentice-Hall, 1990).

Johnson, Harold. *Two Families: Treaties and Government* (Saskatoon, SK: Purich, 2007).

Linklater, D'Arcy, Harry Bone and the Treaty and Dakota Elders of Manitoba with contributions by the AMC Council of Elders. *Ka'esi Wahkotumahk Aski—Our Relations with the Land: Treaty Elders' Teachings Volume 2* (Winnipeg, MB: Treaty Relations Commission of Manitoba and Assembly of Manitoba Chiefs, 2014).

Manitoba Indigenous Cultural Education Centre. *Wahbung: Our Tomorrows* (Winnipeg, Manitoba: Indigenous Cultural Education Centre, 2011).

Morris, Alexander. *The Treaties of Canada with the Indians of Manitoba and the North-West Territories* (Saskatoon, SK: Fifth House, 1991).

Office of the Treaty Commissioner. *Statement of Treaty Issues: Treaties as a Bridge to the Future*, 1998. Accessed October 19, 2019, http://www.jamessmithcreenation.com/downloads/TREATIES%20AS%20A%20BRIDGE.pdf

Pratt, Doris, Harry Bone, and the Treaty and Dakota Elders of Manitoba, with contributions by the Assembly of Manitoba Chiefs Council of Elders and Darren H. Courchene, *Untuwe Pi Kin He-Who We Are. Treaty Elders Teachings*, vol. 1 (Winnipeg: Treaty Relations Commission of Manitoba and Assembly of Manitoba Chiefs, 2011).

Treaty Relations Commission of Manitoba website. Treaty Relations Commission of Manitoba. *Episode 15*, 2018. Accessed December 6, 2019, https://www.youtube.com/watch?v=3PPlxmA0xGU&list=UUygGVnfn4nSuSsONMDVr5-Q&index=2&t=0s

Chapter 8

Reconciliation and Satellite Urban Reserves in Canada

Joseph Garcea[1]

Canadians, like their counterparts in many countries in the world, are living in an era in which there have been and continue to be many reconciliation projects designed to deal with historic wrongs and problems in the relationships between groups and nations, while at the same time other historic wrongs are perpetuated and new ones are created. In the Canadian context there have been several reconciliation projects. One of these projects, and arguably one of the most significant, has been the multifaceted reconciliation project between the First Nations and the Canadian state. An important facet of this reconciliation project has been the creation and operation of satellite urban reserves in conjunction with the *Treaty Land Entitlement* (TLE) and the *Specific Claims* negotiations and compensation processes during the past three decades.[2]

This chapter has two central objectives. The first objective is to provide an overview and analysis of two major alternative perspectives on the relationship between reconciliation and satellite urban reserves, namely the conventional perspective and the critical perspective. The central premise of the conventional perspective is that urban reserves are at once products and facilitators of reconciliation. Those who espouse this perspective suggest that this perspective posits that contemporary economic and social development forces and agendas facilitate productive symbiotic relationships between First Nations governments and municipal governments as well as members of their respective communities, and that such relationships contribute to economic and social development within and beyond the urban communities. By contrast, the central premise of the critical perspective is that satellite urban reserves are neither products nor facilitators of reconciliation. Instead, they are products and facilitators of exploitative parasitic relationships created by contemporary neocolonialism and neoliberalism forces and agendas involving capitalist governments and corporate elites. Moreover, the critical perspective posits that for First Nations the costs outweigh the benefits, and that they bear a disproportionate amount of costs.

The second objective is to provide some observations on the potential means and prospects for addressing what those who espouse the critical perspective deem to be the reconciliation deficit in the creation and operation of satellite urban reserves.

Pursuant to those two objectives, this chapter comprises four major sections. Section 1 provides an overview of key characteristics of satellite urban reserves, the reserve creation processes, and the politics related to the creation of such reserves. Section 2 provides a conceptualization of reconciliation. Section 3 provides an overview of the conventional and critical perspectives on satellite urban reserves. Section 4 provides some observations on potential means and prospects for addressing what those who espouse the critical perspective view as the reconciliation deficit in satellite urban reserves.

URBAN RESERVES

Within the Canadian context, First Nations urban reserves are lands in urban areas that have been officially designated as reserves by the federal government. There are two major types of urban Indian reserves in Canada. The first major type consists of what can be termed original home urban reserves, which historically existed either adjacent to at least one urban municipality or in urbanized region. The second major type, which is the focus of this chapter, consists of what have been termed satellite urban reserves.[3] These are parcels of land located adjacent to an urban municipality that have been added to the land base of existing home reserves officially designated as reserves and that have boundaries which are contiguous with, either in whole or in part, with at least one urban municipality.

Generally, satellite urban reserves have been established to locate commercial, governmental, and community service agencies. To date they have not been used for residential purposes, although bands have consistently insisted on their right to build various types of residential subdivisions or complexes (e.g., conventional single and multiple dwelling housing stock and special care homes) either just for First Nations persons or possibly a mix of First Nations and non-First Nations persons. Residential satellite urban reserves have not been created for a variety of reasons, including opposition by some municipal governments and their communities, and the lack of support by federal officials.[4]

As is the case with the original home reserves both in urban and rural areas, under the *Indian Act* satellite urban reserves are communally owned lands that belong to an entire band, rather than either to one or several band members. They are subject to essentially the same regulations regarding, among other things, land ownership, land use, and financial management as the original home reserves, plus any additional regulations related to land development and use, property maintenance, water and sewer services, and fire and police services, as specified in First Nations-municipal agreements that deal with such matters.

Approximately 130 satellite urban reserves have been created since 1969 in urban communities of various sizes, ranging from villages to large metropolitan centers.[5] Most of those have been created due to the funds made available for First Nations to purchase both urban and rural lands pursuant to the Specific Claims Agreements in various provinces and the comprehensive Treaty Land Entitlement Framework Agreements (TLEFA) signed by First Nations, federal, and provincial governments in the provinces of Saskatchewan and Manitoba.[6]

Creation of Satellite Urban Reserves

Satellite urban reserves have been created by the acquisition of either Crown lands or privately owned lands by First Nations governments for their communities. In several provinces, the acquisition of such lands in urban and rural areas has increased substantially because of the two major categories of negotiation undertaken during approximately the past three decades in honoring the long-standing land transfer commitments promised to First Nations. The first category entailed the negotiations and agreements within the scope of Specific Claims, and the second entailed negotiations involving multiple First Nations within the scope of the TLEFA primarily in the provinces of Saskatchewan and Manitoba.[7]

The policies and processes for creating satellite reserves are outlined in the *Additions to Reserve Policy* (ARP), which applies to lands acquired by bands (whether through land claims agreements or any other means) and earmarked for conversion to reserve status.[8] The general reserve creation process outlined in the ARP consists of six stages.

- The first stage is for the First Nations' council to ratify and submit a Band Council Resolution to the federal department responsible for First Nations relations.
- The second stage is for the federal department and First Nations to discuss all requirements for moving the proposal forward, and determine their respective roles and responsibilities for various matters, including

communication and consultation with municipal governments, and conducting the requisite environmental audits and land surveys.
- The third stage is for the regional Additions to Reserve (ATR) committee to analyze the proposal to ensure all requirements of the ARP were met.
- The fourth stage is for the ATR committee to forward its report to the Regional Director General (RDG) recommending that the proposal for approval in principle (AIP) be either approved or rejected.
- The fifth stage is for the RDG or DM to either agree or refuse recommending the AIP to the minister. An AIP can be granted with or without conditions. If conditions are attached, they must be dealt with fully before the AIP is referred to the Privy Council Office for the governor in Council to consider whether to approve or reject it.
- The sixth stage is for the governor in Council to approve or reject the AIP.

Among the conditions that may be imposed are that after a First Nations acquires a parcel of land and has indicated its intention to have it converted to an urban reserve, it must undertake negotiations for an agreement with any municipality or school board on a number of key issues including: whether compensation will be paid for the loss of municipal and school taxes once the land is placed beyond those taxation domains; the type and financing of municipal services to be delivered to the new reserve; bylaw compatibility between the municipality and the reserve, particularly where reserve development has the potential to affect neighboring municipal lands and residents; and a joint consultative process, especially a dispute-resolution mechanism, for addressing matters of mutual concern. Both the ARP and the TLEFA stipulate that such agreements must be negotiated in good faith and that where a municipality or school board fails to do so in response to the reasonable proposals of a First Nations, the federal government may proceed to create the reserve in question, notwithstanding the objections of the municipality or school board. This is precisely what happened when some municipalities refused to negotiate such agreements.[9] Finally, it should be noted that the creation of reserves, including satellite urban reserves, requires provincial governments to enact statutes that embody policies needed to authorize themselves as well as their respective municipalities and school boards to sign agreements with First Nations on an array of matters required for the creation and operation of reserves.[10]

Political Dynamics Surrounding the Creation of Satellite Urban Reserves

Urban reserves are neither created nor operated either in a political vacuum or in a political context that only involves the governmental actors identified above; it also involves various interest groups and members of the local and regional communities in which they are created and operated. Although members of the public were not directly involved in any negotiations, and were not provided with an opportunity to participate in any aspect of the negotiations through plebiscites or referenda, in some communities they exerted significant influence on the negotiating positions of their respective municipal governments. Such influence was most visible and significant when many municipal government officials and ratepayers were strongly opposed to the creation of urban reserves.

Generally, the political dynamics that involved municipal, First Nations, and federal government officials have taken two forms.[11] Such negotiations have been either collaborative and agonistic, or conflictual and antagonistic. Patterns of collaboration and conflict were evident in negotiations involving all the governments and authorities, albeit to varying extents. The former type of dynamics generally prevailed most often in the negotiations between representatives of First Nations and the federal government. The only notable tensions between them tended to be regarding three key matters: first, the price that First Nations would have to pay for any federally owned urban lands; secondly, decisions on whether properties acquired by First Nations should be converted to reserve status; and thirdly, what some First Nations felt were inexplicable and unacceptable delays in receiving final federal cabinet approval for the creation of reserves. Such tensions were generally muted and did not receive much public or media attention.

By contrast, the dynamics between First Nations and municipal governments have been mixed. Whereas most such dynamics have been relatively collaborative and agonistic, a few have been conflictual and antagonistic. Not surprisingly, as is commonly the case in the political world, the conflictual and antagonistic dynamics received the most public and media attention. Generally, such conflicts did not occur at the negotiating table, they occurred before negotiations even started because municipal governments and influential ratepayers, particularly some in the for-profit sector, were opposed in principle to the creation of such reserves. Invariably the opposition was based on considerations regarding incompatibility of a reserve and municipality coexisting in an urban area. More specifically, it was based on concerns regarding the competitive advantage that First Nations businesses on urban reserves would have vis-à-vis businesses in the municipality; potential problems that would emerge if First Nations would not honor agreements regarding bylaw compatibility and enforcement, and payment of fees for municipal services, rather than paying municipal taxes in lieu of municipal taxes.[12]

CONCEPTUALIZATION AND BASIC TENETS OF RECONCILIATION

The principal objective in this section is to provide a conceptualization of reconciliation and an overview of the tenets of reconciliation between First Nations and non-First Nations governments and people in Canada during the past several decades while satellite urban reserves were being created.[13] For purposes of this chapter, reconciliation is conceptualized both as a public philosophy or, if you will, an instrumental philosophical orientation, and an actual or aspirational political or policy project. Moreover, a public philosophy is conceptualized as an instrumental philosophical orientation consisting of a cluster of norms, values, ethics, and beliefs regarding, among other things, governance, public policy, and public management.[14] A public philosophy is a lens, framework, or narrative that performs a mapping, justificatory, or critiquing function. More specifically, it is a philosophical/normative lens, framework, or narrative used to map, justify, or critique actual or potential policy paths and choices.

It differs from any of the conventional and prevailing ideologies per se in two ways. First, it may contain a mix of selected norms, values, ethics, and beliefs embodied within various ideologies, and it does not necessarily subscribe to the telos of any particular ideology. Secondly, and more importantly, unlike ideologies, which tend to have very broad foci and applications, which generally includes most if not all political and policy matters, public philosophies tend to be more narrowly focused and applied to some particular or distinct facet(s) of public affairs (i.e., governance, public policy, and public management). In other words, a public philosophy may be thought of as a project-based hybridized philosophical or, if you will, ideological orientation that serves the purpose of defining, designing, implementing, and justifying an actual or aspirational historic political, governance or policy project. Finally, a public philosophy is not merely an abstraction or ungrounded construct or vision that exists without history or context; it is a historically based and grounded philosophical orientation focused on a particular historic project. This is what one leading public policy theorist was alluding to in the cogent assertion that "a public philosophy is not something 'thought up' by anybody, it is squeezed out as the end by-product of real strains in society and the unwinding logic of political ideas."[15]

The fundamental aspect of reconciliation both as a public philosophy and as a project is that ideally it entails some notions and actions of (re)conciliation between two or more stakeholders (e.g., groups, nations, governments, etc.). Such (re)conciliation may take different forms depending on precisely what must be (re)conciliated and the goal(s) of (re)conciliation. In the political sphere, the focus of reconciliation in recent decades has been on at least three major types of initiatives, which are often interrelated, namely:

- To reconcile strained or broken relationships resulting from historic wrongs.
- To reconcile strained or broken relationships resulting from fundamental differences in worldviews or values.
- To reconcile strained or broken relations resulting from different or competing goals and objectives.

Faced with strained or broken relationships, the goal of reconciliation projects is generally to improve such relationships by bringing the key stakeholders or their representatives together for two principal purposes. First, to discuss their respective positions as well as their respective goals and objectives regarding their relationship. Secondly, to agree on processes for moving forward in harmonizing or at least aligning their respective positions and in achieving both their respective and their shared goals and objectives. Invariably, the resulting processes may entail negotiations, mediation, mediation, arbitration, accommodation, and even appeasement, Moreover, during the reconciliation processes, generally there is likely to be a much more reliance on agonistic rather than antagonistic modes of communication and relations at least among the leaders involved in negotiators of the parties seeking reconciliation, although historically that has not always been the case. A more common pattern is a mix of agonistic and antagonistic negotiations and other forms of interaction.

What constitutes reconciliation and what are the key tenets of the reconciliation public philosophy regarding relations between First Nations and the Canadian state are highly contested issues? For purposes of this chapter, there is heavy reliance on the basic tenets of reconciliation in Canada involving First Nations and the Canadian state that are cogently articulated by the Truth and Reconciliation Commission of Canada (TRC).[16] Although it was established to deal primarily with the colonial legacy of residential schools, its focus on reconciliation had important implications beyond that particular issue to the entire historic relationship between Indigenous and non-Indigenous governments and people. In articulating the tenets and telos of a public philosophy of reconciliation, the TRC indicated that it was not simply a matter of the reestablishment of a conciliatory Canadian state, because many people do not believe that such a state ever existed in facilitating the relationship between Aboriginal and non-Aboriginal people. With that in mind the TRC asserted that for its purpose's reconciliation entailed "coming to terms with events of the past in a manner that overcomes conflict and establishes a respectful and healthy relationship among people going forward."[17] It added that for that to happen, there has to be awareness of the past, acknowledgement of the harm that has been inflicted, atonement for the causes, and action to change behavior.[18]

> Reconciliation must support Aboriginal peoples as they heal from the destructive legacies of colonization that have wreaked such havoc in their lives. But it must do even more. Reconciliation must inspire Aboriginal and non-Aboriginal peoples to transform Canadian society so that our children and grandchildren can live together in dignity, peace, and prosperity on these lands we now share.[19]

This conceptualization of reconciliation is cogent and important; indeed, as one analyst pointed out, it may well be the TRC's most important contribution to the reconciliation project.[20] In making a case for launching a substantial reconciliation project as soon as possible, the TRC noted that an initial effort toward that end had been made by RCAP approximately a decade earlier, but the effort had not produced the desired results.

> In 1996, the Report of the Royal Commission on Aboriginal Peoples urged Canadians to begin a national process of reconciliation that would have set the country on a bold new path, fundamentally changing the very foundations of Canada's relationship with Aboriginal peoples. Much of what the Royal Commission had to say has been ignored by government; most of its recommendations were never implemented. But the report and its findings opened people's eyes and changed the conversation about the reality for Aboriginal people in this country.[21]

The TRC added that the potential for a positive and productive response to its report constituted a second opportunity to engage in substantive and substantial reconciliation. In imploring governments and their communities to support and sustain the reconciliation project, the TRC stated that: "We live in a twenty-first-century global world. At stake is Canada's place as a prosperous, just, and inclusive democracy within that global world."[22] The TRC served a very important function toward that end, because as noted by one analyst, and echoed by others: "The TRC appears at this point to have attracted attention and support for reconciliation among both interested elite groups and the general public."[23]

In praising the value and work of the RCAP, the TRC could have also credited it for focusing attention on the need and potential for reconciliation in urban areas. The reason for this is that the RCAP understood the importance of focusing on various aspects of the urban experience of First Nations and Metis peoples in recent decades and the likelihood that it would become the experience for a growing number of such people in the future. With that in mind, the RCAP focused on the following major issues in urban areas: the demographics of Aboriginal urbanization, cultural identity, racism, and various governance issues. RCAP devoted attention to all those issues, but in the words of one analyst "some of the commission's most important work centered on urban governance."[24] This is evident in the fact that it established the Urban Governance Working Group (UGWG) to explore various governance issues and options. For its part, the UGWG recognized that the future of Aboriginal and non-Aboriginal people in urban centers was inextricably interrelated, and that to achieve their respective goals they had to agree to a positive, peaceful and productive coexistence. This included coordinating, cooperating and possibly even comanaging many of their joint and their respective undertakings within the shared urban space. In providing some suggestions for moving forward in that way, the UGWG profiled three approaches and three models for improving governance for Aboriginal people in urban areas. The three approaches included: self-government, comanagement, and reform of municipal governments and other local public authorities to make them more representative of Aboriginal people. The three models included: the host-nation model, the extraterritorial model, and the urban reserves model.[25]

ALTERNATIVE PERSPECTIVES ON SATELLITE URBAN RESERVES AND RECONCILIATION

Whereas the previous section has provided an overview of reconciliation as a public philosophy and public policy project, the principal objective in this section is to provide an overview of the conventional and critical perspectives on the linkage between satellite urban reserves and reconciliation. More specifically, the objective is to provide an overview of their respective premises on whether satellite urban reserves are either products and facilitators of reconciliation or products and facilitators of neocolonialism and neoliberalism in which First Nations governments and members of their communities continue to be exploited as they have been heretofore.

Before discussing those alternative perspectives, a caveat is in order. In providing the overview of the alternative perspectives on the relationship between satellite urban reserves and reconciliation, it is important to avoid a conflation of that relationship with the closely related, but distinct, issue of the actual value of such reserves not only for First Nations governments and members of their communities but also for municipal governments and members of the communities in which such reserves are created. The reason it is important to avoid such conflation is that although an initiative may result either in gains or in losses for two or more stakeholders it is not in itself a necessary and sufficient condition to affirm or negate the existence of a reconciliatory relationship between them. The same can be said regarding the negotiating stances and styles of the stakeholders. After all, a reconciliatory relationship depends not just on outputs or outcomes, but also on the spirit or intent that underpins it. More specifically, it depends on a willingness to acknowledge and take responsibility for past policies, postures, and practices that had significant adverse effects on various stakeholders, and to adopt policies, postures, and practices that have significant positive effects on various stakeholders involved in the relationship. This caveat applies equally to the conventional and critical perspectives.

Conventional Perspective

The conventional perspective regarding satellite urban reserves postulates that not only are they products of reconciliation, but that they can also contribute to reconciliation if they are created and operated effectively and responsibly for the mutual benefit of First Nations and municipal governments and their respective communities. This postulation is often implicit rather than explicit in statements or narratives by First Nations, federal, and municipal government officials who have been proponents of the creation of urban reserves, as well as in the extant academic literature, and media coverage on the creation and operation of such reserves.[26]

In cases where this postulation is articulated implicitly, it tends to be embodied in statements that focus primarily on the compensatory or accommodative rather than the reconciliatory aspects of the creation of satellite urban reserves. However, the key unstated assumption in such statements is that compensation and accommodation are important elements of reconciliation.

Generally, this linkage between the compensatory, accommodative, and reconciliatory aspects of the creation of urban reserves occurs within the broader context of the land claims compensation process of the past three decades, which was initiated at the request, indeed insistence, of several First Nations governments. The federal government responded positively to that request based on a combination of compensatory, accommodative, and reconciliatory imperatives vis-à-vis First Nations. The conventional perspective tends to view the land claims compensation process as what might be termed first order compensation, accommodation, and reconciliation, and the creation of satellite urban reserves as second order compensation, accommodation, and reconciliation. The reason for this ordering is that most satellite urban reserves in recent decades were created on urban lands that First Nations acquired either by using money they received as financial compensation through the land claims process for purchasing privately owned land or by requesting they receive some federal Crown land in urban areas as part of such compensation.

The postulation that satellite urban reserves are products of reconciliation is rooted in a belief that the efforts to recognize and honor outstanding land claims through the TLE and the Specific Claims processes were partly a component of the emergent contemporary reconciliation project. Without denying that the land claims process was partly driven by the federal government's interests and imperatives to avoid judicial processes and decisions that could lead to even greater compensation costs for the federal and possibly even for some provincial governments, proponents of the conventional perspective postulate that it has entailed some degree of reconciliation. More specifically, they suggest that whatever degree of reconciliation the land claims settlement process has entailed was rooted in acknowledgments by successive federal governments during recent decades of the historic injustices that were perpetrated by their predecessors on First Nations either by not honoring treaty provisions related to quantum of reserve land or by not respecting inherent rights on nonceded First Nations lands that did not fall within the scope of any treaty. This is not to suggest that successive federal governments have supported the creation of satellite urban reserves either consistently or uniformly. After all, they have facilitated or supported the creation of some satellite urban reserves more than others.

This premise of the link between the creation and operation of satellite urban reserves and the compensatory, accommodative, and reconciliatory dimensions of the TLE and Specific Claims processes on one hand, and economic and community development on the other, is evident in many pronouncements made by federal political and administrative officials. A notable example of this is found in the following statement made by the minister responsible for Indigenous and Northern Affairs in 2016 when the new ARP was approved: "This new Policy Directive will better meet the needs of all our Indigenous and non-Indigenous partners. The goal is to make the Additions to Reserve process more efficient and transparent, helping to advance reconciliation with First Nations, improve treaty relationships, and create new economic opportunities for First Nations communities."[27] A more recent articulation of the federal government's perspective on the relationship between reconciliation and various types of negotiations with First Nations, including negotiations related to resolving outstanding land claims and the creation of reserves is found on the website of the Crown-Indigenous Relations and Northern Affairs Canada (CIRNAC) in a short section titled "Different Paths Toward Reconciliation," which notes that the government has undertaken many different types of negotiations with Indigenous governments in finding solutions to many different types of claims and disputes for advancing reconciliation. In this regard, the website states that:

> The Government of Canada is deeply committed to advancing reconciliation and renewing the relationship with Indigenous peoples based on recognition of rights, respect, co-operation and partnership . . . [and] is working in a spirit of

collaboration and renewal with Indigenous groups and provincial and territorial partners to advance our shared journey toward reconciliation along many different paths. This ongoing joint work includes

- exploring new ways to work together at Recognition of Indigenous Rights and Self-Determination Discussion tables,
- negotiating modern treaties and self-government, and
- resolving specific claims.[28]

It goes on to provide the following reasons why it has opted to undertake negotiations in dealing with its relations with Indigenous peoples and their governments.

Negotiations are taking place across Canada to help right past wrongs, advance reconciliation and shape a new relationship with Indigenous peoples. The Government of Canada believes that negotiations and respectful dialogue are the best ways to resolve outstanding issues. Negotiations lead to shared solutions that work for and benefit everyone. Negotiated agreements strengthen relationships and resolve longstanding disputes in a balanced way that respects the rights of Indigenous people and all Canadians. These co-developed agreements can also be a key path to economic growth, creating new investment opportunities for the benefit of communities today as well as future generations.[29]

Although satellite urban reserves, and the creation of other types of reserves, are not mentioned explicitly in the foregoing passages, implicitly they are because invariably they are codeveloped through various negotiation processes and codeveloped agreements mentioned in those passages that generally involve First Nations, provincial, and municipal governments and in some instances also public authorities such as school boards.

Another premise of the conventional perspective is that generally the creation of satellite urban reserves has been and can continue to be beneficial, rather than detrimental both for First Nations and municipal governments, their respective communities, including those involved in for-profit and not-for-profit agencies. For First Nations governments and members of their communities, they have been beneficial for them not only in the urban areas in which such reserves are located, but also for their members in the longstanding reserves in which some of their members continue to reside. For municipal governments and their respective communities, generally they have been beneficial in fostering economic and community development purposes and for advancing private interests. However, the value of satellite urban reserves is by no means the same for all First Nations and municipal governments and their respective communities. This point was supported by a study of urban reserves in Saskatchewan which concluded that the results on the value of TLE compensation and the creation of urban reserves are mixed. Whereas some urban reserves have not yielded substantial financial or social benefits, a subset of them on which there has been intensive economic development have yielded substantial benefits. In their words, "the improvement has been quite dramatic for a subset of eight First Nations that have used their urban reserves for intensive economic development, including casinos and other recreational facilities, restaurants, shopping centers, and gas stations. Urban reserves appear to be a promising path for improvements in the standard of living for those First Nations that approach them with an entrepreneurial spirit."[30]

The view that satellite urban reserves have been and continue to be useful instruments or mechanism of economic and community development for First Nations and governments, for-profit and nonprofit agencies, and their communities, but also for their municipal counterparts has been articulated by First Nations, federal, provincial, and municipal government officials by proponents of such reserves and the majority of analysts of the creation and operation of such reserves. During the past decade, it has been articulated repeatedly and cogently in a series of statements on the websites of the federal government officials responsible for First Nations issues over time. For example, a 2008 document indicated that urban reserves were "springboards into the mainstream economy" in that they provided "economic opportunities that are generally unavailable in more remote areas."[31] That particular document added that the urban reserves " . . . give First Nations businesses the chance to establish themselves and provide employment and training opportunities."[32] Similarly, a 2014 document stated that satellite urban reserves contribute to the "ability of the First Nations to increase their level of own-source revenues through land development activities, increased employment opportunities for both First Nations and other citizens, and capacity development."[33] A similar assessment of such reserves has been articulated more recently in the following statement on the CIRNAC website:

> Many First Nations in Canada are located in rural areas, far from the cities and towns where most wealth and jobs are created. This geographic remoteness can sometimes pose challenges for First Nations trying to increase their economic self-sufficiency. As a result, urban reserves are one of the most successful ways to address the problem of geographic remoteness of First Nations. Urban reserves offer residents economic opportunities that are generally unavailable in more remote areas. They give First Nations businesses the chance to establish themselves and provide employment and training opportunities. At the same time urban reserves can create jobs for Indigenous and non-Indigenous people and contribute to the revitalization of the host municipality. They reduce operating costs and provide better access to capital markets and transportation routes, enabling First Nations to diversify their economic base.[34]

This premise has been echoed by most, if not all, First Nations and non-First Nations proponents of satellite urban reserves, academic analysts, and an array of media commentators.[35] This is particularly true with reference to satellite urban reserves that have a concentration of commercial and institutional activity that is deemed to render tangible economic and community development benefits either directly or indirectly not only for the First Nations both in the urban areas and their home reserves in the rural and remote areas, but also for the municipal community with which they have contiguous boundaries. This view regarding the mutual benefit of urban reserves for First Nations and non-First Nations stakeholders was articulated recently by an academic analyst based on his observations of the dynamics surrounding the proposed creation of an urban reserve in Winnipeg. In response to concerns and criticisms that were being raised regarding the creation of an urban satellite reserve in Winnipeg, one analyst indicated that "urban reserves are tests of reconciliation,"[36] which are mutually beneficial for First Nations, municipal governments, and their respective communities. For that reason, he implored key stakeholders and the public to enter into constructive negotiations that result in equitable agreements, because negotiations were much more productive than litigation in dealing with challenges in the creation of satellite urban reserves. In his words:

> Everyone must resist the temptation to run to the courts when negotiations become difficult. Economic benefits will slow to a trickle as soon as litigation replaces negotiation. It would be easy for debates on land use to degenerate into a rights contest in which First Nations pit their rights against the NIMBY (not in my backyard) reaction of existing landowners. But the existing landowners and non-Indigenous residents of Winnipeg need to accept urban reserves as a tangible and legitimate expression of reconciliation. First Nations leaders should also view the urban reserve as an important foothold in the urban economy of the future and continue to work with other Winnipeg landowners who have valid interests in how that development proceeds.[37]

It is fair to say that neither the federal government nor others who subscribe to the conventional perspective discuss whether the benefit is equal or unequal between First Nations and municipal governments, and between members of their respective communities. Furthermore, no detailed analysis has been undertaken of the full spectrum of value of all such reserves. The only systematic attempt at quantifying the economic benefits was undertaken by Flanagan and Harding of some satellite urban reserves in Saskatchewan. Their major conclusion was that some satellite urban reserves are more valuable than others for First Nations. More specifically, they concluded that large satellite urban reserves with a high concentration of substantial commercial activity are likely to be more valuable than those which have a paucity of such activity.

In summary, the major postulation of the conventional perspective is that under certain conditions there is a bidirectional causal arrow between reconciliation and the creation and operation of satellite urban reserves and the settlement of land claims related to those satellite urban reserves insofar as they are both products and facilitators of reconciliation. More specifically, the conventional perspective suggests that if they are created and operated effectively and responsibly, satellite urban reserves are reconciliatory initiatives that can result in positive and harmonious symbiotic coexistence and relations between First Nations governments and municipal governments as well as various for-profit and not-for-profit organizations operating within their respective land bases. The conventional perspective suggests that this can even occur if there are any conflicts and residual fears in conjunction with the creation of such reserves because, as noted on a federal government webpage, generally, "any fears subside once the municipality begins to realize the economic benefits."[38]

CRITICAL PERSPECTIVE

The critical perspective in the academic literature regarding the relationship between satellite urban reserves and reconciliation is based on two postulations, which are articulated either explicitly or implicitly. The first postulation is that satellite urban reserves are neither products nor facilitators of the reconciliation project. The second postulation is that regardless of how they are created or operated, satellite urban reserves are not unquestionably reconciliatory initiatives that result in positive symbiotic coexistence and relationships between First Nations governments and municipal governments as well as various for-profit and not-for-profit organizations operating within their respective land base. The third postulation is that insofar as benefits accrue to First Nations from urban reserves, they not necessarily accrue equitably to all members of the First Nations. They may be more beneficial for those directly involved in the management and use of such reserves for their own commercial purposes than for the general membership.

Some of the foundations of a critical perspective on the issue of whether the creation of satellite urban reserves can be considered products and manifestations of reconciliation were laid two decades ago by Michael Gertler.[39] In that article, he raises some important points regarding at least two aspects of the creation of satellite urban reserves. The first aspect is the historic relevance of satellite urban reserves for relations not only between First Nations and the Canadian state's various orders of government, but also for various quasi-governmental and nongovernmental organizations therein. His central contention in this respect is that the creation of urban reserves constitutes a continuation of, rather than a break from, the colonial underpinnings of legacies of such relationships:[40]

> The emergence and development of urban reserves . . . should be recognized as a significant step that involves considerable institutional and organizational renovation. The creation of urban reserves redefines special, social, and political relations. . . . [U]rban reserves have important implications for groups and individuals, as well as for governmental and quasi-governmental organizations at all levels. Yet, urban reserves are not a surgical break with the past. Their development is firmly rooted in the history of relations between Aboriginal Peoples and the Canadian state, and rooted likewise in the conditions and struggles of contemporary life. They do not transcend issues of control, accountability, or equity, nor do they provide easy answers to questions about appropriate models of development, self-government, or community.

The second aspect is the question of who benefits from the creation of urban reserves. In doing so suggested attention should be devoted to considering whether the major benefits accrued to First Nations governments and communities versus the municipal government and communities in advancing their respective economic and social development goals. As well he suggested that attention should be devoted to ascertaining precisely who benefits the most within First Nations communities—is it the First Nations' membership living both in the city in which the reserve is created and the traditional home reserve, or the First Nations' political, administrative and business elites therein?[41]

The themes regarding the opportunities and constraints for First Nations created by satellite urban reserves raised by Gertler have been echoed and amplified more recently by Julie Tomiak in an insightful article which examined those as well as other aspects of such reserves in conjunction with the creation and operation of such reserves in Canada's Prairie Provinces in recent decades.[42] Her principal objective, as revealed in the subtitle of her article, is the relationship between new urban reserves, the neoliberalization of colonialism, and Indigenous self-determination; it is not reconciliation and urban reserves per se. Although she does not address the issue of reconciliation directly or explicitly, implicitly she seems to be saying that any discernable reconciliatory facet of urban reserves is relatively modest in scope. Her major contention regarding the relationship between the creation of urban reserves and colonialism, which echoes one of Gertler's key observations, is that at best the creation and operation of urban reserves constitutes a slight and gradual shift away from, rather than a complete break, with traditional colonialism. She adds that the precise nature of this shift has been heavily influenced more by contemporary neoliberalism than either the reconciliation public philosophy or the reconciliation project.

In substantiating the position that the creation of urban reserves constitutes a gradual shift away from colonialism toward a neocolonialism that is heavily influenced by neoliberalism, she examines their genesis and argues that the creation of such reserves resulted from negotiated land settlement agreements, which entailed the privatization of First Nations' land and the extinguishment of First Nations' historic land rights elsewhere in a province. She asserts that their creation is rooted in a neocolonialism driven by neoliberal capitalist imperatives and agendas, which include dispossessing Indigenous peoples of land through privatization. Furthermore, she suggests that the creation of urban reserves is not merely a matter of privatization of First Nations' lands which they held by inherent right or treaty right, but that it entails what another author described as "the transfer from one type of social system to another: in this case, exchanging colonial regulatory oversight for a more capitalist-oriented real estate market."[43] In making this point, she adds that "reserve creation in cities has not fundamentally disrupted state power and discourses that have constructed Indigeneity as incompatible with urbanism and modernity."[44] Moreover, they have entailed significant losses for First Nations in terms of dispossession of lands and sovereignty. In her words:

> Given that new urban reserves come into existence through treaty land entitlement and the specific land claims process . . . new urban reserves are the direct outcome of the retroactive legalization of dispossession and extinguishment of rights elsewhere, when First Nations, through band-owned development corporations, opt to use cash settlements to purchase land and request reserve status. Indigenous sovereignty is thus converted into private property and framed as "progress" by the settler state. Urban reserve creation speaks to the ongoing and intensifying colonial-capitalist agenda of accumulation by dispossession, in that subsistence and non-capitalist economies and Indigenous title and sovereignty are further undermined.[45]

She adds that an additional loss is that economic development imperatives trump community and social development imperatives. In her words:

> It is also important to note that the federal government continues to insist on the non-residential makeup of urban reserves. That is, in general only economic development proposals are successful, not those focused on creating homes for First Nations citizens and a place for communities in the city.[46]

Nevertheless, Tomiak noted that for First Nations the creation of satellite urban reserves is neither a complete victory nor an unmitigated gain. She notes that the gain is mitigated by the limits created by supplanting colonial regulatory regimes with capitalist regulatory regimes, which are not necessarily beneficial for First Nations governments and communities.

In providing an overall assessment of the merits of the creation of new urban reserves, Tomiak concludes that, notwithstanding the fact that they contribute to the ongoing intensification of the colonial-capitalist agenda of accumulation by dispossession, and entail constraints or limitations in fostering self-determination, they do contribute to a modicum of decolonization and what she terms "place-making" by First Nations in urban areas. In her words:

> Urban reserves, under the current regime, represent limitations in terms of actualizing Indigenous self-determination, because settler law, neoliberal governmentality, and the property regime upon which settler colonialism-capitalism is based are not fundamentally challenged. Rather, Indigenous sovereignty is municipalized and Indigenous title converted into a form of Indian Act private property . . . . The settler state is now positing new authority and land management in cities—First Nations as investors and entrepreneurs—not as rights- and title-holders. At the same time, however, new urban reserves contribute to decolonization and transformative place-making based on First Nations' assertion of sovereignty and self-determination in various ways, including by making visible, politicizing, and reclaiming cities as Indigenous places.[47]

In summary, her basic position is that "new urban reserves are contradictory spaces," insofar as they are both "products and vehicles of settler-colonial state power and Indigenous resistance and place-making."[48] For this reason, she situates "new urban reserves as both expressions of First Nations' struggles to reclaim space and assert inherent rights and, simultaneously, as manifestations of the neoliberalization of settler colonialism."[49]

What is important for this chapter is that she suggests, albeit implicitly, that the creation of new urban reserves is primarily and largely a function of material interests and imperatives by all involved within the context of a colonial-capitalist paradigm which is heavily influenced by neoliberalism, which she suggests is not somewhat separate from colonial rule, but central to it"[50] rather than a public philosophy of reconciliation, a project of reconciliations, or a spirit of reconciliation. Moreover, any discernable reconciliatory features that may exist within the scope of the creation and operation of urban reserves are relatively modest at best and mitigated by neoliberalism forces.

CONCLUSIONS

To reiterate, the central objective of this chapter has been to provide an overview and analysis of two alternative perspectives on the relationship between reconciliation and the creation and operation of satellite urban reserves, which for purpose of this chapter have been labeled the conventional and the critical perspectives. Whereas the premise of the prevailing conventional perspective is that satellite urban reserves are both products and facilitators of reconciliation between First Nations governments and their counterparts at the federal, provincial, and municipal levels, as well as the communities in which the urban reserves are created. By contrast, the central premise of the critical perspective is that new satellite urban reserves are primarily and largely products and facilitators of contemporary neocolonialism influenced by neoliberalism forces and agendas, rather than of the contemporary reconciliation public philosophy or project.

Collectively the two alternative perspectives on the relationship between satellite urban reserves and reconciliation provide us with a fuller explanation of that relationship than either of those two perspectives on their own. After all, these are not necessarily mutually exclusive perspectives. It is possible that the creation and operation of satellite urban reserves entail at once products and facilitators of reconciliation as well as products and facilitators of neocolonialism influenced by neoliberalism. Nevertheless, it is important to keep in mind that the likelihood that the extent to which each of those perspectives applies to the creation and operation of each urban satellite reserve can vary either minimally or substantially. It is also important to keep in mind that a broad brush approach to the analysis of the determinants and effects of the creation and operation of satellite urban reserves based exclusively on either of those perspectives glosses over the complex interplay of factors and forces identified by those two perspectives. Moreover, it is important to keep in mind that in ascertaining the precise mix of determinants and effects of the creation and operation of such reserves, it is imperative to undertake detailed case studies of the creation and operation of each urban satellite reserve.

Of course, in undertaking such case studies, it is also imperative to undertake the very difficult task of finding a conceptualization of reconciliation that is based on sound criteria that resonates and has a substantial level of legitimacy among key stakeholders both within and beyond First Nations communities. Reconciliation is one of those proverbial plastic words that often leads to intense debates on its meaning, methods for determining its existence, and degree to which it exists.

A final question to consider is what would augment the degree of reconciliation sufficiently to satisfy those who espouse the critical perspective on the creation and operation of satellite urban reserves? According to two analysts who addressed the general issue of reconciliation approximately one decade ago, augmenting reconciliation hinges on finding a balance between the notion of Aboriginal self-government (i.e., autonomy) on one hand and Aboriginal self-determination (i.e., sovereignty) on the other. They added that finding the balance is contingent on how much importance the former attaches to the notion of self-government and the degree of emphasis and value that the latter attaches to the self-determination. They implore the two sides to recognize this and to find a balance between those two notions through what might be termed agonistic reciprocity. However, they recognize the challenges that have existed and continue to exist in achieving such a balance. They place much of the blame for the inability to achieve such a balance at the feet of the Canadian state. In their words:

> Unfortunately, there is little evidence of such a balance. The processes associated with self-government negotiations are so powerfully unilateral in their focus that they have all but displaced considerations relating to self-determination . . . . [T]he overall drift of the process has been in the direction of cutting Aboriginal people down to size, which is to say down to the size imagined as manageable by the [Canadian] state. The result has been to diminish the concept of Aboriginality rather than to promote relations that might accommodate complex social and cultural diversity represented by contemporary Aboriginal people in Canada.[51]

They add that for reconciliation to be achieved the "collective singular [Aboriginal] community must be provided with the opportunity to engage in an internal dialogue in order to establish the terms and construct the means of self-determining its own course," and conclude that

> [c]urrently, the support that would enhance and facilitate such dialogue scarcely exists. We contend, however, that it is crucial to the practice of self-government. The evaluative weightings, the guiding principles, the concepts, and the institutional processes will emerge because such a dialogue will form the substance of self-governance. The two sides, self-government and self-determination, must be given the opportunity to co-evolve.[52]

In reading such statements, one is left asking whether a decade later much progress has been made in actual reconciliation as opposed to the intensification of the reconciliation narrative. Regardless how one answers that questions, there is no denying that finding a mutually acceptable balance in various facets of the relationship, including in the creation and operation of satellite urban reserves, between the Canadian state and Aboriginal governments remains a challenge. Undoubtedly, as they look at the same proverbial glass of reconciliation some will focus primarily on how full it is, others will focus on how much fuller it should be.

NOTES

1. The author extends his appreciation to Adrian Aquino for his valuable research assistance in preparing this chapter.

2. Laurie Barron and Joseph Garcea, "Introduction," in *Urban Indian Reserves: Forging New Relationships in Saskatchewan*, ed. Laurie Barron and Joseph Garcea (Saskatoon: Purich, 1999), 1–21; Joseph Garcea, "First Nations-Municipal Relations and the TLEFA in Saskatchewan," in *The Land is Everything: Treaty Land Entitlement*, ed. Tasha Hubbard and Marilyn Poitras (Saskatoon: Office of the Treaty Commissioner, 2014).

3. Joseph Garcea, "First Nations Satellite Reserves: Capacity-Building and Self-Government in Saskatchewan," in *Aboriginal Self-Government in Canada: Current Trends and Issues,* 3rd edition, ed. Yale Belanger (Saskatoon: Purich, 2008), 287–309.

4. Joseph Garcea, "Residential Urban Reserves: Issues and Options for Providing Adequate and Affordable Housing," in *Home in the City: Urban Aboriginal Housing and Living Conditions,* ed. Alan Anderson (Toronto: University of Toronto Press, 2013), 334; Julie Tomiak, "Contesting the Settler City: Indigenous Self-determination, New Urban Reserves, and the Neoliberalization of Colonialism." *Antipode* 49, no. 4 (2017): 928–945.

5. Greg Mason, "The Conversation: Urban Reserves Are Tests of Reconciliation." *University of Manitoba News* (2019), https://news.umanitoba.ca/the-conversation-urban-reserves-are-tests-of-reconciliation/.

6. Canada, Crown-Indigenous Relations and Northern Affairs Canada [CIRNAC], "Specific Claims," last modified August 30, 2019, https://www.rcaanc-cirnac.gc.ca/eng/1100100030291/1539617582343; Idem., "Treaty Land Agreements," https://www.aadnc-aandc.gc.ca/eng/1100100034822/1100100034823

7. CIRNAC, "Specific Claims."

8. Canada, Indian and Northern Affairs Canada [INAC], "Additions to Reserves/New Reserves," in *Land Management and Procedures Manual* (Ottawa: INAC, 1991); Canada, Lands and Trust Services, *Urban Reserves: Presentation to Senior Policy Committee* (1998); Canada, INAC, "Additions to Reserve/Reserve Creation – 2016," in *Land Management Manual* (Ottawa: INAC, 2016), https://www.aadnc-aandc.gc.ca/eng/1465827292799/1465827347934#chpo

9. Garcea, "First Nations Satellite Reserves," 297–298.

10. Treaty Land Entitlement Implementation Act, S.S. 1993, c. T-20.1.

11. Laurie Barron and Joseph Garcea, "Aboriginal Self-Government and the Creation of New Indian Reserves: A Saskatchewan Case Study," in *Aboriginal Self-Government in Canada,* 2nd edition, ed. John Hylton (Saskatoon: Purich Publishing), 301–305.

12. Garcea, "First Nations Satellite Reserves," 287.

13. James Ceaser, "What Is Public Philosophy?" *Perspectives on Political Science* 30, no. 1 (2001): 9–19.

14. Ronald Manzer, *Public Policies and Political Development in Canada* (Toronto: University of Toronto Press, 1985); Brian Howe, "The Evolution of Human Rights Policy in Ontario." *Canadian Journal of Political Science* 24, no. 3 (1991).

15. Hugh Heclo, "Reaganism and the Search for a Public Philosophy," in *Perspectives on the Reagan Years,* ed. John Palmer (Washington, DC: Urban Institute, 1986), 32.

16. Truth and Reconciliation Commission of Canada [TRC], "Honouring the Truth, Reconciling for the Future: Summary of the Final Report of the Truth and Reconciliation Commission of Canada." *Truth and Reconciliation Commission* (2015): 6–8.

17. TRC, "Honouring the Truth," 6–8.

18. Ibid., 6–7.

19. Ibid., 8.

20. James Miller, "Research and Outcomes at the Truth and Reconciliation Commission." *Canadian Historical Review* 100, no. 2 (2019): 181.

21. TRC, "Honouring the Truth," 7.

22. Ibid., 7.

23. Miller, "Research," 181; Matt James, "A Carnival of Truth? Knowledge, Ignorance and the Canadian Truth and Reconciliation Commission." *Canadian Historical Review* 100, no. 2 (2019): 163–181.

24. Katherine Graham, "Urban Aboriginal Governance in Canada: Paradigms and Prospects," in *Aboriginal Self-Government in Canada: Current Trends and Issues,* 2nd edition, ed. John Hylton (Saskatoon: Purich, 1999), 383.

25. Graham, "Urban," 383–385.

26. Laurie Barron and Joseph Garcea, "Aboriginal Self-Government and the Creation of New Indian Reserves: A Saskatchewan Case Study," in *Aboriginal Self-Government in Canada,* 2nd edition, ed. John Hylton (Saskatoon: Purich, 1999), 289–309; Laurie Barron and Joseph Garcea, *Urban Indian Reserves: Forging New Relationships in Saskatchewan* (Saskatoon: Purich, 1999); Leslie Perreaux, "Band Eyes Residential Properties." *Saskatoon StarPhoenix,* January 4, 1999.

27. INAC, "Additions to Reserves."

28. Canada, Crown-Indigenous Relations and Northern Affairs Canada [CIRNAC], "Ongoing Negotiations," last modified May 23, 2018, https://www.rcaanc-cirnac.gc.ca/eng/1100100030285/1529354158736.

29. CIRNAC, "Ongoing Negotiations."

30. Tom Flanagan and Lee Harding, "Treaty Land Entitlement and Urban Reserves in Saskatchewan." *Frontier Centre for Public Policy* (2017): 4.

31. Canada, INAC, "Urban Reserves," last modified April 4, 2017, https://www.aadnc-aandc.gc.ca/eng/1100100016331/1100100016332

32. INAC, "Urban Reserves."

33. Canada, Aboriginal Affairs and Northern Development Canada [AANDC], *Charting a Path for Prosperity: Long Plain First Nation's Urban Reserves Story.* Ottawa: Aboriginal Affairs and Northern Development Canada, 2014. https://www.rcaanc-cirnac.gc.ca/eng/1398180417331/1539954350247.

34. INAC, "Urban Reserves."

35. Evelyn Peters, "Urban Reserves," in *Research Paper for the National Centre for First Nations Governance,* 2007; Barron and Garcea, "Urban Indian Reserves."

36. Mason, "The Conversation."

37. Ibid.

38. AANDC, "Charting a Path."
39. Michael Gertler, "Indian Urban Reserves and Community Development: Some Social Issues," in *Urban Indian Reserves: Forging New Relationships in Saskatchewan,* ed. Laurie Barron and Joseph Garcea (Saskatoon: Purich, 1999), 263–279.
40. Gertler, "Indian Urban Reserves," 263.
41. Ibid., 277.
42. Tomiak, "Contesting," 931.
43. Pasternak Shiri, "How Capitalism Will Save Colonialism: The Privatization of Reserve Lands in Canada." *Antipode* 47, no. 1 (2015): 185.
44. Tomiak, "Contesting," 930.
45. Ibid., 934.
46. Ibid., 934.
47. Ibid., 940.
48. Ibid., 928.
49. Ibid., 930.
50. Ibid., 933.
51. R. F. McDonnell and R. C. Depew, "Aboriginal Self-Government and Aboriginal Self-Determination in Canada: A Critical Commentary," in *Aboriginal Self-Government in Canada: Current Trends and Issues,* 2nd edition, ed. John Hylton (Saskatoon: Purich, 1999), 353.
52. McDonnell and Depew, "Aboriginal Self-Government," 370.

BIBLIOGRAPHY

Barron, Laurie and Joseph Garcea, eds. *Urban Indian Reserves: Forging New Relationships in Saskatchewan* (Saskatoon: Purich, 1999a).

Barron, Laurie and Joseph Garcea. "Introduction." In *Urban Indian Reserves: Forging New Relationships in Saskatchewan.* Edited by Laurie Barron and Joseph Garcea, 1–21. (Saskatoon: Purich, 1999b).

Barron, Laurie, and Joseph Garcea. "Aboriginal Self-Government and the Creation of New Indian Reserves: A Saskatchewan Case Study." In *Aboriginal Self-Government in Canada,* 2nd ed. Edited by John Hylton, 289–309 (Saskatoon: Purich, 1999d).

Canada. Lands and Trust Services. *Urban Reserves: Presentation to Senior Policy Committee* (1998).

Canada. Aboriginal Affairs and Northern Development Canada. *Land Management Manual.* (Ottawa: Aboriginal Affairs and Northern Development Canada, 2001).

Canada. Aboriginal Affairs and Northern Development Canada. *Charting a Path for Prosperity: Long Plain First Nation's Urban Reserves Story.* Ottawa: Aboriginal Affairs and Northern Development Canada, https://www.rcaanc-cirnac.gc.ca/eng/1398180417331/1539954350247 (2014).

Canada. Indian and Northern Affairs Canada. "Additions to Reserves/New Reserves." In *Land Management and Procedures Manual* (Ottawa, ON: INAC, 1991).

Canada. Indian and Northern Affairs Canada. "Additions to Reserve/Reserve Creation – 2016," in *Land Management Manual Ottawa* (Ottawa: INAC, 2016), https://www.aadnc-aandc.gc.ca/eng/1465827292799/1465827347934#chpo.

Canada. Indigenous and Northern Affairs Canada. "Urban Reserves." Last modified April 11, 2017. Accessed November 29, 2019, https://www.aadnc-aandc.gc.ca/eng/1100100016331/1100100016332.

Canada. Crown-Indigenous Relations and Northern Affairs Canada. "Ongoing Negotiations." Last modified May 23, 2018. Accessed November 29, 2019, https://www.rcaanc-cirnac.gc.ca/eng/1100100030285/1529354158736.

Canada. Crown-Indigenous and Northern Affairs Canada. "Treaty Land Agreements." Last modified April 11, 2017. Accessed November 29, 2019, https://www.aadnc-aandc.gc.ca/eng/1100100034822/1100100034823.

Canada, Crown-Indigenous Relations and Northern Affairs Canada. "Specific Claims." Last modified August 30, 2019. Accessed November 29, 2019, https://www.rcaanc-cirnac.gc.ca/eng/1100100030291/1539617582343.

Ceaser, James. "What Is the Public Philosophy?" *Perspectives on Political Science* 30, no. 1 (2001): 9–19, https://doi.org/10.1080/10457090109600715.

Flanagan, Tom. *Treaty Land Entitlement and Urban Reserves in Saskatchewan* (Winnipeg, MB: Frontier Centre for Public Policy, 2017).

Garcea, Joseph. "First Nations Satellite Reserves: Capacity-Building and Self-Government in Saskatchewan." In *Aboriginal Self-Government in Canada: Current Trends and Issues*, 3rd ed., edited by Yale Belanger, 287–309 (Saskatoon: Purich, 2008).

Garcea, Joseph. "Residential Urban Reserves: Issues and Options for Providing Adequate and Affordable Housing." In *Home in the City: Urban Aboriginal Housing and Living Conditions,* edited by Alan Anderson, 334–354 (Toronto: University of Toronto Press, 2013).

Garcea, Joseph. "First Nations-Municipal Relations and the TLEFA in Saskatchewan." In *The Land Is Everything: Treaty Land Entitlement*, edited by Tasha Hubbard and Marilyn Poitras, 111–127 (Saskatoon: Office of the Treaty Commissioner, 2014).

Gertler, Michael. "Indian Urban Reserves and Community Development: Some Social Issues." In *Urban Indian Reserves: Forging New Relationships in Saskatchewan*. Edited by Laurie Barron and Joseph Garcea, 263–279 (Saskatoon: Purich, 1999).

Graham, Katherine. "Urban Aboriginal Governance in Canada: Paradigms and Prospects." In *Aboriginal Self-Government in Canada,* 2nd ed., Edited by John Hylton, 377–392 (Saskatoon: Purich, 1999).

Heclo, Hugh. "Reaganism and the Search for a Public Philosophy." In *Perspectives on the Reagan Years*. Edited by John Palmer, 31–58 (Washington, D.C.: Urban Institute, 1986).

Manzer, Ronald. *Public Policies and Political Development in Canada* (Toronto: University of Toronto Press, 1985).

Mason, Greg. "The Conversation: Urban Reserves Are Tests of Reconciliation." *University of Manitoba News*, https://news.umanitoba.ca/the-conversation-urban-reserves-are-tests-of-reconciliation/ (2019).

McDonnell, R.F., and R.C. Depew. "Aboriginal Self-Government and Aboriginal Self-Determination in Canada: A Critical Commentary." In *Aboriginal Self-Government in Canada: Current Trends and Issues,* 2nd ed. Edited by John Hylton, 370 (Saskatoon: Purich, 1999).

Miller, James. "Research and Outcomes at the Truth and Reconciliation Commission." *Canadian Historical Review* 100, no. 2 (2019): 163–181.

Pasternak, Shiri. "How Capitalism Will Save Colonialism: The Privatization of Reserve Lands in Canada." *Antipode* 47, no. 1 (2015): 179–196

Perreaux, Leslie. "Band Eyes Residential Properties." *Saskatoon StarPhoenix* (January 4, 1997).

Peters, Evelyn. "Urban Reserves." Research Paper for the National Centre for First Nations Governance, http://fngovernance.org/ncfng_research/e_peters.pdf, 2007.

Tomiak, Julie. "Contesting the Settler City: Indigenous Self-determination, New Urban Reserves, and the Neoliberalization of Colonialism." *Antipode* 49, no. 4 (2017): 928–945.

Treaty Land Entitlement Implementation Act, S.S., c. T-20.1 (1993).

Truth and Reconciliation Commission of Canada. *Honouring the Truth, Reconciling for the Future: Summary of the Final Report of the Truth and Reconciliation Commission of Canada*. Winnipeg: Truth and Reconciliation Commission of Canada (2015).

Chapter 9

Business and Reconciliation

Call to Action 92

Ronald G. Evans

Reconciliation is much more than improving understanding and relationships, it is good for business. Serious attention to the social world is becoming more and more widely seen as critical to long-term sustainability and profitability. In December 2015, The *Truth and Reconciliation Commission of Canada* (TRC)[1] issued its *Calls to Action*, a set of ninety-four recommendations. These recommendations span virtually all of Canadian society from the public to private sectors. They are in large part intended to assist in developing understanding and cross-cultural relationships as well as in the overall purpose of community and nation building in health, housing, education, family support, childcare, and social programming. These are important and they are all connected within the community and within the country. These *Calls to Action* affect how we build our families, express our skills and talents, care for our health, and more fully participate with the world around us. The following exploration of the potential implementations of Call to Action 92 for the business community is drawn from, and a reflection on, my experiences.

Experience only has meaning in context, and for context the reader needs to know that I speak from the perspective of a First Nations person; an Ayisiniwok and Nehiyawok, from KinosaoSipi (Norway House Cree Nation) in the north-central part of Manitoba, Canada in Treaty 5 territory. My perspective has also been informed through my work as an ordained Anglican minister, an employee for a number of businesses, small business owner, commercial fisherman, a Band Councilor, and chief of Norway House Cree Nation, and as the grand chief of the Assembly of Manitoba Chiefs. I hold an honorary Doctorate of Divinity. I bring many perspectives to the potential shared future offered by the Business and Reconciliation

Call to Action 92. This chapter explores how "business and reconciliation" may unfold toward a more sustainable and profitable future—for the benefit of all of us.

Call to Action 92 focuses on reconciliation and business. Business relationships, employment, economic development, and finances are important to communities and individuals. These factors are among the most important factors for the overall improvement in quality of life as well as for securing the financial resources necessary for community services and for providing a strong foundation for true self-government. Economic and business relationships, and opportunities and development are vitally important for building our future as a community and as a country.

From one point of view, business and reconciliation may appear to be a politically based process that is generally aimed at restoring positive or friendly relations, or bringing together differing or divergent ideas or conceptions. While this may hold true, having the private sector engage in the reconciliation efforts identified by the TRC is simply good for business. Typically, primary business concerns are in managing resources to provide services and goods to the marketplace, and not in social justice activities. This profit-led focus work in the economy, but it is becoming clear that increasing attention to the social context is good for organizational operations, efficiencies, effectiveness, profitability, and sustainability. It is equally clear that implementing Call to Action 92 can serve as an excellent tool for attracting investment, solidifying long-term business sustainability, expanding the range of possibilities for hiring skilled talent, and increasing the effective management of a positive workplace within a human resources context.

The TRC recommendations are clear and instructive. The "Call to Action 92: For Business and Reconciliation" directs the following:

> 92. We call upon the corporate sector in Canada to adopt the United Nations Declaration on the Rights of Indigenous Peoples as a reconciliation framework and to apply its principles, norms, and standards to corporate policy and core operational activities involving Indigenous peoples and their lands and resources.
> This would include, but not be limited to, the following:
> i. Commit to meaningful consultation, building respectful relationships, and obtaining the free, prior, and informed consent of Indigenous peoples before proceeding with economic development projects.
> ii. Ensure that Aboriginal peoples have equitable access to jobs, training, and education opportunities in the corporate sector, and that Aboriginal communities gain long-term sustainable benefits from economic development projects.

iii. Provide education for management and staff on the history of Aboriginal peoples, including the history and legacy of residential schools, the United Nations Declaration on the Rights of Indigenous Peoples, Treaties and Aboriginal rights, Indigenous law, and Aboriginal–Crown relations. This will require skills based training in intercultural competency, conflict resolution, human rights, and anti-racism.[2]

A CHALLENGING CONTEXT

In order to consider our pathways forward, and how Call 92 may be implemented, it is important to look at some of the challenges. Since before Confederation in 1867, Canada has actively disempowered, disengaged, and marginalized Indigenous people and their participation in the "mainstream" economy. These actions were guided and legitimated through the 1869 *Indian Act*, legislation that clearly defines the relationship of First Nations people with Canada's central government, and which redefined and restricted all relationships and economic transactions within Indigenous communities. Despite regular promises of change by politicians, the legislation remains primarily in its original state 150 years later. Under the *Indian Act*, the establishment of land reserves and "confining" Indigenous people on those reserves moved Indigenous people off their land to remote areas so that immigrant populations could establish homesteads, towns, businesses, develop resources, and build railways. This coincided with overhunting and the decline of the buffalo from the prairies, opening uninhabited land for development. The result of this policy has been marginalization, resulting in starvation, abject poverty, inadequate housing, poor health, and substandard education for the majority of Canada's First Nations people.[3] Perhaps most devastating of all this process for many is that it has virtually extinguished hope.

In today's world it seems that historical understanding has little to do with how we live out our lives day to day and it is understandable if Canadians do not understand the need for reconciliation. However, history does inform our current understandings, our presuppositions, or even prejudices. So, even if people believe that they are not actively involved in marginalizing Indigenous peoples, our systems, institutions, legislation, and established habits just continue on, unquestioned and unabated, and still serve to marginalize. There are current factors that disempower the current barriers to change and how the *Calls to Action* might help to build a new way forward. When we recognize Indigenous marginalization and challenge our thinking to find a new understanding, a new way to move forward together is possible.

COLONIZATION AND DISEMPOWERMENT

To understand how Call 92 applies, a discussion of colonization and disempowerment as roots to marginalization may be helpful. By its very definition, colonization is "the action or process of settling among and establishing control over the indigenous people of an area."[4]

Dispossession of the Land

Along with the end of the Seven Years War in 1755 between the Kingdoms of Great Britain and France, the need for land and for a more orderly method of transferring land provided the foundation for the *Royal Proclamation* of 1763 of King George III of England.[5] As well as the recognition of Indigenous land rights, the proclamation formed the foundation for the Crown acquiring and holding title for the land that then resulted in the creation and existence of "Indian land reserves."[6] It is almost beyond belief that a document produced over 250 years ago has any impact today. However, the proclamation is the underpinning of the process of dispossessing First Nations individuals and communities of their own land through the subsequent *British North America Act*, treaties, and the *Indian Act*. Together, these established the barriers that prevent economic development, and the generation of wealth and jobs.

As European arrival and settlement increased and expanded, colonists needed more and more territory for homes, buildings, businesses, woodlots, or farms.[7] There was little consideration of the original inhabitants. Land seemed to be seen as endless with no owners or users that needed any consideration.[8]

Location

Added to the challenges of economic and job development are the factors of dislocation, remoteness and community population, or market size. The smaller the market, the less economic activity and the less opportunity. As the "settlement" of Canada continued to grow, First Nations were required to sign treaties to cede their rights to the land and be located in much smaller holdings and on marginal lands that were not suited for development. If one looks at a map of Canada to discover where most First Nations are located, one will find that most are not in economically viable locations.

Those few First Nations that are currently located in economically viable locations occurred as a matter of unanticipated economic growth—almost as mistakes by the government of the day. For instance, across the country, the reserve location for the Osoyoos Indian Band was not selected with foresight because it was an ideal location for vineyards and wine production; it was not the discovery of oil that motivated the location of the Samson Cree Nation, Louis Bull Tribe, or Montana First Nation among others south of Edmonton. In Manitoba, the reserve locations of Nisichawayasihk Cree Nation, Tataskweyak Cree Nation, War Lake First Nation, York Factory First Nation, and Fox Lake Cree Nation were not chosen for their potential in partnering in hydroelectric projects. All of these land reserves were meant to be small and as far out of the way as possible, as it is with most other First Nations across the country.

Remoteness

It has been often argued that another important contributing factor for entrenching marginalization and limiting economic development is remoteness. For the purposes of this discussion, let us define remoteness as the severely limited ability to travel freely to and from the community. This would include fly-in communities or those accessed by winter roads. Along with being outside of the mainstream economic wheel, these communities have remarkably few choices and in many ways are an isolated market. Typically, in these conditions, the employment of local people is rare.

Outside of "traditional" activities like fishing, trapping, or the seasonal work of guiding anglers and hunters, opportunities are often limited to activities like periodic public works, projects, or custodial jobs. While this is a broad generalization of the lack of opportunities, the fact is that few local people have sustainable, long-term, or stable employment.

In my experience, historically people from outside the community have staffed professional job opportunities in our communities. These usually include teachers, police officers, nurses, and social workers. To illustrate the pervasiveness of this, a few years back a colleague related to me a story of a friendly contest that asked young students in First Nations schools to submit artwork or drawings about the importance of education. The drawings that were submitted solely depicted the same four professions, and no others whatsoever. Those students did not see any other professions as options for their potential careers. Of course this would have been predictable as these were generally the only decent paying and stable professions they actually saw in the community and hoped to do one day. Their exposure to a greater spectrum of opportunity was limited and their imagined futures fairly narrow.

When thinking about engaging First Nations individuals in ways that use innate talent and drive, it is more difficult to look beyond "home ground" to a world of other possibilities; this is disempowering. Remoteness may be less an issue for individuals as the digital world grows. Opportunities seem more possible when the roles of teacher, police officer, nurse, and social worker are increasingly staffed by local or Indigenous people. When this happens, the sense of opportunity expands. It is good to see these changes, but change has only just begun. Unimagined or unrealized hope for opportunities allows marginalization to remain.

The remote and isolated markets of our communities are also disempowering. From my experience, remote communities are often very small and cannot sustain a variety of competitive businesses. Many times there is only one supplier of goods and services in a community. These businesses tend to provide many services. They are at one time the seller of food, hardware, clothing, appliances, furniture, and other goods, as well as the providers of banking services and even in some cases the providers of health care and prescription drugs. They are truly a one-stop shop. In these cases, the consumer has no choice and must patronize the one local establishment. With little or no competition, consumers can feel trapped because they have no power to choose otherwise. Some may think this a small point, but it reinforces the belief that one really has no value or importance except as a consumer, but it is as a consumer with no choices. This can powerfully impact a person's self-image, engagement, and enthusiasm. It can be yet another disempowering barricade to people finding their voice or vocation, and marginalization continues.

The factors of location, remoteness, and size also impact the business and service practices that are often used within First Nations. In these conditions, the community has a relative lack of working capital, human resource capacity, and has very limited options. From my work at the Assembly of Manitoba Chiefs, it was clear that many of our First Nations communities were generally in need of more support for infrastructure, potable water, housing, health care, education, and social services. The lack of local resources and the ultimate dependence on government programs and funding combine to make a significant opportunity. In my experience as chief, the demand for infrastructure works, construction materials, and goods and services creates a great and profitable marketplace for contractors, engineers, designers, suppliers, builders, consultants, managers, accountants, teachers, health care professionals, and lawyers. It seems to me that First Nations in Canada provide an excellent business opportunity benefiting a number of varied providers across the land. While this sounds cynical, it points to the fact that First Nations communities and individuals are not significantly engaged or involved in the tasks to be done in bringing solutions to their own challenges in their own home communities.

Inaccessibile Capital

Under the *Indian Act*, Canada's federal government is obligated to provide financial support for First Nations communities from the public purse. This also means that First Nations people are discouraged and prohibited by law from owning reserve land. As an example of how this has impacted First Nations negatively, not owning assets (land) prevents using collateral to secure capital, which thwarts the building of houses, businesses, or even community infrastructure. To understand how impactful this can be, imagine the housing or business capital markets in Canada if it was virtually impossible to borrow money for homes or businesses, and the only way to secure a home or to start a business depended on the decisions of an unelected government department—as it is for First Nations people. We must contend with the bureaucracies of the federal department, the *Indian Act*, and a figurehead Cabinet minister appointed by the prime minister of Canada, whose job is not to lobby for us, but to ensure that the goals of his or her elected political party are met. It is very, very hard to grow or move forward economically if individuals have severely restricted access to capital. In discussions on economic development in my time at the Assembly of Manitoba Chiefs, we recognized from UNESCO Case Studies[9] and from the development work done by the London School of Economics that restricted access to capital is often at the root of similar problems faced by developing countries. There is no mystery why some First Nations communities exhibit "Third-World" conditions.

Education

In addition to the land and its geographical implications, it is important to consider education's colonizing role and the marginalization of Indigenous peoples. Depending on the province and depending on the analogous programming, First Nations education and schools are funded at rates that are significantly less as compared to the amount expended in non-First Nations education systems, and allegedly justified because First Nations reserves and people do not pay taxes.[10] This is an unreasonable rationale.

In my discussions with educators, poor funding allocations have had a significant impact, resulting in a lack of learning resources, overcrowded schools, and limited spaces available to First Nations community students. As a direct result, educational outcomes suffer. In addition, the reliability and availability of internet access is inconsistent in remote areas where most reserves are located. Difficulties with teacher recruitment and retention, and limited exposure to educational experiences such as field trips all combine to result in First Nations students being at significant educational risk. In this way, First Nations student experiences fall far short of the educational benefits and opportunities afforded to students outside First Nations communities. This is a huge problem with a huge literature. For those interested, the gaps and solutions are well articulated by reports from the Senate of Canada.[11]

While academic success does happen on occasion despite these conditions, it is not uniform. Nor does rare First Nations student success compare fully to the outcomes realized by non-First Nations community students. As an example of current federal government funding measures, there has been a funding cap imposed on First Nations postsecondary student support that does not keep pace with inflation or population growth.[12] This has effectively and increasingly reduced the number of First Nations students that are able to undertake educational opportunities for career acquisition or development, and such policies are not something communicated by government to the general Canadian public. Again, government policies restrict opportunities for our people to rise from marginalized obscurity, through education and training for careers.

Outmigration and Employment

Considerable outmigration of First Nations community members from their home communities to urban centers has been occurring for years. In part, this has been a result of the lack of opportunities at home outlined above. All in all, the urban population of First Nations individuals has been increasing. In the 2016 Canadian Census, Statistics Canada reported that:

> In 2016, 867,415 Aboriginal people lived in a metropolitan area of at least 30,000 people, accounting for over half (51.8%) of the total Aboriginal population. From 2006 to 2016, the number of Aboriginal people living in a metropolitan area of this size increased by 59.7%.[13]

Unfortunately, unemployment follows many to the city. Again, Statistics Canada has reported that "around half (52% or 240,960 individuals) of First Nations people living off reserve aged 15 or older were employed in 2016."[14] Conversely, this means that the unemployment rate is 48%. Compare this to the national unemployment rate of 7.0%[15] boasted by the central government, and clearly First Nations employment significantly trails that of other Canadians. This gap needs significant work.

First Nations and Financial Resources

There is no question that First Nations people as a group are among the poorest in Canada. Statistics Canada finds that about 29% of the First Nations people are identified as low income. The employment rate has consistently been just over 57%.[16] While these numbers may not seem alarming at first, imagine if these statistics were true for all Canadians in all of Canada.

A countrywide 43% unemployment rate would be catastrophic. During the worst economic downturn in the county's history—the Great Depression—the national unemployment rate in Canada in 1933 was 19.3%.[17] Imagine the conditions in Canada today if this rate was doubled in the main workforce. Not surprisingly then, many First Nations leaders describe First Nations marginalization and poverty as a crisis, an epidemic, and even a matter of life and death. This is particularly so as life, health, water, food, and shelter all depend on acquiring the resources necessary for their provision.

Solutions need to be implemented now. For these reasons alone, it is arguable that one of the most important functions of reconciliation is the building of economic and job opportunities for First Nations. As a brief review, elements that have historically and currently contributed to or affected First Nations marginalization include: colonization and disempowerment, dispossession of the land, inaccessible capital, location, remoteness, education, outmigration and employment, and First Nations and financial resources. While this list may not be exhaustive, it serves as an excellent starting point for application of TRC's Calls to Action.

A WAY FORWARD TO RECONCILIATION

While TRC recognizes the importance of First Nations' empowerment and engagement in "mainstream" economic opportunities, it also reports that "the government of Canada is not the lead on a response for Call to Action 92."[18] This does not mean that the government is not responsible to support First Nations and private sector business relationships and activities. The support for building these relationships must be real from government and other sources, and offer a tangible, practical pathway to implementation, and not merely become another "symbolic" pronouncement, for which the Canadian government has a long and documented history.[19]

Recognizing First Nations' rights and responsibilities to the land and using these for the foundation of building meaningful relationships between First Nations, Canada, and the private sector can positively address colonization and disempowerment. The words of the Call to Action 92: For Business and Reconciliation, TRC, are the following:

> 92. We call upon the corporate sector in Canada to adopt the United Nations Declaration on the Rights of Indigenous Peoples as a reconciliation framework and to apply its principles, norms, and standards to corporate policy and core operational activities involving Indigenous peoples and their lands and resources.[20]

The *United Nations Declaration on the Rights of Indigenous Peoples* (UNDRIP) articulates a number of principles in its preamble building a foundation for its forty-six articles. Of particular interest to empowerment, the UNDRIP preamble states the following:

> *Concerned* that indigenous peoples have suffered from historic injustices as a result of, inter alia, their colonization and dispossession of their lands, territories and resources, thus preventing them from exercising, in particular, their right to development in accordance with their own needs and interests,
>
> *Recognizing* the urgent need to respect and promote the inherent rights of indigenous peoples which derive from their political, economic and social structures and from their cultures, spiritual traditions, histories and philosophies, especially their rights to their lands, territories and resources.[21]

Following these principles, together with the protection of rights enshrined in Section 35 of the *Canadian Constitution Act*, will establish the foundation for the empowerment of First Nations governance and stewardship of land and traditional territory, as well as overall development. When addressing First Nations marginalization through these concerns and recognitions, it is clear that the action taken would support and enhance economic and job development. Once established, empowered, and demarginalized, First Nations can then search out and build partnerships with private sector interests for development.

This promising process, stemming from the TRC and the United Nations, encourages the empowerment of the First Nations. When engaged, this will establish a fairer division of the value and benefits that would derive from the relationship or partnership. One example is the Attawapiskat First Nation,[22] who has a mutual benefit agreement with diamond miners De Beers Canada. This secures local participation in the venture of extracting resources. Adopting this approach across Canada could spur local capacity building, training opportunities, employment, and "own-source" community revenues that could in turn be invested in housing, education, health facilities, or any other community infrastructure needed to grow and improve local living standards. The potential is more than exciting.

Furthermore, when the right to land and management of that land is entrusted back to First Nations, communities will be able to structure themselves to create a more meaningful expression of self-government. This type of development is currently happening with the creation of the Cree Nation Government (self-government) in northern Quebec's James Bay area.[23] After negotiating agreements with the federal and provincial governments, the Cree Nation Government is making significant progress for its members.

For instance, they develop, manage, and deliver a number of services to their people. These include a Cree public tendering process; justice and correctional services; child and family services; emergency services; management of environmentally protected areas; mining; forestry; land use and planning; wildlife management and conservation; environmental and social impact assessments; trade and commerce agreements; business incubators; and overall socioeconomic development and management. The Cree Nation Government is truly and fully engaged in determining their future development and their relationships with government and the private sector. They are showing leadership and how true success can be replicated by other First Nations. This kind of development can and should be available to all First Nations across the country and effectively address the elements of marginalization.

Investment and Social Responsibility

As outlined in this chapter, First Nations empowerment is also good for business development, on which our economies rely. Corporate social responsibility as well as a stable predictable method for successful Indigenous engagement is critical to attracting new business and investment, and is globally recognized as an indicator of business sustainability. This is becoming more and more important as both consumers and the investment communities are becoming more sensitive to the importance of the role of corporate social responsibility.

A new term has been coined to describe corporate social responsibility: the double bottom line.

> What does that mean? Essentially the emerging field of impact investing seeks to get more out of capital. Beside a healthy financial return, many investors—large and small—are seeking ways for their money to contribute back to a social cause, save resources, or contribute to an effort they care about that betters society in some way. The possibilities are endless from poverty alleviation to affordable housing to natural resource conservation to building needed infrastructure in a city or state.[24]

This sense of corporate social responsibility closely aligns with Call to Action 92. The Call states that in order to facilitate reconciliation, business communities and governments must:

i. Commit to meaningful consultation, building respectful relationships, and obtaining the free, prior, and informed consent of Indigenous peoples before proceeding with economic development projects.

ii. Ensure that Aboriginal peoples have equitable access to jobs, training, and education opportunities in the corporate sector, and that Aboriginal communities gain long-term sustainable benefits from economic development projects.[25]

Clearly when implemented by the larger business community, these measures are very likely to be recognized as measures that make society and the world a better, more socially responsible place, and will benefit First Nations people—especially those on reserves. In turn, this is more likely to attract positive attention, brand loyalty, and investment.

A number of organizations and indexes recognize that there is value in investment. That is, corporate social responsibility for providing business sustainability and long-term operations. The International Organization for Standardization, *ISO 26000 Social Responsibility*, statement says that "business and organizations do not operate in a vacuum. Their relationship to the society and environment in which they operate is a critical factor in their ability to continue to operate effectively. It is also increasingly being used as a measure of their overall performance."[26] Considering the focus of ISO 26000, it seems that implementing Call to Action 92 can align with the standards for doing good business. Following the same theme, another example is the S&P 500 Environmental and Socially Responsible Index that "is designed to measure the performance of securities from the S&P 500 that meet environmental and social sustainability criteria."[27]

Finally, as an example of Consumer sensitivity and brand loyalty applies to good corporate social responsibility. After news of inappropriate staff racist behavior was recorded in one of the stores of a popular coffee chain, the business implemented a company-wide program aimed at identifying bias and building awareness. Again, this fits with Call to Action 92:

iii. Provide education for management and staff on the history of Aboriginal peoples, including the history and legacy of residential schools, the United Nations Declaration on the Rights of Indigenous Peoples, Treaties and Aboriginal rights, Indigenous law, and Aboriginal–Crown relations. This will require skills based training in intercultural competency, conflict resolution, human rights, and anti-racism.[28]

To conclude, the *Truth and Reconciliation Commission*'s Call to Action 92: For Business and Reconciliation is not some kind of reparation for past wrongs but it is the practical road forward. It is recognition of First Nations' land, territory, and development rights, as well as a call for active engagement with the private and public sectors of Canada. Implementation will significantly reduce the impacts of colonization and marginalization and promote self-determination and partnerships. For business and commerce, the implementation of Call to Action 92 will provide opportunities to enhance their ability to attract investment capital, and to more positively connect with their customer base. This will also improve human resources management. The development of a respectful workplace for First Nations people gives the chance for businesses to draw from a larger set of potential employees that in turn can bring richer skill sets that might otherwise not be available for their operations.

Reconciliation, as outlined in Call to Action 92, is much more than improving understanding and relationships, it is good for defeating colonization and marginalization and for building strong and profitable business opportunities.

NOTES

1. Truth and Reconciliation Commission, *Truth and Reconciliation Commission of Canada, Final Report*, 2015, accessed December 8, 2019, www.trc.ca.

2. Truth and Reconciliation Commission, *Truth and Reconciliation Commission of Canada: Calls to Action*, 2015, accessed December 8, 2019, www.trc.ca.

3. Statistics Canada, *The Daily, Aboriginal Peoples in Canada: Key Results From the 2016 Census*(2017), accessed September 15, 2019, https://www150.statcan.gc.ca/n1/daily-quotidien/171025/dq171025a-eng.htm.

4. Oxford English Dictionary, s. v. "Colonization," accessed December 8, 2019, https://www.oxfordlearnersdictionaries.com/definition/english/colonization.

5. Government of Canada, *Royal Proclamation of 1763*, accessed December 8, 2019, https://www.aadnc-aandc.gc.ca/eng/1379594359150/1379594420080.

6. Government of Canada, Royal Commission on Aboriginal Peoples, *Report of the Royal Commission on Aboriginal Peoples, Volume 1 – The Imposition of a Colonial Relationship*, Ottawa, Canada, October, 1996: 134.

7. Government of Canada, Royal Commission on Aboriginal Peoples, *Report of the Royal Commission on Aboriginal Peoples, Volume 1*, 107–112, 130–133.

8. Government of Canada, *Royal Proclamation of 1763*.

9. UNESCO webpages, accessed December 8, 2019, https://en.ccunesco.ca/

10. Government of Canada, Office of the Parliamentary Budget Officer, *Federal Spending on Primary and Secondary Education on First Nations Reserves*, Ottawa, Canada, 2016: 25–27.

11. Government of Canada, *Senate of Canada Report of the Standing Committee on Aboriginal Peoples, Reforming First Nations Education: From Crisis to Hope*, Ottawa, Canada, December 2011.

12. Assembly of First Nations webpage, *Fact Sheet, First Nation Education Funding*, accessed September 15, 2019, https://www.afn.ca/uploads/files/education/fact_sheet_-_fn_education_funding_final.pdf.

13. Statistics Canada, *The Daily, Aboriginal Peoples in Canada: Key Results From the 2016 Census*(2017), accessed September 15, 2019, https://www150.statc an.gc.ca/n1/daily-quotidien/171025/dq171025a-eng.htm

14. Statistics Canada, *Aboriginal Peoples Survey, 2017,Labour Market Experiences of First Nations People Living Off Reserve: Key Findings from the 2017 Aboriginal Peoples Survey* (2018), accessed September 15, 2019, https://www150. statcan.gc.ca/n1/pub/89-653-x/89-653-x2018003-eng.htm

15. The Conference Board of Canada, *Provincial and Territorial Ranking, Unemployment Rate*(2017), accessed September 15, 2019, https://www.conferenceboard.ca /hcp/provincial/economy/unemployment.aspx

16. Statistics Canada, *Aboriginal Statistics at a Glance: 2nd Edition*, accessed September 15, 2019, https://www150.statcan.gc.ca/n1/pub/89-645x/2015001/ employment-emploi-eng.htm.

17. Dave Gower, Statistics Canada, "Labour and Household Surveys Analysis Division, Perspectives on Labour and Income," 4, no. 3(1992).

18. Government of Canada, *Delivering on Truth and Reconciliation Commission Calls to Action*, accessed September 15, 2019, https://www.aadnc- aandc.gc.ca/eng /1524494530110/1524494579700.

19. Consider, for example, the recommendations from the Royal Commission on Aboriginal Peoples from 1996, which were ignored until a change of government and the Harper Apology of 2008; see, for example, the campaign promises of the Justin Trudeau government to implement all ninety-four Calls to Action of the *Truth and Reconciliation Commission of Canada's Final Report* in 2015—unfulfilled and without mention in his 2019 election campaign.

20. Truth and Reconciliation Commission of Canada, *Truth and Reconciliation Commission of Canada: Calls to Action,*10.

21. United Nations, *United Nations Declaration on the Rights of Indigenous Peoples*, Adopted September 13, 2007, accessed September 15, 2019, https:// www.un.org/development/desa/indigenouspeoples/wp-content/uploads/sites/19/201 8/11/UNDRIP_E_web.pdf,3

22. Attawapiskat First Nation, home page, accessed September 15, 2019, http:// www.attawapiskat.org/

23. The Grand Council of the Crees (EeyouIstchee),*Where We Share*, accessed September 15, 2019, https://www.cngov.ca/.

24. Lori Kozlowski, *Impact Investing: The Power of Two Bottom Lines*, modified October 2, 2012, accessed September 15, 2019, https://www.forbes.com.

25. Truth and Reconciliation Commission of Canada, *Truth and Reconciliation Commission of Canada: Calls to Action,* 10.

26. International Organization for Standardization, *ISO 26000 Social Responsibility*, accessed September 15, 2019, https://www.iso.org/iso-26000-social-responsibilit y.html.

27. S&P Dow Jones Indicies, *S&P 500 Environmental & Socially Responsible Index,* accessed September 15, 2019, https://ca.spindices.com/indices/equity/sp-50 0-environmental-socially-responsible-index.

28. Truth and Reconciliation Commission of Canada, *Truth and Reconciliation Commission of Canada: Calls to Action,*10.

BIBLIOGRAPHY

Assembly of First Nations. "Fact Sheet, First Nation Education Funding." Accessed September 15, 2019, https://www.afn.ca/uploads/files/education/fact_sheet_-_fn_education_funding_final.pdf.

Attawapiskat First Nation, home page. Accessed September 15, 2019, http://www.attawapiskat.org/.

Government of Canada. "Delivering on Truth and Reconciliation Commission Calls to Action." Accessed September 15, 2019, https://www.aadnc-aandc.gc.ca/eng/1524494530110/1524494579700

Government of Canada, Office of the Parliamentary Budget Officer. "Federal Spending on Primary and Secondary Education on First Nations Reserves." Modified December 6, 2016, accessed December 8th, 2019, https://www.pbo-dpb.gc.ca/en/blog/news/First_Nations_Education.

Government of Canada, Royal Commission on Aboriginal Peoples. *Report of the Royal Commission on Aboriginal Peoples, Volume 1—Looking Forward, Looking Back*. Ottawa, Canada, October, 1996.

Government of Canada. *Royal Proclamation of 1763*. Accessed December 8th, 2019, https://www.aadnc-aandc.gc.ca/eng/1379594359150/1379594420080.

Government of Canada. Senate of Canada, Report of the Standing Committee on Aboriginal Peoples, "Reforming First Nations Education: From Crisis to Hope." Ottawa, Canada, December 2011.

Gower, Dave. "Statistics Canada, Labour and Household Surveys Analysis Division, Perspectives on Labour and Income." *Autumn 1992A Note on Canadian Unemployment since 1921* 4, no. 3 (1992).

International Organization for Standardization. "ISO 26000 Social Responsibility." Accessed September 15, 2019, https://www.iso.org/iso-26000-social-responsibility.html.

Kozlowski, Lori, "Impact Investing: The Power of Two Bottom Lines." Modified October 2, 2012, accessed September 15, 2019, https://www.forbes.com.

Oxford English Dictionary, s. v. "Colonization." Accessed December 8, 2019, https://www.oxfordlearnersdictionaries.com/definition/english/colonization.

S&P Dow Jones Indices. "S&P 500 Environmental & Socially Responsible Index." Accessed September 15, 2019, https://ca.spindices.com/indices/equity/sp-500-environmental-socially-responsible-index.

Statistics Canada. "Aboriginal Peoples Survey, 2017, Labour Market Experiences of First Nations People Living Off Reserve: Key Findings from the 2017 Aboriginal Peoples Survey." Modified November 26, 2018, accessed September 15, 2019, https://www150.statcan.gc.ca/n1/pub/89-653-x/89-653-x2018003-eng.htm.

Statistics Canada, "Aboriginal Statistics at a Glance: 2nd Edition." Accessed September 15, 2019, https://www150.statcan.gc.ca/n1/pub/89-645x/2015001/employment-emploi-eng.htm.

Statistics Canada. "The Daily, Aboriginal Peoples in Canada: Key Results From the 2016 Census." Released October 25, 2017, accessed September 15, 2019, https://www150.statcan.gc.ca/n1/daily-quotidien/171025/dq171025a-eng.htm.

The Conference Board of Canada, Provincial and Territorial Ranking. "Unemployment Rate" June 2017, accessed September 15, 2019, https://www.conferenceboard.ca/hcp/provincial/economy/unemployment.aspx.

The Grand Council of the Crees (EeyouIstchee)."Where We Share." Accessed September 15, 2019, https://www.cngov.ca/.

Truth and Reconciliation Commission of Canada. *Truth and Reconciliation Commission of Canada: Calls to Action*, 2015. Accessed December 8, 2019, http://trc.ca/assets/pdf/Calls_to_Action_English2.pdf.

United Nations. *United Nations Declaration on the Rights of Indigenous Peoples,* 3.Adopted September13, 2007, accessed September 15, 2019, https://www.un.org/development/desa/indigenouspeoples/wp-content/uploads/sites/19/2018/11/UNDRIP_E_web.pdfpp.

Chapter 10

Reconciliation and the Evolution of Canadian Policing

Dale McFee with Robert Chrismas

The relationship between police and Indigenous people is one of the oldest in Canada, dating back to the fur trade. The association has been a volatile one as the role of the police has historically been mainly law enforcement. Often it is the police that Indigenous people (and others) blame for laws created and enforced by governments. Overcoming a troubled past, building, and maintaining trust may be one of the most profound challenges and priorities confronting modern policing. In this chapter, the authors[1] explore the evolution of this very old relationship and the practical ways today's police leaders can advance justice, respect, and contribute to Canada's reconciliation journey.

HISTORICAL CONTEXT

Canadian police services have a shared history with early law enforcement. In the centuries between the 1600s and Confederation in 1867, Canada's staple-based economy grew out of European demand for beaver pelts.[2] Among the first laws to be enforced were those that regulated the fur trade. The British Army enforced regulations and legislation that authorized the HBC and the North West Company to control beaver trapping throughout what was then called Rupert's Land, to export pelts to Europe.[3] Modern interpretations of history hold that the police-community relationship started as a primarily positive one.

With the advent of the Industrial Revolution in Europe, an insatiable need for natural resources in the British and French markets grew, and the relationship with Indigenous people in British North America began to change and deteriorate. King George III of Britain issued a *Royal Proclamation* in 1763 to claim all of what is now North America for Britain and wrote within it protections of Indigenous people across the continent.[4] These provisions are now protected in Section 25 of Canada's *Constitution Act*. However, while the continent was slowly populating with European settlers, the eruption of the American Revolution between 1765 and 1783 introduced fear and intimidation as Indigenous people south of the 49th parallel suffered under American policies of annihilation. Within one hundred years, Canada was formed, and government policies and the laws of Britain and France were collected within one piece of legislation to efficiently control Indigenous people and define their relationship with government.

The *Indian Act* officially received Royal Assent in 1879 and remains primarily intact today. One early provision formally marginalized Indigenous people away from mainstream society onto remotely located parcels of land called reserves. Although it is federal legislation, one of the roles of the police at all levels of government has been to monitor and enforce the provisions of the *Indian Act*. In this way, the police became an agent for law enforcement for the British and Canadian governments, and the goodwill partnerships of the fur trade all but disappeared. The roots of these contentious roles are evident in today's relationship between the Canadian police and Indigenous people, who rightly or wrongly blame the police for systemic oppression. The desire to return to a more respectful community within the context of contemporary realities drives strategies for community service and engagement that characterize many Canadian police services today.

While organized citizens patrolled Quebec City as early as 1651, most municipal police forces in what was later known as Canada were not established until the mid-1800s. The earliest law enforcement systems followed French and English traditions. In the early 1800s in Eastern Canada, citizens were appointed magistrates and the military was called on during rare times of civil unrest when force was needed.[5] In the west, the HBC played a large part in Canada's settlement, and its legal system and regulations served as the first body of enforceable laws until they were replaced by federal statutes in 1869.[6]

With Canadian Confederation in 1867, Canada was officially established as a federal system with two levels of government. Canada's governing constitution at the time, the *British North America Act* of 1867, gave each of Canada's provinces the authority to establish police forces within their jurisdictions. Canada's first prime minister, Sir John A. Macdonald, established the North-West Mounted Police (NWMP) in 1873. They had a military-based structure and discipline, but constables acted as both police and magistrates, enforcing the laws and also acting as prosecutors. Sir John A. Macdonald defended the NWMP structure as needed in the wild expanses of Western Canada that they had to patrol. In 1904 the Royal prefix was added, and the NWMP was renamed the Royal Canadian Mounted Police (RCMP).[7] The

RCMP was meant to be a temporary force, but the model was deemed so successful that in 1905 the newer provinces of Alberta and Saskatchewan convinced Prime Minister Wilfrid Laurier to leave the RCMP in place. Its jurisdiction was extended to Manitoba in 1912 and to British Columbia in 1918.[8] However, law enforcement remains constitutionally a provincial responsibility to this day, meaning that it is ultimately provincial governments and provincial budgets that guide police work, with significant support from the RCMP in matters of federal jurisdiction.[9]

The work and challenges of contemporary policing have changed significantly over the century and a half of Canada's "official" history. During the fur trade and the American Revolution, the European introduction of alcohol initially as trade for assistance in trapping for beaver pelts is attributed at least in part to the legacy of substance abuse that is now inherent in many of Canada's Indigenous communities. For many reasons related to settlement and colonization outlined in other chapters of this volume, in the early decades of the twenty-first century Canada's police services are overwhelmingly occupied with extreme behavioral implications of alcohol and substance abuse among Indigenous people.[10] The links between alcohol abuse and crime, victimization and diminishing community order and safety are well documented and understood.[11] We are now in an era of some of the most significant challenges, yet some of the most effective and transformative policing strategies Canada has ever seen.

NEW ANSWERS FOR OLD PROBLEMS

There are valuable lessons to be learned from other areas of the world. There is a growing and effective common theme in modern policing and that is the role of community engagement and respect toward all citizens. For example, recent work in Glasgow, Scotland, provides a relevant and intriguing model for Canada. There, the police have learned the craft of community mobilization and bringing multiple service sectors together for effective crime reduction.[12] When I was the Prince Albert's police chief, we recognized that high crime rates tied to antecedents, such as alcohol abuse, were on an unsustainable trajectory and called for a new approach and focus on intervention. I learned about positive advances made in Glasgow, Scotland, and led a delegation from Canada to explore and better understand their approach. We returned with a plan, and those changes produced positive results that we implemented first in the city of Prince Albert, Saskatchewan, and have since then been modeled in various jurisdictions and across Canada. Adopting a version of the Glasgow model, we created spaces for influence and collective multisectoral work. While as police we are not entirely accountable for crime rates and social problems, as a police service we demonstrated that we can wield a great deal of influence in bringing the right parties together around social issues.

For Prince Albert we developed the Prince Albert Hub model.[13] This model brought various sectors together around risks that were identified in the community, in many cases intervening before issues became more inflamed policing problems. This model of community mobilization around social problems had a 37% reduction in violent crime between 2010 and 2014.[14] The main lesson learned from the Saskatchewan initiative is that the police are only one element in the spectrum of government services, including health, child and social welfare and education, sectors that are also significant to crime prevention, and, more broadly, community safety and well-being. As these services work together in a concept well known in Canada as horizontal governance, positive change takes place. Our leadership role as police services has been to influence these different service sectors to work together for a common and positive goal.

The more we looked at this, the more quickly we began to realize that police in most instances were the front-facing service arm for our vulnerable populations. Police services across North America work tirelessly to help equip and prepare their frontlines in dealing with the complexity of the issues. In many instances, we thought success in community safety could be measured in how quickly we could get to a call for service and what additional training we could give our same frontline personnel to better deal with the issues they were facing. What we found in Scotland was something I believed had the essential components of success in driving change and dealing with wicked problems that were plaguing police in dealing with vulnerable populations. The four pillars that appeared to be at the heart of the various delivery models in Scotland were (1) local solutions, (2) data-driven, (3) partnerships, and (4) collective outcomes.

These four elements have been known to police for many years, yet we have been unable to break through many of the barriers that seem to focus on the barriers, versus the lens that starts with the art of the possible. How to share private data, competing budgets, lack of measurement, and horizontal outcomes had been issues no one seemed to be able to figure out. Numerous death inquests made recommendations to change the way we worked with vulnerable populations, and many demanded that professional services must do better in sharing information and working collectively toward better, client-centered, outcomes. To bridge the gap and overcome these very real challenges, the Hub concept was born. It brought joint ownership to the outcome of connecting people to services.

The Hub model, based on what we had learned in Scotland, formalized joint ownership where the partners put the situation and the needs of the person at the center of the intervention, rather than the needs of the service agencies. It was designed to formally have discussions through a framework to get services quickly to those displaying characteristics that multidisciplined trained professionals could make a team decision in reducing risk in close to real time. What it was not going to be was a study or an inquiry that gives us many of the same recommendations every time we hold them; it was not going to be an academic table where we debate what to do; it was not designed to take away from these essential functions, but it was to remain as an action table that helped connect people and reduce risk with informed processes that contained focused discipline on how it was to be done.

The Hub was designed as part of an ecosystem for change. It is based on professional services recognizing the acutely elevated risk of individuals, designing the appropriate intervention based on their professional expertise with a goal to connect them to the right services based on circumstances in close to real time. The critical parts were that everyone had access to their own data to get a better picture of the full circumstances to better treat and deal with the individual. As a result, and as an additional piece of multidisciplinary service, we now have the ability to see trending issues across the country that are disproportionately driving work across human services delivery providers. With this knowledge, we are better able to work on priorities at a community level in directing the right programs and policies while at the same time, removing the long-standing problem of siloed service delivery that is often led by who owns a budget versus what is needed for the individual and or community facing the problem. Additionally, the creation of the Hub model now allows governments and organizations to focus human and financial resources into the areas where we can make the most significant impact increasing our value for money proposition.

The main lesson learned from the Saskatchewan initiatives is that the police, along with courts and prisons, are only one element in the spectrum of government services important to crime prevention, including health, child and social welfare, and education. However, the Hub has been a hugely significant contributor to improved community relations and improved community engagement.

A BRIEF OVERVIEW OF CANADIAN POLICING

People now ask the police for assistance with very different matters from those that were seen as parental responsibility at the turn of the century. Such minor service calls can be overwhelming for police agencies in the context of the ever-growing queue of calls for service and limited police resources. We found that 81% Saskatchewan police calls for service are for noncriminal antisocial behavior; similarly, 92.7% of Edmonton police service's calls for low-priority circumstances.[15] These numbers are reflective across Canada as people have increasingly turned, in recent decades, to the police for all manner of complaints—often far outside the mandate of policing.

Police agencies in the modern context are also perpetually challenged by demands to fill systemic gaps in adjacent service sectors. In 2014, the Canadian Association of Chief of Police issued a statement declaring "that the growing frequency, severity, human risks, business risks, and resource levels associated with police responses and interactions with persons with mental health issues collectively represent the number one emerging issue facing police services in Canada."[16] Some of the main issues showing up consistently in over 140 service hubs in Canada and the United States are mental health and addictions, domestic violence, trauma, and literacy-absenteeism-parenting, with lack of employment appearing as a potential root cause. Also, as a result of the history described earlier, distrust of the police, the justice system, and government, in general, is endemic among many Indigenous people.[17]

Establishing, rebuilding, and maintaining trusting relationships with Indigenous people is an ongoing concern for Canada's law enforcement agencies. The principles of good policing that were initially set out by Sir Robert Peel, when establishing London's first Metropolitan Police Force in 1829, are a doctrine for professional policing in the Western world that remains apposite to this day.[18] These principles, if properly applied, can stand as a guide for police agency transformation and improved trust and respect of Indigenous people. Principle 7, commonly stated as "the police are the people and the people are the police," highlights the role of the community in public safety. Peel's principles define the police as an extension of the public, not as a replacement of them. The idea that the police are one of many stakeholders, and not solely responsible for crime reduction and public safety, is an underpinning principle in the collaborative approaches to policing now being undertaken across Canada.

The RCMP are the most visible police service on Canada's reserves. Their association with enforcing laws like those surrounding the *Indian residential school policy* has been nurtured in the minds of Indigenous people by the continued relationship that the RCMP have maintained providing contract policing in rural reserves and communities in several provinces and territories across Canada to this day. Many Indigenous people saw the RCMP as assisting Indian agents (now expanded as the federal department of Crown-Indigenous Relations) to enforce assimilation policies that included government bans prohibiting Indigenous people from consuming liquor, hunting, or participating in the traditional pow wows, sun dances, and ceremonies that are critical to their culture and heritage.[19] In 2004, RCMP Commissioner

Zacardelli officially apologized for the RCMP's involvement in the "Indian residential school legacy."[20]

The RCMP provides federal enforcement across Canada and to this day are involved in provincial contract policing in all provinces except Ontario and Quebec. The Ontario Provincial Police, Sûreté du Québec, and Royal Newfoundland Constabulary are the only provincial police forces, to date, in Canada. In Ontario and Quebec, the RCMP serves only federal functions such as national security and smaller municipalities often contract police services from provincial agencies, while larger ones maintain their own forces. Newfoundland's provincial police force is responsible only for its larger urban areas; the province has contracted the RCMP to patrol the rest of the province.[21] In other provinces, the RCMP handle policing except where regional forces have been set up. Many Indigenous communities have their own police forces, funded through tripartite agreements between the government of Canada, the provinces, and Indigenous communities. Currently, Aboriginal policing is supported through 168 policing service agreements for the policing of 408 Indigenous communities across Canada.[22]

As Canadian cities have grown, so too have municipal police forces. Currently, Canada's 222 police organizations include one federal police force (the RCMP), three provincial police forces, 150 municipal police services, over 50 Indigenous police services, and some specialized agencies such as the two national railway police services. These police organizations are comprised of 12 police services with over 1,000 employees, 15 larger police services with 300–999 employees, 27 medium-sized police services with 100–299 employees, and 65 small police services with 25–99 employees in each. There are 103 small police services employing fewer than 25 employees. In Canada, there are over 61,050 police officers and 23,391 civilian support staff, which amounts to one officer for every 528 Canadian citizens.[23] Each police organization also has a unique culture that is molded by its specific circumstances, history, regional characteristics, and cultural context, affected in part by the differences in each region, city, and town. They also all have unique relationships with Indigenous people.

CALLED TO SERVE

The police have been thrust into the center of some of Canada's most inflamed conflicts. The significance of land to Indigenous people is now better understood as scholars have found that their oral traditions are story-based, and strongly linked to geographic landmarks and areas.[24] The trauma of being separated from traditional lands onto reserves is now better understood. Physical landmarks are a significant part of Indigenous identity. Canadian conflicts over land use and land rights, such as the protracted siege by the Mohawk tribe near the Quebec town of Oka, in 1990, have defined police-community relationships.[25] The list of land-related conflicts between Indigenous and mainstream Canada goes on.[26] The police remain a crucial stakeholder in Canada's reconciliation of these deep historical conflicts. At the same time, many look to the police to solve problems that are well beyond their capabilities and mandates. One of the first lessons learned in Prince Albert, brought back from Glasgow, is the disproportionate involvement of people with justice and other service sectors in the absence of appropriate cross-sectoral intervention.[27]

Another broad trend in Canadian politics is the recent tendency of our political leaders to acknowledge and apologize for past injustices. Much like the politically correct practice of acknowledging treaties at public gatherings, apologies appear to be a growing trend and may or may not have substance behind them. Research has demonstrated that there are elements that must characterize apologies for them to be deemed—and more importantly to be received—as authentic.[28] These elements are true of the June 11, 2008 *Statement of Apology to Former Students of Canadian Residential Schools* by Stephen Harper, the prime minister of Canada.[29] However, the many recent apologies of the Trudeau government (elected in 2015) for apparently any Canadian offence toward parties who have perceived injustice, but actually making no meaningful structural change to address those wrongs, build false hope, erode public trust, and may drive us backward in efforts to improve relationships.

On occasion, the Canadian government establishes public inquiries to signal to people (voters) that they take events seriously and are looking for recommendations for current policy positions.[30] In Canada, the federal government has established and received recommendations from a number of federal inquiries, but it is important to note that inquiry recommendations are not binding. For example, Manitoba's Aboriginal Justice Inquiry that followed the shooting of Indigenous man J. J. Harper by a Winnipeg police officer in 1988 recommended increased consultation with Indigenous communities in the areas of education, justice, law enforcement, the courts and prison system, and increased recruitment of Indigenous people in policing.[31] Despite numerous development and recruitment programs in Manitoba and across Canada, Indigenous people are still generally underrepresented in policing.[32] In Prince Albert, we learned quickly that building a police service that is reflective of community demographics alone is not enough. Each member of the police service must be a champion for change and act accordingly, or risk being accused of making empty promises.

WHEN THE POLICE MUST PERFORM OTHER PUBLIC SERVICES

Policing has taken on a disproportionate amount of the burden that all of society must share in the current state of Indigenous relations in Canada. Currently, the police service is the default for other social services that, according to legislation, are the responsibility of the federal government under the *Indian Act* and the Canadian *Constitution*. For example, the police are often asked to perform services that are not part of their training, role, or responsibilities. It is generally believed within the policing community that armed police officers are not the appropriate resource to assist nonviolent people who need to be brought in for examination by a doctor under mental health legislation. Yet, the police are used for this task continually and massive resources are tied up that are intended to be available for emergency response or positive community engagement.

In prior generations in Canadian homes, parents and community played more significant roles in raising children, but this role, too, has defaulted in many circumstances to the police. There was less need for formal education, as farming was a hands-on trade passed on father/mother to son/daughter. As industry progressed and people left the house for work in factories and nonfarming industries, much childcare responsibility was shifted to public schools. According to some historians,[33] learning to function in the newly emerging agrarian society was part of the rationale for the federal residential school policy. In prior generations, public officers also took on more significant roles in security, safety, justice, and social regulation. Some people now look to child welfare agencies and the police to solve problems that were historically handled adequately and appropriately in the home.

Another policing challenge, and likely a close second behind mental health calls,[34] is child welfare and missing persons. Police agencies across Canada have been challenged in recent decades by the growing reliance of child welfare systems on the police to return chronic runaway youth. For example, the Winnipeg Police Service had a problem with chronic missing person reports. They found that 70% of the 5,000–7,000 missing person calls handled per year involved chronic repeat runaways, and three-quarters or more of those were Indigenous youth.[35] Chronically overwhelmed and under-resourced child welfare systems often look to the police as a default resource. The police are forced to develop proactive approaches (and find the appropriate resources) to reduce the strain on police resources engaged in protecting vulnerable youth.[36]

The challenge missing persons has had for policing is highly relevant to understanding contemporary policing in Canada. The prairie province of Manitoba, for example, has been in a continuous child welfare crisis for decades, with 12,000 children in the care of the state, the highest per capita in Canada, and three-quarters of these seized children are Indigenous. Among the missing person cases that overwhelm police resources are the vulnerable population of troubled youth who are targeted and exploited in the sex industry.[37] Police resources being overwhelmed and overused to fill systemic gaps in other social agencies is a problem across Canada.

Popular media often complicates the public understanding of the role of Canadian police services, frequently suggesting that the police or government agencies are responsible for crime rates, or the failure to correct social problems. Rarely is the focus on the root causes of problems or the social structures that perpetuate them. The reality is that no amount of money could make government agencies so effective that they alone can correct major societal ills, such as poverty. The entire community and multisectoral system of resources must work together to address complex social problems; which explains the shift in recent decades to multisystem approaches and public engagement. In many ways, current challenges have driven police to revert to their historical origins, placing resources back in the community, walking beats, and engaging in community problem-solving. We have also learned that people do not want to be policed; rather, they want to participate in the safety of their own neighborhoods. This requires trusting partnerships.

BUILDING TRUST FOR A BETTER FUTURE

For there to be genuine reconciliation in Canada between police services and Indigenous people, authentic trust will have to be built; it is a challenge that will need constant attention. Indigenous-police relationships have ebbed and flowed throughout Canadian history. Trust is earned; people need to feel that they are on a level playing field, know that justice is fair, and that they have control over their choice to obey the laws and support the system. If people feel that they can be arbitrarily detained, searched, and arrested, or that the laws are enforced differentially, favoring elites or only certain people, they will likely not see why they should accept and abide by the laws. Why would people cooperate with a civil authority that does not appear to represent their interests? Research conducted in sixteen different countries found that the perception of government corruption is directly correlated with decreased public trust in the police.[38] These findings are relevant to Indigenous Canadians' criminal involvement problems, as government and the police in both rural and urban settings are likely to be seen, by some, as contributing to the problems in the community. The Canadian government has invested large amounts of money, often without improving the quality of life for Indigenous people and with a long-standing backlog of unresolved treaty claims. Many have lived for decades with mostly ineffective government support as well as infighting and ineffective Indigenous leadership.[39]

Other research has found that trust is improved when the police are perceived as being competent and fair.[40] In order to trust the justice system and its agents, Indigenous people, and all citizens, must feel that the system protects all parties' interests equally.[41] These findings generalize from the police to other government agencies as well; perceived unfairness creates distrust. One study of communities in England determined that the trust of police is improved by community-based approaches that engage the public. It found that citizens generally want more input into police priorities and decisions. The police, on the other hand, are generally cautious about people's motives and are often uncomfortable with sharing information and decision-making authority unless they are sure the citizens involved are competent and able to make valuable and informed contributions.[42] The police, as well as the public, need to earn trust in a two-way relationship in order to work effectively together.

The effectiveness of Canada's emerging governance structures may depend mainly on Indigenous people and mainstream governments learning to trust each other.

Achieving and maintaining trust is a delicate balance as government agencies can lose trust through attempts to manipulate whom they work with, while simultaneously losing credibility and effectiveness by attempting to work with people who are not considered representatives of the community at large. For decades now, Canadian police agencies have strived to engage citizens and be seen as responsive to changing community needs through various reiterations of community policing. Community-oriented policing developed as a formal concept in the 1950s and 1960s in Canada, seeking to improve the interaction between police and the communities they serve.[43] One historian cites, "Community policing represents a fundamental shift in police services management and has replaced the military model as the dominant service delivery model in Western Countries."[44]

The Halton Regional Police Service, in Ontario, Canada, was one of the earliest comprehensive community policing programs implemented in North America.[45] Halton's experience revealed that implementation and change to community-oriented policing approaches can be challenging. Substantial change requires commitment and momentum. One expert wrote that community policing has been defined in different ways. It is a philosophy designed to reduce crime through community partnerships, problem-solving, and the decentralization of decision-making authority to frontline officers.[46] Community-oriented policing has been pursued due to the mass of evidence that conventional reactive practices in overall crime reduction are generally less effective. We need approaches that seek to address the root causes of crime, rather than just reacting to them. While community-oriented policing is widely endorsed by those involved in it, one expert points out that the term means different things to different people. For example, various police departments have emphasized different aspects, including crime prevention seminars, satellite community-based storefronts, newly designed uniformed patrol beats and foot patrols, community advisory groups and forums, neighborhood watch programs, and plans designed to make the police more visible in neighborhoods.[47]

Improved communication and engagement fosters trust between police agencies and the communities that they serve. Peacebuilding scholars have emphasized the need for citizen empowerment to participate in solving societies' problems.[48] The narrative across society needs to evolve to engage whole communities working together to reduce crime and improve quality of life.[49] However, increased citizen engagement and inclusion requires police willingness to accept input and share power.

Nilson points out that "Advocates of the Hub model are driven by the notion that the 'human service disconnect' in our contemporary bureaucracies makes it difficult for some individuals and families to get the supports they need."[50] Manitoba's Block by Block, Community Safety and Wellbeing Initiative was initially modeled after Prince Albert's Hub (multisector committee of frontline service providers) and COR (center of responsibility), which is comprised of decision-makers from the involved government and nongovernment organizations.[51] As a serving member on the COR of the Thunderwing, which is the first initiative under Manitoba Block by Block Initiative, Chrismas observed Nilson's finding first hand. Many families come up against bureaucratic barriers that can be fixed. It is a simple concept; however, bureaucratic challenges are often surprisingly difficult to rectify. We saw the same thing in Prince Albert.

The value of collaborative multisectoral approaches has been proven over and over again. In fact, the discourse in justice, and in government in general, has now shifted such that the idea of any one agency tackling any major issue alone now seems ludicrous. The question now is where is the leadership to bring the right parties around the table? Our current crisis, in both the United States and Canada, with methamphetamines is a case in point. The question will not be what the police are doing, but more who is bringing the right parties to the table to find collaborative solutions.[52]

THE WAY FORWARD: LESSONS FROM
PRINCE ALBERT AND EDMONTON

Now we know what we know, so now what? My biggest lessons were to focus on what drives the work and use reverse engineering to chart a course for change. It means bridging a gap between data, literature, and focused practical application. This means finding a consortium of the willing that are prepared to be vulnerable or open to criticism to improve the current path. For me it means to find smart people, empower them, and be willing to be the buffer to the critics that are most often protecting their own interests. In addition, it means giving those smart people the chance to fail in a safe environment while they work to make things better for those facing the current crisis on the frontlines.

As an individual of Metis ancestry, the most glaring example of this for me is the identification of problems by race versus vulnerabilities, then further running multiple parallel studies based on race or culture versus risk factors. These actions were predictable and would most often end with multiple inquiries or studies on the same topic without any change to service delivery. If reconciliation in its purest form is to be an action word that helps people, then it must be as much about the path forward as it was in recognizing that whatever happened was not right. The path forward needs courage which means protecting the things we are good at with measured relevance and being relentlessly committed to innovation in finding new practical ways that work in reducing the demand of the services that are needed. In policing, a simple translation of this is that police control 100% of intake into the justice system, meaning the system does not exist if we do not lay a charge.

Now, we know it is critical that we work to capitalize on recruitment, training, data, and partnerships ensuring that we properly sort intake and capitalize on that first contact with a client. We must differentiate our first decision between individuals we are afraid of versus those that we are mad at when utilizing the criminal justice system. Overall the prognosis is favorable for Canada's future. While we still have a long way to go to achieve true reconciliation, the culture of Canadian policing is generally about compassion and problem-solving. We (in policing) are generally concerned about community well-being, and playing our part in mobilizing the right sectors around improved safety for all the citizens we serve. Community engaged policing worked in Prince Albert, and it is working in Edmonton. Nationally, Canadian police services are committed to models that engage with people we serve, partnering rather than keeping adversarial relationships of the past. Shared responsibility and partnership is perhaps what reconciliation is.

NOTES

1. The authors have both been involved in Canadian policing for over thirty years each. Chief Dale McFee was instrumental in redefining community-oriented policing, first by creating more collaborative models as chief of the Prince Albert Police

Service and currently as chief of the Edmonton Police Service. Bob Chrismas is a Staff Sergeant in the Winnipeg Police Service and completed his Master of Public Administration and PhD in peace and conflict studies with a focus on police–community engagement.

2. Harold AdamsInnis, *The Fur Trade in Canada: An Introduction to Canadian Economic History* (New Haven, CN: Yale University Press,1930).

3. Lloyd Duhaime, "Canada's Criminal Code: A History" 2008, accessed December 6, 2019,http://www.duhaime.org.

4. See https://indigenousfoundations.arts.ubc.ca/royal_proclamation_1763/ for a discussion of the provisions of the *Royal Proclamation* and a verbatim copy of the original document.

5. Craig Brown, *The Illustrated History of Canada* (Toronto, ON: Key Porter Books, 2002); Duhaime, "Canada's Criminal Code: A History."

6. Brown, *The Illustrated History of Canada*.

7. RCMP, "History of the Royal Canadian Mounted Police," *Mounted Police Post*, modified 2012, accessed December 6, 2019, http://www.mountieshop.com/new /history.asp.

8. Brown, *The Illustrated History of Canada*.

9. Jeffrey Ross, "The Historical Treatment of Urban Policing in Canada: A Review of the Literature."*Urban History Review*24, no. 1 (1995): 36–43.

10. Robert Chrismas, *Canadian Policing in the 21st Century*; *A Frontline Officer on Challenges and Changes* (Montreal, QB: McGill-Queens University Press. 2013); Chrismas, Robert, "The People Are the Police: Building Trust with Aboriginal Communities in Contemporary Canadian Society," *Canadian Public Administration* 55, no3 (September 2013): 451–70.

11. Dale McFeeand Norm Taylor, "The Prince Albert Hub and the Emergence of Collaborative Risk-driven Community Safety," Toronto, ON: Canadian Police College, modified 2014, accessed December 6, 2019, http://www.cpc-ccp.gc.ca/sites / default/files/pdf/prince-albert-hub-eng.pdf.

12. Govanhill webpage, "Three-month Review of the Govanhil Operational Hub." Glasgow Centre for Population Health," modified 2010, accessed December 6, 2019, http://www.glasgow.gov.uk/councillorsandcommittees/viewSelectedDocumen t.asp?c=P62AFQZ3T1DXT10G;McFee and Taylor, "The Prince Albert Hub and the Emergence of Collaborative Risk-driven Community Safety."

13. See McFee and Taylor, "The Prince Albert Hub and the Emergence of Collaborative Risk-driven Community Safety."

14. Ibid.

15. Edmonton Police Service business intelligence data, provided by the author-Dale McFee.

16. Canadian Association of Chiefs of Police, accessed December 6, 2019,https:// www.cacp.ca/resolution.html?asst_id=389.

17. Chrismas, *Canadian Policing in the 21st Century*; Chrismas, "The People Are the Police."

18. Susan Lentz and Robert Chaires, "The Invention of Peel's Principles: A Study of Policing 'textbook' History." *Journal of Criminal Justice* 35, no. 1 (2007): 69–79.

19. Marcel-Eugène LeBeuf, "The Role of the Royal Canadian Mounted Police during the Indian Residential School System," RCMP webpages, modified October 29, 2011, accessed December 6, 2019, http://www.rcmp-grc.gc.ca/ aboriginal-autochtone/irs-spi-eng.htm.

20. RCMP webpage, accessed December 6, 2019, http://www.rcmp-grc.gc.ca/aboriginal-autochtone/apo-reg-eng.htm.

21. Chrismas, *Canadian Policing in the 21st Century.*

22. Public Safety Canada webpages, "Trends in Indigenous Policing Models: An International Comparison," accessed December 6, 2019, https://www.publicsafety.gc.ca/cnt/rsrcs/pblctns/trnds-ndgns-plc-mdl/index-en.aspx

23. Police Sector Council webpage, modified 2012, accessed December 6, 2019, www.policecouncil.ca/ pages/policing.html.

24. John Paul Lederach, *The Moral Imagination:The Art and Soul of Building Peace* (New York: Oxford University Press, 2005).

25. Kiera Ladner and Leanne Simpson, *This Is an Honour Song: Twenty Years Since the Blockades* (Winnipeg, MB, Canada: Arbeiter Ring Press, 2010);

26. Maria Campbell, *Halfbreed: A Proud and Bitter Canadian Legacy* (Toronto, ON:McClelland and Stewart Limited, 1974); IlaBussidor and stuñBilgen-Reinart, *Night Spirits: The Story of the Relocation of the Sayisi Dene* (Winnipeg: University of Manitoba Press, 1997).

27. Govanhill, "Three-month Review of the Govanhil Operational Hub."; McFee and Taylor, "The Prince Albert Hub."

28. Robert Weyeneth, "The Power of Apology and the Process of Historical Reconciliation," *The Public Historian* 23 no. 3 (2001): 9–38.

29. See chapter 1 for a full explanation of the apology process. The 2008 Apology may be read at https://www.aadnc-aandc.gc.ca/eng/1100100015644/1100100015649.

30. Ed Ratushny, *The Conduct of Public Inquiries: Law, Policy, and Practice* (Toronto, ON: Irwin Law, 2009).

31. Alvin Hamilton and Murray Sinclair, *Report of the Aboriginal Justice Inquiry of Manitoba: The Justice System and Aboriginal People* (Manitoba, MB: Queen's Printer, 1991).

32. Geoffrey Li, "Private Security and Public Policing," modified 2008, accessed December 6, 2019, http://www.statcan.gc.ca/pub/85-002-x/2008010/article /10730-eng.htm.

33. James Miller, *Shinwauk's Vision; A history of Native Residential Schools* (Ontario: University of Toronto Press Incorporated. Toronto, 1996).

34. Chrismas, *Canadian Policing in the 21st Century.*

35. Ibid.

36. Ibid.

37. Robert Chrismas, *Modern Day Slavery and the Sex Industry: Raising the Voices of Survivors and Collaborators While Confronting Sex Trafficking and Exploitation in Manitoba, Canada,* University of Manitoba, MSpace, entered 2017, accessed December 6, 2019, http://hdl.handle.net/1993/32586.

38. Juha Tapio Kaariainen, "Trust in the Police in 16 European Countries: A Multilevel Analysis." *European Society of Criminology* 4, no. 4 (2007): 409–35.

39. Mary Agnes Welch and Mia Rabson, "Contentious Cleanup." *Winnipeg Free Press* (December 30, 2011).

40. Jonathan Jackson and Ben Bradford, "What Is Trust and Confidence in the Police?"*Policing* 4, no. 3 (2010): 241–248.

41. Katrina Hohl, Ben Bradford, and Elizabeth A. Stanko, "Influencing Trust and Confidence in the London Metropolitan Police." *British Justice and Criminology* 50 (2010): 491–513; Tank Waddington, "Policing with Trust and Confidence." *Policing* 4, no. 3 (2010): 197–198.

42. Louise Westmarland, "Dodgy Customers? Can the Police Ever Trust the Public?" *Policing* 4, no. 3 (2010): 291–297.

43. Jack R. Greene, "Foot Patrol and Community Policing: Past Practices and Future Prospects." *American Journal of Police* 6 (1987): 1–15.

44. Lori A. Cooke-Scott, "Community–Based Policing in Ontario: Lessons from the Halton Regional Police Service." *Canadian Public Administration* 41 (1998): 120–146.

45. Cooke-Scott, "Community–Based Policing in Ontario."

46. Mathew Scheider, Robert Chapman and Amy Schapiro, "Towards the Unification of Policing Innovations under Community Policing." *Policing: An International Journal of Police Strategies and Management* 32, no. 4 (2009): 694–718.

47. David Bayley, "Community Policing: A Report from the Devil's Advocate." In J. R. Green, and S. D. Mastrofski (Eds.), *Community Policing—Rhetoric or Reality* (New York: Praeger, 1988): 225–237.

48. John Paul Lederach, *The Moral Imagination: The Art and Soul of Building Peace* (New York: Oxford University Press, 2005).

49. Sean Byrne, Dennis Sandole, Ingrid Sandole-Staroste and Jessica Senehi, *Handbook of Conflict Analysis and Resolution* (Oxford: Routledge, 2009).

50. Chad Nilson, "Risk-Driven Collaborative Intervention: A Preliminary Impact Assessment of Community Mobilization Prince Albert's Hub Model," Saskatoon, SK: Centre for Forensic Behavioural Science and Justice Studies. The University of Saskatchewan, entered2014, accessed December 6, 2019, https://cfbsjs.usask.ca/documents/Hub%20PIA%20Synopsis%20Handout.pdf.

51. Nilson, "Risk-Driven Collaborative Intervention."

52. Dylon Robertson and Aldo Santin, "Meth Task Force Report Passing the Baton to Each of the Three Levels of Government." *Winnipeg Free Press* (June29, 2019).

BIBLIOGRAPHY

Bayley, David. "Community Policing: A Report from the Devil's Advocate." In J. R. Green and S. D. Mastrofski (Eds.),*Community Policing—Rhetoric or Reality* (New York: Praeger, 1988).

Brown, Craig. *The Illustrated History of Canada* (Toronto, ON: Key Porter Books, 2002).

Bussidor, Ila and stüñBilgen-Reinart. *Night Spirits: The Story of the Relocation of the Sayisi Dene* (Winnipeg: University of Manitoba Press, 1997).

Byrne, Sean, Dennis Sandole, Ingrid Sandole-Staroste, and Jessica Senehi. *Handbook of Conflict Analysis and Resolution* (Oxford: Routledge, 2009).

Campbell, Maria. *Halfbreed: A Proud and Bitter Canadian Legacy* (Toronto, ON: McClelland and Stewart Limited, 1974).

Canadian Association of Chiefs of Police. "Safety and Security for all Canadians through Innovative Police Leadership." Accessed December 6, 2019, https://www.cacp.ca/resolution.html?asst_id=389.

Chrismas, Robert. *Canadian Policing in the 21st Century: A Frontline Officer on Challenges and Changes* (Montreal QB: McGill-Queens University Press, 2013).

Chrismas, Robert. *Modern Day Slavery and the Sex Industry: Raising the Voices of Survivors and Collaborators While Confronting Sex Trafficking and Exploitation in Manitoba, Canada.* University of Manitoba, MSpace, entered 2017, accessed December 6, 2019, http://hdl.handle.net/1993/32586.

Chrismas, Robert. "The People Are the Police: Building Trust with Aboriginal Communities in Contemporary Canadian Society." *Canadian Public Administration* 55 (2013): 451–470.

Cooke-Scott, Lori A. "Community–Based Policing in Ontario: Lessons from the Halton Regional Police Service." *Canadian Public Administration* 41 (1998): 120–146.

Duhaime, Lloyd. "Canada's Criminal Code: A History," modified 2008, accessed December 6th, 2019, http://www.duhaime.org.

Fenno, Jason. "Prince Albert Youth Drug and Alcohol Use: A Comparison Study of Prince Albert, Saskatchewan and Canada Youth." *Journal of Community Safety and Well-being* 1, no. 3, 2016, accessed December 6, 2019, https://journalcswb.ca/index.php/cswb/article/view/18/52.

First Nations and Indigenous Studies. "Royal Proclamation (of 1763)," University of British Columbia webpages, accessed December 6, 2019, https://indigenousfoundations.arts.ubc.ca/royal_proclamation_1763/

Geoffrey, Li. "Private Security and Public Policing," Statistics Canada webpages, last modified2008, accessed December 6, 2019, http://www.statcan.gc.ca.

Govanhill."Three-month Review of the Govanhill Operational Hub. Glasgow Centre for Population Health." Community Mobilization Prince Albert, last modified 2010, accessed December 6, 2019, http://www.glasgow.gov.uk/councillorsandcommittees/viewSelectedDocument.asp?c=P62AFQZ3T1DXT10G.

Government of Canada. "Edmonton Police Service Business Intelligence Data". Public Safety Canada, last modified2015, accessed December 6, 2019, https://www.publicsafety.gc.ca/cnt/cntrng-crm/plcng/cnmcs-plcng/ndx/dtls-en.aspx?n=134.

Greene, Jack. R. "Foot Patrol and Community Policing: Past Practices and Future Prospects." *American Journal of Police* 6 (1987): 1–15.

Hamilton, Alvin and Murray Sinclair. *Report of the Aboriginal Justice Inquiry of Manitoba: The Justice System and Aboriginal People* (Manitoba: Queen's Printer, 1991).

Hohl Katrina, Ben Bradford, and Elizabeth A. Stanko. "Influencing Trust and Confidence in the London Metropolitan Police." *British Justice and Criminology* 50 (2010): 491–513.

Indigenous and Northern Affairs Canada. "Statement of Apology to Former Students of Indian Residential Schools." Government of Canada, modified 2008, accessed December 6, 2019.https://www.aadnc-aandc.gc.ca/eng/1100100015644/1100100015649.

Innis, Harold Adams. *The Fur Trade in Canada: An Introduction to Canadian Economic History* (New Haven, CN: Yale University Press, 1930).

Jackson, Jonathan and Ben Bradford. "What Is Trust and Confidence in the Police?" *Policing* 4, no. 3 (2010): 241–248.

Kaariainen, JuhaTapio. "Trust in the Police in 16 European Countries: A Multilevel Analysis." *European Society of Criminology* 4, no. 4 (2007): 409–435.

Ladner, Kiera and Leanne Simpson. *This Is an Honour Song: Twenty Years since the Blockades* (Winnipeg, MB, Canada: Arbeiter Ring Press, 2010).

LeBeuf, Marcel-Eugène. "The Role of the Royal Canadian Mounted Police during the Indian Residential School System," entered 2011, accessed December 6, 2019, http://www.rcmp-grc.gc.ca/ aboriginal-autochtone/irs-spi-eng.htm.

Lederach, John P. *The Moral Imagination: The Art and Soul of Building Peace* (New York: Oxford University Press, 2005).

Lentz, Susan and Robert Chaires. "The Invention of Peel's Principles: A Study of Policing 'textbook' History." *Journal of Criminal Justice* 35, no. 1 (2007): 69–79.

McFee, Dale and Norm Taylor. "The Prince Albert Hub and the Emergence of Collaborative Risk-driven Community Safety," Toronto, ON: Canadian Police College webpages, entered 2014, accessed December 6, 2019, http://www.cpc-ccp.gc.ca/sites/default/files/pdf/prince-albert-hub-eng.pdf.

Miller, James. *Shinwauk's Vision; A History of Native Residential Schools* (Toronto, ON: University of Toronto Press, 1996).

Nilson, Chad. "Risk-Driven Collaborative Intervention: A Preliminary Impact Assessment of Community Mobilization Prince Albert's Hub Model." Saskatoon, SK: Centre for Forensic Behavioural Science and Justice Studies. The University of Saskatchewan, entered2014, accessed December 6, 2019, https://cfbsjs.usask.ca/documents/Hub%20PIA%20Synopsis%20Handout.pdf.

Paulson, Bob. "Indian Residential School Apologies." Royal Canadian Mounted Police webpages, accessed December 6, 2019, http://www.rcmp-grc.gc.ca/aboriginal-autochtone/apo-reg-eng.htm.

Police Sector Council. Canadian Police Knowledge Network, entered 2012. Accessed December 6, 2019,www.policecouncil.ca/ pages/policing.html.

Public Safety Canada. "Trends in Indigenous Policing Models: An International Comparison." Government of Canada webpages, entered 2018, accessed December 6, 2019, https://www.publicsafety.gc.ca/cnt/rsrcs/pblctns/trnds-ndgns-plc-mdl/index-en.aspx.

Ratushny, Ed. *The Conduct of Public Inquiries: Law, Policy, and Practice* (Toronto, ON: Irwin Law, 2009).

Robertson, Dylon and Aldo Santin. "Meth Task Force Report 'passing the baton to each of the three levels of government.'" *Winnipeg Free Press*, June 29, 2019.

Ross, Jeffrey. "The Historical Treatment of Urban Policing in Canada: A Review of the Literature." *Urban History Review* 24, no. 1 (1995): 36–43.

Royal Canadian Mounted Police. "History of the Royal Canadian Mounted Police." *Mounted Police Post*, entered 2012, accessed December 6, 2019, http://www.mountieshop.com/new/history.asp.

Scheider, Mathew, Robert Chapman and Amy Schapiro. "Towards the Unification of Policing Innovations under Community Policing." *Policing: An International Journal of Police Strategies and Management* 32 no. 4 (2009): 694–718.

The Case for a Prince Albert and Region Alcohol Strategy. "A Call to Action for All Community Sectors to Collectively Develop and Implement a Comprehensive Alcohol Strategy." Prince Albert, SK webpages, entered 2012, accessed December 6, 2019, http://paalcoholstrategy.ca/wp-content/uploads/2018/03/2018-Alcohol-Strategy.pdf.

Waddington, Tank. "Policing with Trust and Confidence." *Policing* 4, no. 3 (2010): 197–198.

Welch, Mary Agnes and Mia Rabson. "Contentious Cleanup." *Winnipeg Free Press* (December 30, 2011).

Westmarland, Louise. "Dodgy Customers? Can the Police Ever Trust the Public?" *Policing* 4, no. 3 (2010): 291–297.

Weyeneth, Robert. "The Power of Apology and the Process of Historical Reconciliation." *The Public Historian* 23, no. 3 (2001): 9–38.

Our Shared Future

Conclusions from the Windows

Robert Chrismas and Laura E. Reimer

Canada's contested history weaves the experiences and stories of the past around how we live together today and shapes how we will live together in the future. We step into the lives of others, knowing that on this reconciliation journey we must walk into the unknown, together. Notably, six of the twelve contributors identify Indigenous heritage. We all represent the rich diversity of Canada's cultural history, which reaches around the globe; the settlers who came in the 1600s walked out their lives in the vast wilderness and extreme weathers of the land with each other and with their Indigenous neighbors. The newcomers who have come since and who are yet to come represent important dimensions of Canada's reconciliation journey. There is much work to be done as we create an ethical and honoring Canadian culture, together. We are challenged to meet in spaces of reconciliation, "where truth and mercy, justice, and peace meet."[1] The chapters of this volume represent those spaces, and inspire hope for Canada's shared future.

We acknowledge that not everyone is on this journey; some deny it, some are just awakening, others have struggled in silence across their generations, others are curious but are uncertain of their role. We cannot trust the promises of our governments that reconciliation is a priority because despite some genuine political effort early in the twenty-first century, there is no real change and the *Indian Act* still ensures that the Canadian government has a firm and official colonized relationship over First Nations and First Nations people. The contributors to this volume have provided windows into their reconciliation journeys by sharing their stories, their visions, and their understandings that reconciliation is about relationships, courage, and action. Perhaps, then, reconciliation cannot be the work of governments alone. This journey is one of compassion, empathy, and understanding; one that individual Canadians must consider, and we submit, one that we all should enter.

To set the context for Canada's current reconciliation journey, Dr Laura Reimer outlined the long road of Indigenous relations in Canada through the windows of British, and then Canadian federal government policies. The roots of relationship are found in the early years of contact between the Original People and those whose heritage originated in Europe, primarily France and Britain. The roots of reconciliation are in the policies and purposes of the governments of Canada, from its fledging beginnings as a tiny geographical area in 1867 to its establishment as a coast-to-coast Dominion in 1949, and through to modern day. However, the *Indian Act* of 1869 and its dire repercussions remain central in the story of Indigenous relations in Canada, and today's need for reconciliation.

Dr Brian Rice shared with readers the intimate journey of the heart and mind that accompanied his footsteps as he reconciled the conflicts of identity known to many Canadians. By talking with others, he gained understanding and made peace: "What better way for reconciliation to begin," he concluded.[2]

Determining common interests is a long-recognized and most effective form of transformative change. Father Peter Bisson shared his deeply personal reconciliation journey and as a leader among the Jesuit brothers of the Catholic Church. Through his journey we learn that the "spiritual dimension of reconciliation and decolonization makes for a lot of lived common ground between Indigenous people and the churches."[3] He leaves us with hope that although the past cannot be undone, there is sincerity in the early fragile bonds of a shared future.

In her carefully researched chapter on trauma and the effects of vicarious trauma in the classroom, Christa Yeates confronts us with the very real challenges of teaching and learning in the reconciliation context: deep pain and broken hearts that require healing. Despite difficult work that requires so much beyond typical teacher training, and that often escapes the resource planning of education systems, we see the effort and life-changing results of trauma-informed education for Indigenous students and their teachers.

Leading the University of Winnipeg as president and vice-chancellor, Dr Annette Trimbee outlined the innovative journey of reconciliation and indigenization taking place in the academic context of one Central Canadian prairie university. Engaging the framework of Gaudry and Lorenz to categorize and assess the work, Trimbee and her colleagues know that what they are doing is having an impact and contributing to a more positive future. They also acknowledge that there is more to be done, and will continue the journey in partnership with Indigenous peoples, so that all may succeed together.

Loretta Ross is one of Canada's prairie Treaty Relations Commissioners, and shared the principles of treaties in her chapter. Recognizing that there is a context of renewed interest in reconciling the past wrongs, she focused on the treaties and the unique relationship between First Nations peoples and the Crown (now the government of Canada) to challenge what we think we know about treaties. Ross compels readers to explore with her how a First Nations perspective of the treaties can guide approaches to stronger relationships.

As a recognized authority in the area of urban reserves, Dr Joe Garcea provided a comprehensive overview and analysis of the critical and conventional perspectives on the relationship between reconciliation and the creation and operation of satellite urban reserves.

Chief Ron Evans provided a highly practical response to Canada's *Truth and Reconciliation Commission's* (TRC) Call to Action 92, business and reconciliation, and proclaims that it is simply good business to take up the call. Drawing upon his long experience and perspectives as a chief, leader, and business owner among First Nations communities, Chief Evans explained how reconciliation can take shape in the market economy to ensure a more sustainable and profitable future for all.

As leaders in law enforcement, Edmonton Police Chief Dale McFee and coeditor of this volume, Staff Sergeant (Dr) Bob Chrismas of Winnipeg provided a unique window into reconciliation through the work being done in many Canadian cities. With expertise in different aspects of leadership, McFee and Chrismas outlined the evolution of the very old relationship between Indigenous people and law enforcement and the practical ways that police leaders are advancing justice and respect, and contributing significantly to Canada's reconciliation journey.

Each chapter represents a different facet of the relationship being lived out today in Canada, and a different way that reconciliation has become a place where truth and mercy, justice, and peace meet—for us as individuals, as neighbors, as community members, and as leaders. The pages of this book are windows into diverse, thoughtful, and intentional contributions to Canada's reconciliation journey. There are very real barriers to reconciliation. Until these are dismantled, we must find our way around them. In the pages of this book, readers have learned how Canadians have a united interest and a responsibility to work together and reconcile tensions of our past and of our present in order to ensure our future is just.

The wampums on the cover are intentionally poignant reminders of the covenants of intended peaceful relationships among the Original Peoples, the Europeans who established colonies here, and their descendants. Symbolically, the wampums are wrapped around the land that we all share and where our journey is taking place. Hopefully what has been shared here inspires readers to contemplate their role in the reconciliation journey for Canada's shared future, and to step onto the path with us.

NOTES

1. John Paul Lederach, *Building Peace: Sustainable Reconciliation in Divided Societies* (Washington, DC: United States Institute of Peace, 1997), 29.
2. See chapter 3.
3. See chapter 4.

Afterword and Dedications

In the pages of this book are the thoughts and deeds of dedicated and respected reconciliation practitioners in our country. They quietly do their work, and it makes a difference each and every day. I am grateful for the effort and time they prioritized to produce the thoughtful chapters that comprise this collection. I hold a deep respect for each of them. Though the book is finished, our journey is far from over.

This project was quite personal for me, and had landed in my mind when I awoke one morning in late 2018. I was a young child in Nelson, British Columbia, when I first learned that there were Indigenous people in Canada, and that they had been here long before anyone else. I have been captivated by the relationship ever since; my heart has always leaned with a desire to understand Indigenous ways in Canada; many years later, my doctoral research was with Indigenous people. I continue to learn that I am still learning. I am astounded at how the book that has emerged—from the cover sketch to the topics of our contributors—mirrors the reconciliation journey for knowledge and understanding that I am still walking.

My family heritage runs deep into the histories of Canada; the fur trade of the 1600s and 1700s, and before. My mother's story is a remarkable Manitoba story and when she died suddenly in 2012, we lost our family historian—a role I have assumed with a growing sense of wonder. She was always eager to learn more about her family, and was both irritating and infectious with exuberant blurtings of her latest findings about her ancestors. It is amazing to think that she traced her family lines to the earliest days of contact. Her diligent and vivacious enthusiasm has left us with a remarkable story that, in many ways, typifies that of many Canadians. We know that our story is much older than the arrival of young George Robertson from the

Orkney Islands to York Factory in the 1600s with the HBC. We know he married a Dene washerwoman and that her name has come through our family stories as Katherine Lindsay; I often wonder what her name really was, so that I could learn about that part of our family. Mom traced the descendants of the Robertsons south, and eventually into Winnipeg around 1870, when Manitoba joined Canadian Confederation. The family names animate stories of early Canada: Wilson, Lindsay, Frobisher, Forbister, Christie, Robertson…..Our grandmother was raised by her Cree aunt and a few cultural traditions from Métis heritage, including baking traditions (best on a wood stove) were passed down to us from Nana. We know from my Mom's photos, records, and family Bibles that Dene, Cree, Scots/Irish, and British blood runs in our veins. We know that our family includes the Ukrainian, German, Polish, Icelandic, Mennonite, French, and English settler stories. We know that on her French (Pariseau) father's side, Mom's ancestors lived among the Iroquois, fought the British on the Plains of Abraham, joined the Voyageur, and eventually settled near La Broquerie, Manitoba. They moved into Winnipeg around 1900. My Dad's family were settlers in the Marlbank area of Ontario from County Fermanagh in Ireland in the early 1800s, learning the ways of the land from local Mohawk people; Dad's father was from Nottingham, England.

I used to think that my story was that of Canada's two solitudes (French and English) but I know now that our story is so much more and I am aware that I, too, am striving to understand what that means for me. My mother was fiercely proud of her Métis/Scots/Irish heritage, and I am grateful to her for her tireless dedication to understand what it means to really know how we are all connected and how we must work that hope to stay connected in the fullest meanings of friendship, in this great land we call Canada.

And so this book is for my Mom. As the years without her go by, I realize how fully and fearlessly she stood on the foundations of truth, mercy, peace, and justice—and gave me early footing for my own reconciliation journey.

There are many people who made this book possible, and I wish to first thank the team at Lexington Books. They are unequaled in the field for support and guidance, and working with them continues to be a pleasure. I am thankful to Bob Chrismas for agreeing to coedit this book with me—it has been fun and I have greatly appreciated his willingness to share the load! Thank you to the people who stood with the authors of these chapters—families, friends, colleagues—yours is a quiet and unrecognized role, but as scholars, we cannot do what we do, and produce the writing that we do, without you.

I also want to thank my adult children, Graham, Jayne, Jill, and Jenna, and my daughter-in-law, Danielle, each of whom live out love in their unique spheres of influence and inspire others—including me—by their pursuit of excellence. Their lives give me much hope for Canada's shared future.

Finally, I thank my husband Rick. When I told him I wanted to do this book, he did what he always does—stood quietly at the helm and held our course steady, while my work with the book filled the sails of our life with new friends, new adventures, and another new horizon to ponder.

Laura E. Reimer
Winnipeg 2019

Gratitude is the feeling I had as I worked with Laura and all of the learned authors while creating this volume. It is humbling and also inspiring that so many are so willing to share their vast personal experiences and knowledge, just for the asking. For my own personal journey, I am thankful for the experiences and teachers I have had, developing my own voice on issues I feel passionate about. Having worked in the justice system for over thirty-five years, first in the courts and then starting in policing during Manitoba's Aboriginal Justice Inquiry, in 1989, I have lived and worked intimately with the challenges faced by Indigenous people in Canada. I have had a lot of impactful experiences through my policing career and met so many passionate and inspiring leaders both within and outside the Indigenous community. I want to acknowledge those leaders, and in particular those in justice and in policing, too many to list, who have worked publicly putting themselves out there. Even more significantly, I appreciate those who work in the shadows, doing the right thing when no one is watching; those have been my true role models and inspiration for continuing my work striving to contribute to improved social justice in Canada.

In my own family, I wish to acknowledge my recently deceased brother, Doug (and his supporting wife Star), for his work protecting Canada in a career in the Canadian Airforce during the Cold War, followed by his twenty-seven-year career with the Calgary Police Service. Doug and Star were passionate about helping Indigenous people. In his policing career and in retirement as well, Doug taught me about integrity, compassion, and justice.

Last but not least, I wish to acknowledge my ever-supportive, tolerant, and encouraging wife, Barb, and all of our children, Crystal, Chelsea, Brandi, and Bobby. They have all encouraged and inspired me in different ways. Bobby is a kind, compassionate, and nonjudgmental young man who has taught me about tolerance. Chelsea is a yoga teacher and trainer who continually gives to the community, whether it be free yoga lessons in the park or feeding the homeless. Brandi, a Winnipeg Police Cadet, is starting her law enforcement career on the right foot, engaging and working with the community at every opportunity and publishing on justice issues. Crystal and Barb, both nurses, provide medical care with blind compassion. All have inspired the idea in me that reconciliation can take many forms; it comes down to individual acts and personal relationships, regardless of how big or small our sphere of influence is.

Robert Chrismas
Winnipeg, 2019

Appendix A

Full Text of the Official Apology from Hansard, the official record
of the Government of Canada Parliamentary proceedings.
11 June 2008
House of Commons, Ottawa, Canada
Right Hon. Stephen Harper (Prime Minister, CPC)

I stand before you today to offer an apology to former students of Indian residential schools. The treatment of children in these schools is a sad chapter in our history.

For more than a century, Indian residential schools separated over 150,000 Aboriginal children from their families and communities.

In the 1870s, the federal government, partly in order to meet its obligations to educate Aboriginal children, began to play a role in the development and administration of these schools.

Two primary objectives of the residential school system were to remove and isolate children from the influence of their homes, families, traditions, and cultures, and to assimilate them into the dominant culture.

These objectives were based on the assumption that Aboriginal cultures and spiritual beliefs were inferior and unequal.

Indeed, some sought, as was infamously said, "to kill the Indian in the child."

Today, we recognize that this policy of assimilation was wrong, has caused great harm, and has no place in our country. 132 federally supported schools were located in every province and territory, except Newfoundland, New Brunswick, and Prince Edward Island.

Most schools were operated as joint ventures with Anglican, Catholic, Presbyterian, and United churches.

The Government of Canada built an educational system in which very young children were often forcibly removed from their homes and often taken far from their communities.

Many were inadequately fed, clothed, and housed. All were deprived of the care and nurturing of their parents, grandparents, and communities.

First Nations, Inuit, and Métis languages and cultural practices were prohibited in these schools.

Tragically, some of these children died while attending residential schools, and others never returned home.

The government now recognizes that the consequences of the Indian residential school policy were profoundly negative and that this policy has had a lasting and damaging impact on Aboriginal culture, heritage, and language.

While some former students have spoken positively about their experiences at residential schools, these stories are far overshadowed by tragic accounts of the emotional, physical, and sexual abuse and neglect of helpless children, and their separation from powerless families and communities.

The legacy of Indian residential schools has contributed to social problems that continue to exist in many communities today.

It has taken extraordinary courage for the thousands of survivors who have come forward to speak publicly about the abuse they suffered. It is a testament to their resilience as individuals and to the strengths of their cultures.

Regrettably, many former students are not with us today and died never having received a full apology from the Government of Canada.

The government recognizes that the absence of an apology has been an impediment to healing and reconciliation. Therefore, on behalf of the Government of Canada and all Canadians, I stand before you, in this chamber so central to our life as a country, to apologize to Aboriginal peoples for Canada's role in the Indian residential school system.

To the approximately 80,000 living former students and all family members and communities, the Government of Canada now recognizes that it was wrong to forcibly remove children from their homes, and we apologize for having done this.

We now recognize that it was wrong to separate children from rich and vibrant cultures and traditions, that it created a void in many lives and communities, and we apologize for having done this.

We now recognize that in separating children from their families, we undermined the ability of many to adequately parent their own children and sowed the seeds for generations to follow, and we apologize for having done this.

We now recognize that far too often these institutions gave rise to abuse or neglect and were inadequately controlled, and we apologize for failing to protect you.

Not only did you suffer these abuses as children, but as you became parents, you were powerless to protect your own children from suffering the same experience, and for this we are sorry.

The burden of this experience has been on your shoulders for far too long. The burden is properly ours as a government, and as a country. There is no place in Canada for the attitudes that inspired the Indian residential school system to ever again prevail.

You have been working on recovering from this experience for a long time, and in a very real sense we are now joining you on this journey. The Government of Canada sincerely apologizes and asks the forgiveness of the Aboriginal peoples of this country for failing them so profoundly.

We are sorry.

Nimitataynan.

Niminchinowesamin.

Mamiattugut.

In moving toward healing, reconciliation, and resolution of the sad legacy of Indian residential schools, the implementation of the IRSSA began on September 2007. Years of work by survivors, communities, and Aboriginal organizations culminated in an agreement that gives us a new beginning and an opportunity to move forward together in partnership.

A cornerstone of the settlement agreement is the Indian residential schools' truth and reconciliation commission. This commission represents a unique opportunity to educate all Canadians on the Indian residential school system. It will be a positive step in forging a new relationship between Aboriginal peoples and other Canadians, a relationship based on the knowledge of our shared history, a respect for each other, and a desire to move forward with a renewed understanding that strong families, strong communities and vibrant cultures and traditions will contribute to a stronger Canada for all of us.

God bless all of you. God bless our land.[1]

NOTE

1. Statement of Apology to former students of Indian Residential Schools. Accessed December 8, 2019. https://www.aadnc-aandc.gc.ca/eng/1100100015644/1100100015649

Index

abuse, 20, 68, 71–72, 74, 89, 95–97, 110, 112–14, 116, 118–19, 207, 234
accountable, 20, 24, 207
addictions, 110, 112, 115, 210
adolescent, 113, 119
alcoholism, 96, 103
ancestors, 49, 56, 58, 64–65, 77, 142, 149, 229–30
anishinabe, 68, 73, 146, 152, 155, 159–60
apology, vii, 3, 5, 7–8, 22–27, 30–32, 34, 67, 69, 71, 73, 75, 77, 79–83, 85, 87–89, 91, 202, 212, 219, 222–23, 233–35
arbitration, 169
assimilation, 16, 26, 81, 95–96, 112, 115, 210, 233
Attawapiskat, 198, 202–3

Canada, vii–19, 22–32, 35–36, 38, 41–46, 56, 59, 68–69, 73–76, 79–80, 82, 84–91, 95–97, 100, 104, 106, 111–12, 115, 117–19, 121–22, 124, 126, 129–30, 132–33, 135–37, 139, 141–44, 147–48, 151–53, 158–60, 163–65, 167–71, 173–75, 177–79, 181–87, 189–92, 194–98, 200–208, 210–22, 225–31, 233–35

Canadian, viii–1, 3–6, 9, 11–17, 19–29, 31, 33–34, 41–42, 49, 56, 68, 70, 73, 76, 80–81, 86, 90, 93, 96–98, 111–14, 116–18, 123–26, 133, 135–37, 139, 141–42, 144–45, 147, 150, 152, 157–59, 163–64, 169–70, 178, 182–84, 187, 189, 196–98, 203, 205–7, 209–15, 217–23, 225–27, 230–31
catholic, 5, 56, 61, 64, 67–68, 70, 73, 76–77, 79, 83–89, 226, 233
ceremony, 14, 20, 51, 112, 118, 151, 153, 160
colonialism, 4, 12, 30, 32, 73, 116, 133, 178–80, 183, 185, 187
colonization, 4, 11, 20, 29, 34, 68, 71, 75, 77, 80–81, 85, 130, 170, 192, 197–98, 201, 203, 207
colonized, 3–4, 25, 78, 225
colonizer, 73, 78
conflict, 1–2, 7–8, 11–13, 15–34, 75, 111, 132, 167, 169, 191, 218, 220–21
covenant, 11, 16, 59
cree, 88, 116, 127, 132, 189, 193, 198–99, 230
crime, 207–10, 214–16
criminology, 219–22
crown, 11, 14–15, 26, 28, 89, 141–45, 148–54, 157, 165, 172–73, 183–84, 186, 192, 200, 227

decolonization, 4, 7–8, 70, 75–76, 79, 81–85, 89, 123–25, 135–36, 139, 180, 226
democracy, 13, 20, 25, 27–28, 31, 45–46, 111, 114, 170
depression, 113, 117, 197
dialogue, 47, 70, 125, 131, 174, 182
disadvantaged, 106
discipline, 146, 206, 209
disease, 49, 103, 114, 116
dislocation, 192
displaced, 20, 182
diversity, 9, 124, 133, 182, 225
doctrine, 42, 84, 89, 210
drugs, 97–98, 103, 112, 116, 194

economy, 13, 15, 175–76, 190–91, 205, 227
Edmonton, 125, 193, 210, 216–18, 221, 227
elders, 28, 32, 59, 76, 85, 108, 126, 129, 131–32, 136, 141, 145, 154–55, 158–61
empathy, 5, 43, 45, 225
employment, 42, 75, 95, 109, 127–28, 175, 190, 193, 196–98, 202, 210
enforcement, 6, 16, 167, 205–7, 210–12, 227, 231
England, 6, 12–13, 148, 159, 192, 215, 230
entrenched, 18, 20–22, 42
environment, 93, 96, 100–101, 105, 107, 128–29, 154, 200, 217
equality, 27, 155
equally, 40, 151, 172, 190, 215
ethnic, 14, 21, 25, 28–32, 34
europe, 4, 9, 12–13, 148, 205, 226
european, 3, 10–11, 17, 19, 68, 89, 144, 146–47, 151, 159–60, 192, 205–7, 219, 222
expertise, 129, 133, 209, 227
exploitation, 219, 221
exploration, 102, 133, 189

family, 18, 43, 50–51, 53, 56, 65, 70, 78, 95, 98–99, 106–7, 109, 112, 115, 118, 121, 127–28, 135, 146, 155–56, 189, 199, 229–31, 234
federal, 5, 17–18, 21, 23–26, 40, 79, 96, 133, 136, 143, 164–67, 172–73, 175–77, 179, 181, 194–96, 198, 201, 203, 206–7, 210–13, 226, 233
financial, 72–73, 87, 131, 152, 165, 172, 175, 190, 194, 196–97, 199, 209
force, 96, 121, 206–7, 210–11, 220, 222
framework, 2, 12, 19, 42, 97, 111–12, 117, 122–25, 134, 136, 144, 165, 168, 190, 197, 209, 226
France, 12–13, 111, 117, 149, 192, 206, 226
funding, 42, 98, 108, 134–35, 144, 194–96, 201, 203

gangs, 98
gathering, 44, 70–71, 73–75, 79, 89, 147, 149, 157
gender, 39, 89
generations, 3, 73, 94, 96, 174, 213, 225, 234
genocide, 73–74
geographic, 9, 175, 211
geriatric, 113, 117
global, 1, 22, 26, 28, 34, 39, 111, 132, 170
governance, 14–15, 17, 20, 36, 38–40, 42, 45–46, 68, 101, 114, 117, 124, 126, 132, 142, 146, 152, 158, 168, 170–71, 182, 184, 186–87, 198, 208, 215
government, 2, 5–7, 9–28, 35–40, 43, 49, 56, 68, 78–80, 88, 111, 122, 133, 136, 142–45, 147, 152, 157–58, 160, 164, 166–67, 170–79, 182–87, 190–92, 194–99, 201–3, 206, 208–16, 220–22, 225–27, 233–35
grassroots, 44, 135
grief, 49, 71, 116
guidance, 76, 78, 93, 100, 126, 128, 154, 230

Halifax, 113, 118

harm, 18, 21, 24, 26, 52–53, 79–80, 170, 233
harmony, 115, 146
hate, 27
heal, 27, 30, 34, 73, 80, 110, 118, 170
healing, 1, 3, 10, 18, 24, 37, 43, 58, 72, 75, 80, 85, 87, 89, 95, 105, 107, 111–18, 226, 234–35
health, vii, 14, 18, 21, 24, 39, 87, 94, 96–97, 99, 103–4, 106, 109–14, 116–19, 146, 189, 191, 194, 197–98, 208–10, 213, 218, 221
help, viii, 38, 48, 53, 56, 61–62, 64, 70, 77, 84, 94, 98–99, 105, 107–9, 128, 132–33, 157–58, 174, 191, 208
honour, 150, 219, 222
hope, viii–1, 12, 19, 26–27, 48, 53, 76, 81–82, 85, 94, 108, 191, 194, 201, 203, 212, 225–26, 230–31
huron, 68, 72–73, 75, 153
hydroelectric, 79, 193

identity, 5, 13–15, 18–23, 25–26, 29–33, 36, 41, 43–45, 69, 78, 81, 84, 93–94, 96, 105, 112, 117, 122, 127, 132, 134–35, 170, 212, 226
immigration, 153
imperialism, 11, 26, 29, 32
inclusion, 122–26, 135–39, 151, 216
indicators, viii, 13, 87, 103
indigenizing, 124, 136, 139
industry, 37, 213–14, 219, 221
inequality, 20, 36, 39
infrastructure, 136, 194–95, 198–99
inhabitants, 3, 9, 11, 13, 111, 192
injustice, 2, 30, 32, 82, 212
inquests, 208
inquiries, 30, 34, 212, 217, 219, 222
intergenerational, 16, 39, 82, 110–12, 114–15, 117–18, 128
intractable, 22, 31, 33, 39
Inuit, 27, 87, 111, 128, 159, 234
investment, 174, 190, 199–201
Iroquois, 11, 27, 29, 34, 65–66, 230

jail, 95

Kahnawakē, 56–57, 64–65
Kelowna, 21–22, 26, 30, 33

Lakota, 112, 116
leadership, 5–6, 14, 20, 22–23, 25–26, 35–41, 43–45, 50, 69, 72–74, 76, 84, 114, 117, 122, 125–28, 130–33, 135, 199, 208, 215–16, 221, 227
legacy, vii, 41, 73, 97, 117, 169, 191, 200, 207, 211, 219, 221, 234–35
legislation, 11–15, 20, 27, 97, 111, 143, 191, 205–6, 213
literacy, 98, 104, 210
longhouse, 50–51, 53, 65

management, 23, 35, 37, 39, 114, 117, 165, 168, 177, 180, 183, 185–86, 190–91, 198–201, 215, 220, 223
marginalization, 80, 96, 134, 191–95, 197–99, 201
market, 179, 192–93, 202–3, 227
marketplace, 190, 194
Maskawatisiwin, 93, 96–102, 109–10
media, 14, 21, 24, 39–40, 42, 87, 167, 172, 176, 214
mediation, 169
mercy, 2–3, 25, 225, 227, 230
Métis, viii, 27, 43, 73, 111, 121, 128, 134–35, 230, 234
military, 13, 147, 151, 206, 215
mining, 152, 199
missionary, 28, 33, 67–69, 74
Mohawk, 5, 27, 32, 47, 58–64, 212, 230
monument, 58
multidisciplinary, 132, 209
multigenerational, 116
multisectoral, 207, 214, 216
museum, 62, 133

narrative, 2, 41–42, 47, 113, 122, 168, 182, 216
nationhood, 4, 155
native, 10, 30, 34, 51, 59, 86, 90, 116–17, 125, 219, 222

negotiations, 30, 33, 80, 146, 153–54, 163, 165–67, 169, 173–74, 176, 182, 184, 186
neocolonialism, 164, 171, 179, 181
neoliberalism, 164, 171, 179–81
newcomers, 1, 9, 151, 154, 225
Niagara, 3, 5, 12–14, 16, 27–28, 149–50
nongovernmental, 38, 40, 178
nonIndigenous, 10–11, 16, 25, 72
norms, 168, 190, 197

Ojibway,Ojibwe, 68, 127, 132, 152
Oneida, 27, 58
organizations, 1, 6–8, 29, 33, 37–38, 40, 43, 45, 74, 76–77, 114, 117–18, 121, 126, 128, 133, 136, 177–78, 200, 209, 211, 216, 235
outcomes, vii, 2, 42, 93, 95–96, 103–4, 172, 184, 187, 195–96, 208
oversight, 101, 179

paradigm, 15, 25, 35, 111, 117, 180
parents, 99, 213, 234–35
parliament, 9, 12, 16, 21, 25, 30, 33
partnership, 10, 73, 81–82, 101–2, 125, 127, 132–33, 136, 173, 198, 217, 226, 235
paternalism, 76
peacebuilding, 7–8, 30, 33, 216
peaceful, 17, 61, 146, 150–52, 171, 227
peacemaker, 5, 47, 49, 51–59, 61, 63–65
pedagogy, 76, 104, 113, 116–17, 124
perpetrators, 80
phenomenological, 111, 119
philosophy, 48, 168–69, 171, 179–81, 183–84, 186, 215
policies, 5, 9, 16, 18, 20, 26, 29, 38, 43, 77, 95–96, 105, 121, 124, 142–43, 157–58, 165–66, 172, 183, 186, 196, 206, 209–10, 226
politics, 15, 19, 89, 115, 132, 164, 212
population, 10, 16, 22, 101, 117, 121, 129, 159, 192, 196, 214, 218, 221
postcolonialism, 91
postmodern, 88
potlatch, 14–15, 20, 28, 31, 33

poverty, 14, 39, 63, 95, 97–98, 100, 132, 191, 197, 199, 214
protection, 12–13, 51, 148, 198
provincial, 6, 40, 69–70, 73, 75–76, 81, 86–87, 98, 102, 136, 165–66, 173–75, 181, 198, 202, 204, 207, 211

Québec, 68, 73, 79, 86, 88, 198, 206, 211–12

racism, 10–11, 98, 100, 109–10, 130–31, 134, 170, 191, 200
RCMP, 206–7, 210–11, 218–19, 222
recolonized, 4
recommendations, 5, 9, 17–18, 21, 24, 82, 97, 104, 110, 130–31, 170, 189–90, 202, 208–9, 212
reform, 38, 41, 171
reframing, 89
Regina, 73, 75
regional, 29, 32, 67, 166–67, 211, 215, 220–21
religion, 83, 85, 88–89, 91, 132
religious, 67, 69–70, 72, 78, 85–86, 88
relocated, 68
relocation, 219–20
reparation(s), 4, 11, 22–26, 30–34, 77, 200
reserve, 20, 24, 42, 53, 142, 164–67, 173, 176, 178–79, 181, 183, 185–87, 192–93, 195–96, 202–3
resilience, 37, 109, 116, 151, 234
resistance, 76, 78, 98, 180
resolution, 2, 29–33, 132, 148, 165–66, 191, 200, 220–21, 235
respect, vii, 3, 6, 10–11, 27, 42, 44, 52, 72, 81–82, 88, 94, 102, 106, 108, 125, 133–34, 150–51, 157, 173, 178, 198, 205, 207, 210, 227, 229, 235
restitution, 7–8, 80, 82
restoring, 115, 190
risk, 73, 94, 98, 102, 195, 209, 212, 217–18, 220, 222
river, 2, 11–12, 29, 32, 55, 58, 60–64, 68
rural, 165, 175–76, 210, 214

Index

sacred, 51–55, 128, 147, 154–55
Sakokwenionkwas, 61, 64, 65
Saranac, 29, 34
Saskatchewan, vii, 28, 32, 75, 126, 159–60, 165, 174, 176, 183–86, 207–9, 220–22
Saskatoon, 159–60, 183–87, 220, 222
Sawiskera, 47–50, 52–53, 55–58, 61, 65–66
settlers, 3, 5, 12, 20, 61, 77, 81–82, 150–52, 155, 159, 206, 225, 230
shame, 43, 71–73, 96, 105
shared, viii–1, 3–4, 6, 9–10, 26–27, 43–45, 68, 73, 75, 79, 82, 85, 93, 95, 129, 146–47, 150, 169, 171, 174, 189, 205, 217, 225–28, 231, 235
slavery, 23, 219, 221
solutions, 9, 36, 39, 44, 173–74, 194–95, 197, 208, 216
sovereignty, 19, 38, 148–50, 152, 179–80, 182
spirit, vii, 28, 32, 37, 44, 49, 52, 54, 56, 69–70, 74, 79, 108, 148, 154–58, 172–73, 175, 180
spirituality, 60, 67, 71, 74, 86, 146
standardization, 200, 202–3
statistics, 21, 136, 139, 196, 201–3, 221
status, 17, 27, 98, 117, 123, 143, 165, 167, 179
stewardship, 6, 15, 155, 198
storytelling, 22, 76, 106
structural, 13, 19, 22, 25–26, 29–30, 32, 82, 212
sustainability, 25, 100, 189–90, 199–200

territory, 48–49, 51, 53, 58–59, 63, 65, 71, 85, 121, 125, 135, 152, 155–56, 189, 192, 198, 200, 233
theology, 85, 87–88, 90
tobacco, 51, 54–55, 57–60, 62–64
traditional, 14, 20, 35, 47–49, 65–66, 78, 97–99, 101, 108, 110, 124, 126, 133, 135–36, 145, 155, 158, 178, 193, 198, 210–11
transformation, 19, 22, 24–25, 27, 29, 31, 33, 35, 69, 72, 75, 81–82, 85–86, 111, 123, 210

transition, 15, 73, 76, 80, 126, 131, 157
traumainformed, 95, 105, 113–14
traumatic, 7–8, 71, 96, 103, 105, 110, 118
Treaty, viii, 3–6, 11–17, 25, 27–28, 30–32, 85, 121, 124–25, 135, 141–42, 144–47, 149–61, 163, 165, 173, 179, 183–84, 186–87, 189, 214, 227
tribes, 10, 148
tribunals, 2
Truth and Reconciliation Commission (TRC), vii, 24, 29, 31, 34–36, 40–46, 69–70, 72–73, 75–78, 80, 85–87, 89, 112, 122–23, 125–26, 133, 137, 139, 141, 143, 169–70, 184, 189–90, 198, 201, 204

UNESCO, 111, 117, 195, 201
United Nations Declaration on the Rights of Indigenous Peoples (UNDRIP), 198

values, 4, 71, 79, 87–88, 145–46, 156, 159, 168–69
Vatican, 70, 79
victimization, 94–95, 105, 207
violence, 20–21, 25, 61, 78–79, 81, 84, 94–98, 210
virtue, 44, 69
vision, 1, 6, 37–38, 168, 219, 222

Wahbung, 142, 157–58, 160
Wampum, 3, 5, 11–16, 27–28, 51, 125, 146, 149–50, 160
wealth, 12, 175, 192
weapons, 72
welfare, 19, 100, 115, 128, 143, 208–9, 213
wellbeing, 146, 216
western, 4, 6, 151, 156, 159–60, 206, 210, 215
whiteman, 56, 59, 157
wisdom, 7, 70, 132, 146
women, 50, 68, 74, 82, 85, 88, 90, 109, 112, 118, 136
wrongs, 3, 25, 27, 44, 82, 141, 163, 169, 174, 200, 212, 227

About the Contributors

Laura E. Reimer, MPA, PhD
Dr Laura Reimer is currently a research associate and faculty member with the Arthur V. Mauro Institute for Peace and Justice in Winnipeg, Manitoba. She is a former assistant professor of public administration and public policy at the University of Winnipeg, where she was awarded the prestigious Clifford J. Robson Memorial Award for Teaching Excellence. Upon completion of her PhD, Laura held an administrative teaching postdoctoral fellowship at the University of North Carolina Greensboro. Her research interests explore the intersection of theory and practice, and her expertise merges peacebuilding practices with policy, governance, and leadership. She has particular interest and expertise in practical conflict resolution skills, education policy, and Indigenous education. Laura is a former elected school trustee, an experience which in part drives her passion for excellence in public service and leadership. She is the author of two leading books on education governance entitled *Guarding the Trust: Leadership and School Boards* (2008) and *Leadership and School Boards in an Era of Community Engagement* (2015). She was the lead author for the popular *Transformative Change: An Introduction to Peace and Conflict Studies*, also published by the Lexington Group (2015). This is the third book on which Laura has been the lead editor, all of which explore diverse enquiries and practices of positive transformative change and reconciliation. She is a certified mediator and has been a leadership and strategic planning consultant. Visit Laura's professional website at www.drlauraereimer.com.

Robert Chrismas, MPA, PhD
Dr Bob Chrismas is an author, scholar, consultant, passionate speaker, and social justice advocate, with thirty-five years of law enforcement experience

and broadly recognized expertise in community engagement and crime prevention. A graduate of peace and conflict studies at the University of Manitoba, Bob was awarded the University of Manitoba Distinguished Dissertation Award for his doctoral thesis, *Modern Day Slavery and the Sex Industry: Raising the Voices of Survivors and Collaborators while Confronting Sex Trafficking and Exploitation in Manitoba*, Canada. Bob is an advocate for social reform and has written and speaks on innovative trends in social justice, policing, community partnerships, and governance. His first book *Canadian Policing in the 21st Century: A Frontline Officer on Challenges and Changes* (McGill-Queens U. Press, 2013) is a widely used text on modern policing. His next book *Sex Industry Slavery: Protecting Canada's Youth* (2020, U. Toronto Press) aims to raise awareness and bring tangible solutions to modern-day slavery in the sex industry. Visit Bob at BChrismas.com.

David Barnard, PhD, OM

Dr David Barnard studied computer science (University of Toronto: BSc, MSc, PhD), Christian studies (Regent College, UBC: Dip.CS) and law (Osgoode Hall, York University: LLM). After his doctorate he joined the faculty of Queen's University and had various administrative roles. He became vice-president, then president at the University of Regina, and is now president and vice-chancellor at the University of Manitoba. He has served on several boards: CentreVenture, St Boniface General Hospital, Bank of Canada (lead director), Greystone Capital Management, SaskPower (Chair), Manitoba Electoral Divisions Boundary Commission; and is currently on boards of Payments Canada, CentrePort Canada and UMProperties. He is a member of the Order of Manitoba and a fellow of the Royal Society of Canada. He likes to read about many things—leadership advice, politics, theology, mysteries, poetry, history, literary criticism, and so on.

Peter Bisson, PhD

Dr Peter Bisson, S.J., is a Roman Catholic priest in the Catholic religious order known as the Jesuits (the Society of Jesus), and has strong interests in the relationships between spirituality and social justice, and in communal forms of spirituality. He now lives in Ottawa, with the task of encouraging relations of Canadian Jesuit organizations with Indigenous peoples and organizations. Dr Bisson had leadership roles for the Jesuits from 2008 to 2018, and before that was an assistant professor of religious studies at Campion College in the University of Regina. He holds degrees in humanities, religious studies, philosophy, and theology, including a doctorate in theology from the Pontifical Gregorian University in Rome.

Ronald G. Evans, DDhc

Dr Ronald G. Evans is an Ayisiniwok and Nehiyawok, from Kinosao Sipi (Norway House Cree Nation) in Treaty 5 Territory in North-Central Manitoba. He has held leadership positions and worked extensively within the First Nations' context in the public and private sectors. Dr Evans was educated in Canada's residential school system and has attended schools in Quebec, Alberta, and Manitoba. He was conferred a Doctor of Divinity, honoris causa by Providence Theological Seminary in Manitoba. Mr Evans is an ordained Anglican minister, has held the elected offices of Band Councilor and chief of Norway House Cree Nation for a combined thirty years, and has served as the Grand Chief of the Assembly of Manitoba Chiefs. Presently Mr Evans is a private business owner working to bring truth and reconciliation initiatives to businesses and institutions within Manitoba and across Canada. He also remains active in his home community of Norway House as a small business owner and commercial fisherman. Chief Evans can be reached atinfo@rgevans.ca.

Joseph Garcea, PhD

Dr Garcea is a political studies professor at the University of Saskatchewan. His areas of teaching include Canadian public policy, public management, public-private partnerships, multiculturalism, and local governance. His research agenda includes the analysis of First Nations satellite urban reserves in Canada; public-private partnerships; and Canadian immigration, integration, intercultural, and citizenship issues andoptions. He has coedited a volume and written several articles on Indian satellite urban reserves. Dr Garcea has coedited two volumes on local government reforms, one focusing on such reforms in Canada and another focusing on such reforms in Canada, United States, Australia, New Zealand, Britain, and Ireland. He has served as chair of the Task Force on Municipal Government, and as a member of a Task Force on Métis elections in the province of Saskatchewan. Dr Garcea may be contacted at joe.garcea@usask.ca.

His Doctoral Dissertation can be viewed at:
https://curve.carleton.ca/8f8f681a-c348-456b-9a38-1961f428e458.

Dale McFee, OOM

Dale McFee was sworn in as the Edmonton Police Service's 23rd chief of Police in February 2019. He has an extensive background in policing, including nine years as chief of Police in Prince Albert, Saskatchewan and six years as the deputy minister of Corrections and Policing for the Saskatchewan Government's Ministry of Justice. He has been involved in various provincial and national policing associations. Chief McFee has Métis heritage, and believes that a willingness to learn from the past informs future success, and that embracing diversity can transform modern policing. Dale was awarded the Officer of the Order of Merit (OOM) which recognizes outstanding meritorious service in duties of responsibility over an extended period. When he is not leading police service in one of Canada's cities, Dale is an active member of his community. In addition to serving on boards throughout Alberta and Saskatchewan, he speaks and lectures provincially, nationally, and internationally on the topics of leadership, data usage, and change management.

Mikayla Leanne Plett, BA

Mikayla Leanne Plett is a self-taught visual artist based in Winnipeg, Manitoba who specializes in realistic colored pencil and graphite drawings. Mikayla has been drawing since a young age, and has always had a natural talent for bringing her subjects to life through the tip of her pencil. While she has drawn a variety of subject matter, her favorites include people and wildlife. Mikayla is specifically intrigued by the challenge of photorealism and the meticulous attention to detail it demands, and this is a skill she continues to develop and perfect to this day. Each and every drawing exerts a lifelike vitality, and is a product of many hours of careful and diligent work. Mikayla currently sells originals and prints of her artwork, and also takes commission work. Visit her professional website at https://mikaylaleanne.art/, or view her Instagram profile: @artbymikaylaleanne.

Brian Rice, PhD

Dr Brian Rice is a professor in the Faculty of Kinesiology and Recreation Management as an Indigenous global land-based researcher. He is an enrolled member of the Indigenous Mohawk Nation at Kahnawaké, Quebec, Canada. Besides being a teacher and an interim principal for a year in an Indigenous band-operated school, he has previously taught full time in the departments of native studies, religious studies, continuing education, and education over a thirty-year period. He holds a PhD in Traditional Knowledge. Dr Rice continues teaching courses in Indigenous history and culture: both national and global. Over the years he has been asked to participate in many workshops as well as being asked to be a keynote speaker at several conferences. His most recent work has been in Japan and Kenya making connections in preparing for interviewing the elders on land-based education. He has published three books *Seeing the World with Aboriginal Eyes; The Rotinonshonni: A Traditional Iroquoian History Though the Eyes of Sawiskera and Tehronhia:wako;* and *A History of Newcomer and Indigenous First Encounters from the East to the Mid-west for Educators*. He has also published various chapters and articles on Indigenous issues, history, and culture.

Loretta Ross, LLB

Loretta Ross is a member of the Hollow Water First Nation in Manitoba and obtained her law degree from Queen's University, Canada. She has practiced law for over twenty-five years providing legal counsel to numerous First Nations people, governments, and organizations, including the Assembly of Manitoba Chiefs and the Assembly of First Nations. She has worked with the Manitoba Aboriginal Justice Inquiry and was as a Commissioner on the First Nations Circle on the Constitution. Her grandfather, George Barker, who served for forty-four years as chief of Hollow Water, taught her from an early age that she would always carry the responsibility of advocating and educating on behalf of First Nations people. This responsibility fits with her position as Treaty Commissioner in Manitoba, in Central Canada, where she educates about the treaties, and challenges our understanding of treaties and their significance in facilitating the change required in the relationship between First Nations and non-First Nations people.

Annette Trimbee, PhD

Dr Annette Trimbee is president and vice-chancellor of the University of Winnipeg, which has approximately 10,000 students. The University is located in downtown Winnipeg on Treaty 1 territory in the heart of the Métis homeland. Developed under her leadership, the University's strategic directions articulate a deep commitment to growing leaders through a focus on excellence and accessibility—especially for traditionally underrepresented groups such as Indigenous, new Canadian, and refugee students. In 2016, University of Winnipeg affirmed its role as a leader in reconciliation when it became one of the first universities in Canada to introduce an Indigenous course requirement. The initiative was led by Dr Trimbee, who is of Métis heritage, and seeks to ensure that all students have baseline knowledge of Indigenous people and culture. Dr Trimbee holds a BSc from the University of Winnipeg, an MSc from the University of Manitoba, and a PhD from McMaster University in aquatic ecology.

Paul E. Vogt, MPhil

Paul Vogt was president of Red River College in Manitoba from 2015 to 2019. Prior to that, he served for eight years as the head of the Manitoba Civil Service and Deputy Minister to the Premier, and for six years as cabinet policy secretary. An alumnus of the University of Manitoba, Vogt also did graduate work at Oxford and Princeton University. He has taught politics, philosophy, and public administration at the University of Manitoba and the University of Winnipeg, and Canadian Mennonite University.

Christa Yeates, BEd

Christa Yeates began teaching 1997. First stop was Flin Flon, in Manitoba's north. Next stop West Africa where she had the amazing opportunity to work with math and science educators for three years. She has been working as a teacher with adults in Winnipeg's North End since 2005. Returning from West Africa with a new language, new friends, and family, and in awe of a beautiful culture and its people, Christa was inspired to learn more about the rich cultures and traditions from the Indigenous people who are her neighbors. Her work, her colleagues, and her students have helped to open her eyes, heart, and mind to the lives and culture of some of Winnipeg's First Peoples. Christa is very passionate about having her adult students' stories heard. In her students she sees strength, caring, tolerance, perseverance, hope, pain, sadness, and joy. Her work toward a master's degree in counseling at the University of Manitoba is helping her to see their trauma and its effects in people's lives.

Lightning Source UK Ltd.
Milton Keynes UK
UKHW051353181221
395884UK00005B/27